WRITER'S WORD HANDBOOK

Practical Phrases, Expressions & Similes
To Enhance Your Writing

© 2018 Typewriter Publishing.

All Rights Reserved.

"One cannot always live in the palaces and state apartments of language, but we can refuse to spend our days in searching for its vilest slums." —William Watson

"Words without thought are dead sounds; thoughts without words are nothing. To think is to speak low; to speak is to think aloud." —Max Muller

"The first merit which attracts in the pages of a good writer, or the talk of a brilliant conversationalist, is the apt choice and contrast of the words employed. It is indeed a strange art to take these blocks rudely conceived for the purpose of the market or the bar, and by tact of application touch them to the finest meanings and distinctions." —Robert Louis Stevenson

"It is with words as with sunbeams, the more they are condensed, the deeper they burn." —Southey

"No noble or right style was ever yet founded but out of a sincere heart." —Ruskin

"Words are things; and a small drop of ink, falling like dew upon a thought, produces that which makes thousands, perhaps millions, think." —Byron

"A good phrase may outweigh a poor library." —Thomas W. Higginson

Table of Contents

FOREWORD 3

INTRODUCTION 4

HOW TO USE THIS BOOK 6

PLAN OF STUDY 7

SECTION I 9

USEFUL PHRASES 9

SECTION II 58

SIGNIFICANT PHRASES 58

SECTION III 86

FELICITOUS PHRASES 86

SECTION IV 102

IMPRESSIVE PHRASES 102

SECTION V 115

PREPOSITIONAL PHRASES 115

SECTION VI 137

BUSINESS PHRASES 137

SECTION VII 147

LITERARY EXPRESSIONS 147

SECTION VIII 180

STRIKING SIMILES 180

SECTION IX 215

CONVERSATIONAL PHRASES 215

SECTION X 235

PUBLIC SPEAKING PHRASES 235

SECTION XI 297

MISCELLANEOUS PHRASES 297

FOREWORD

Although this is a reproduction of a book published in the early 1900s, the exhaustive list of phrases and wording is a goldmine for authors that are equally seasoned or new to the craft of writing. Use the enclosed invaluable lists, broken down by categories, as a reference for when you have writer's block or want to spice up a character's dialogue. At last count, there are approximately fifteen thousand useful phrases included from the English language.

INTRODUCTION

The most influential and the most suitable expression of thought and feeling through the medium of oral language is traced to the mastery of words. Nothing is better suited to lead speakers and readers of English into an easy control of this language than the command of the phrase that expresses the thought. Every speaker's aim is to be heard and understood. A clear, crisp articulation holds an audience as by the spell of some irresistible power. The choice word, the correct phrase, are instruments that may reach the heart, and awake the soul if they fall upon the ear in melodious cadence; but if the utterance is harsh and discordant they fail to interest, fall upon deaf ears, and are as barren as seed sown on fallow ground. In language, nothing conduces so emphatically to the harmony of sounds as perfect phrasing—that is, the emphasizing of the relation of a clause to clause, and of the sentence to sentence by the systematic grouping of words. The phrase comprises a few words which denote a single idea that forms a separate part of a sentence. In this respect, it differs from the clause which is a short sentence that forms a distinct part of a composition, paragraph, or discourse. The correct phrasing is regulated by rests, such rests as do not break the continuity of a thought or the progress of the sense.

GRENVILLE KLEISER dedicated years of his industrious life to imparting the art of correct expression in speech and writing has provided many aids for those who would know not merely what to say, but how to say it. He has taught also what the great HOLMES taught, that language is a temple in which it enshrines the human soul, and that it grows out of life—out of its joys and its sorrows, its burdens and its necessities. To him, and to the writer, the deep strong voice of man and the low sweet voice of woman are never heard at a finer advantage than in the earnest but mellow tones of familiar speech. In the present volume, Mr. Kleiser furnishes an additional and an exceptional aid for those who would have a mint of phrases at their command from which to draw when in need of the golden mean for expressing thought. Few are the books fitted today to impart this knowledge, yet two centuries ago phrase-books were revered as supplements to the dictionaries, and have not by any manner of means lost their value. The guide to familiar quotations, the index to similes, the grammars, the readers, the machine-made letter-writer of perfect letters of congratulation or condolence—none are sententious enough to supply the need. By the compilation of this praxis, Mr. Kleiser has not only supplied it, but has afforded a means for the expansion of one's vocabulary by practical methods. There are thousands of persons who may profit by the systematic study of such a publication as this if they will familiarize themselves with the author's purpose by an attentive reading of the preliminary pages of his book. To speak in public pleasingly and readily and to read well are accomplishments acquired only after many days, weeks even, of practice.

Foreigners sometimes reproach us for the asperity and discordance of our speech, and in general, this reproach is just, for there are many persons who do scanty justice to the vowel-elements of our language. Although these elements constitute its music, they are continually mistreated. We flirt with and pirouette around them constantly. If it were not so, English would be found full of beauty and harmony of sound. Familiar with the maxim, "Take care of the vowels and the consonants will take care of themselves,"—a maxim that when put into practice has frequently led to the breaking-down of vowel values—the writer feels that the common custom of allowing "the consonants to take care of themselves" is pernicious. It leads to suppression or to an imperfect utterance and thus produces indistinct articulation.

The English language is so complex in character that it can scarcely be learned by rule, and can best be mastered by the study of such idioms and phrases as are provided in this book; but just as care must be taken to place every accent or stress on the proper syllable in the pronouncing of every word it contains, so must it must place the stress or emphasis on the proper word in every sentence spoken. To read or speak pleasingly, one should resort to constant practice by doing so aloud in private, or, in the presence of such persons as knowing good reading when they hear it and are masters of the melody of sounds. It was Dean Swift's belief that the common fluency of speech in many men and most women was due to a scarcity of matter and scarcity of words. He claimed a master of language possessed a mind full of ideas, and that before speaking, such a mind selected the choice word—the phrase best suited to the occasion. "Common speakers," he said, "have only one set of ideas, and one set of words to clothe them in," and these are always ready on the lips. Because he holds the Dean's view sound to-day, the writer will venture to warn the readers of this book against a habit that, growing far too common among us, should be checked, and this is the iteration and reiteration in a conversation of "the battered, stale, and trite" phrases, the like of which were credited by the worthy Dean to the women of his time.

Human thought elaborates itself with the progress of intelligence. Speech is the harvest of thought, and the relation which exists between words and the mouths that speak them must be carefully observed. Just as nothing is more beautiful than a word fitly spoken, so nothing is rarer than the use of a word in its exact meaning. There is a tendency to overwork both words and phrases that are not restricted to any class. The learned sin in this respect even as do the ignorant, and the practice spreads until it becomes an epidemic. The epidemic word with us yesterday was unquestionable "conscription"; several months ago it was "preparedness." Before then "efficiency" was heard on every side and superseded "vocational teaching," only to be displaced by "life extension" activities. "Safety-first" had a long run which was brought almost to an abrupt end by "strict accountability," but these are mere reflections of our cosmopolitan life and activities. There are others that stand out as indicators of brain-weariness. These are most frequently met in the work of our novelists.

English authors and journalists are abusing and overworking the word intrigue today. Sir Arthur Quillercouch on page 81 of his book "On the Art of Writing" uses it: "We are intrigued by the process of manufacture instead of being wearied by a description of the ready-made article." Mrs. Sidgwick in "Salt and Savour," page 232, wrote: "But what intrigued her was Little Mamma's remark at breakfast," From the Parliamentary news, one learns that "Mr. Harcourt intrigued the House of Commons by his sustained silence for two years" and that "London is interested in, and not a little intrigued, by the statement." This use of intrigue in the sense of "perplex, puzzle, trick, or deceive" dates from 1600. Then it fell into a state of somnolence, and after an existence of innocuous desuetude lasting till 1794 it was revived, only to hibernate again until 1894. It owes its new lease of life to a writer on The Westminster Gazette, a London journal notorious for its competitions in aid of the renewing of the lost meanings of words.

One is almost exasperated by the repeated use and abuse of the word "intimate" in a published work of fiction, by an author who aspires to the first rank in his profession. He writes of "the intimate dimness of the room;" "a fierce intimate whispering;" "a look that was intimate;" "the noise of the city was intimate," etc. Who has not heard, "The idea!" "What's the idea?" "Is that the idea?" "Yes, that's the idea," with an increased inflection at each repetition. And who is without a friend who at some time or another has not sprung "meticulous" upon him? Another example is afforded by the endemic use of "of sorts" which struck London while the writer was in that city a few years ago. Whence it came no one knew, but it was heard on every side. "She was a woman of sorts;" "he is a Tory of sorts;" "he had a religion of sorts;" "he was a critic of sorts." While it originally meant "of various kinds," as hats of sorts; offices of sorts; cheeses of sorts, etc., it is now used disparagingly, and implies something of a kind that is not satisfactory, or of a character that is rather poor. This, as Shakespeare might have said, is "Sodden business! There's a stewed phrase indeed!"

The abuse of phrases and the misuse of words rife among us can be checked by diligent exercises in good English, such as this book provides. These exercises, in conjunction with others to be found in different volumes by the same author, will correct careless diction and speech, and lead to the art of speaking and writing correctly; for, accuracy in using words is more a matter of habit than of theory, and once it is gained, it becomes just as easy to speak or to write good English as bad English. It was Chesterfield's resolution not to speak a word in a conversation which was not the fittest he could recall. All persons should avoid using words whose meanings they do not know, and with the correct application of which they are unfamiliar. The best spoken, and the best written English is that which conforms to the language as used by men and women of culture—a high standard, it is true, but one not so high that it is unattainable by any earnest student of the English tongue.

HOW TO USE THIS BOOK

The study of words, phrases, and literary expressions is a highly interesting pursuit. There is a reciprocal influence between thought and language. What we think molds the words we use, and the words we use react upon our thoughts. Hence a study of words is a study of ideas, and a stimulant to deep and original thinking.

We should not, however, study "sparkling words and sonorous phrases" with the object of introducing them consciously into our speech. To do so would inevitably lead to stiltedness and superficiality. Words and phrases should be studied as symbols of ideas, and as we become thoroughly familiar with them they will play an unconscious but effective part in our daily expression.

We acquire our vocabulary largely from our reading and our personal associates. The words we use are an unmistakable indication of our thought habits, tastes, ideals, and interests in life. In like manner, the habitual language of a people is a barometer of their intellectual, civil, moral, and spiritual ideals. A great and noble people express themselves in great and noble words.

Ruskin earnestly counsels us to form the habit of looking intensely at words. We should scrutinize them closely and endeavor to grasp their innermost meaning. There is an indefinable satisfaction in knowing how to choose and use words with accuracy and precision. As Fox once said, "I am never at a loss for a word, but Pitt always has the word."

All the great writers and orators have been diligent students of words. Demosthenes and Cicero were indefatigable in their study of language. Shakespeare, "infinite in faculty," took infinite pains to embody his thought in words of crystal clearness. Coleridge once said of him that one might as well try to dislodge a brick from a building with one's forefinger as to omit a single word from one of his finest passages.

Milton, master of majestic prose, under whose touch words became as living things; Flaubert, who believed there was one and one only best word with which to express a given thought; De Quincey, who exercised a weird-like power over words; Ruskin, whose rhythmic prose enchanted the ear; Keats, who brooded over phrases like a lover; Newman, of pure and melodious style; Stevenson, forever in quest of the scrupulously precise word; Tennyson, graceful and exquisite as the limpid stream; Emerson, of trenchant and epigrammatic style; Webster, whose virile words sometimes weighed a pound; and Lincoln, of simple, Saxon speech,—all these illustrious men were assiduous in their study of words.

Many persons of good education unconsciously circumscribe themselves within a small vocabulary. They have a knowledge of hundreds of desirable words which they do not put into practical use in their speech or writing. Many, too, are conscious of a poverty of language, which engenders in them a sense of timidity and self-depreciation. The method used for building a large vocabulary has usually been confined to the study of single words. This has produced good results, but it is believed that eminently better results can be obtained from a careful study of words and expressions, as furnished in this book, where words can be examined in their context.

It is intended and suggested that this study should be pursued in connection with, and as a supplement to, a good standard dictionary. Fifteen minutes a day devoted to this subject, in the manner outlined, will do more to improve and enlarge the vocabulary than an hour spent in desultory reading.

There is no better way in which to develop the mental qualities of clearness, accuracy, and precision, and to improve and enlarge the intellectual powers generally, than by regular and painstaking study of judiciously selected phrases and literary expressions.

PLAN OF STUDY

First examine the book in a general way to grasp its character, scope, and purpose. Carefully note the following plan of classification of the various kinds of phrases, and choose for initial study a section which you think will be of the most immediate value to you.

There are many advantages in keeping before you a definite purpose in your study of this book. A well-defined plan will act as an incentive to regular and systematic effort, and incidentally develop your power of concentration.

It is desirable that you set apart a certain convenient time each day for this study. Regularity tends to produce maximum results. As you progress with this work your interest will be quickened and you will realize the desirability of giving more and more time to this important subject.

When you have chosen a section of the book which particularly appeals to you, begin your actual study by reading the phrases aloud. Read them slowly and understandingly. This tends to impress them more deeply upon your mind, and is in itself one of the best and most practical ways of acquiring a large and varied vocabulary. Moreover, the practice of fitting words to the mouth rapidly develops fluency and facility of speech.

Few persons realize the great value of reading aloud. Many of the foremost English stylists devoted a certain period regularly to this practice. Cardinal Newman read aloud each day a chapter from Cicero as a means of developing his ear for sentence-rhythm. Rufus Choate, in order to increase his command of language, and to avoid sinking into mere empty fluency, read aloud daily, during a large part of his life, a page or more from some great English author. As a writer has said, "The practice of storing the mind with choice passages from the best prose writers and poets, and thus flavoring it with the essence of good literatures, is one which is commended both by the best teachers and by the example of some of the most celebrated orators, who have adopted it with signal success."

This study should be pursued with pencil in hand, so that you may readily underscore phrases which make a special appeal to you. The free use of a pencil in marking significant parts of a book is good evidence of thoroughness. This, too, will facilitate your work of subsequent review.

The habit of regularly copying, in your own handwriting, one or more pages of phrases will be of immense practical value. This exercise is a great aid in developing a facile English style. The daily use of the pen has been recommended in all times as a valuable means of developing oral and literary expression.

A helpful exercise is to pronounce a phrase aloud and then fit it into a complete sentence of your own making. This practice gives added facility and resourcefulness in the use of words.

As an enthusiastic student of good English, you should carefully note striking and significant phrases or literary expressions which you find in your general reading. These should be set down in a note-book reserved for this exclusive purpose. In this way you can prepare many lists of your own, and thus greatly augment the value of this study.

The taste for beauty, truth, and harmony in language can be developed by careful study of well-selected phrases and literary expressions as furnished in this book. A good literary style is formed principally by daily study of great English writers, by careful examination of words in their context, and by a discriminating use of language at all times.

SECTION I

USEFUL PHRASES

A

abandoned hope

abated pride

abbreviated visit

abhorred thraldom
[thraldom = enslaved or in
bondage]

abiding romance

abject submission

abjured ambition

able strategist

abnormal talents

abominably perverse

abounding happiness

abridged statement

abrogated law

abrupt transition

absolutely irrevocable

absorbed reverie

abstemious diet
[abstemious = eating and
drinking in moderation]

abstract character

abstruse reasoning

absurdly dangerous

abundant opportunity

abusive epithet

abysmally apologetic

academic rigor

accelerated progress

accentuated playfulness

accepted littleness

accessible pleasures

accessory circumstances

accidental lapse

accommodating temper

accomplished ease

accredited agent

accumulated burden

accurate appraisement

accursed enemy

accusing glance

accustomed lucidity

aching desire

acknowledged authority

acoustical effects

acquired timidity

acrid controversy

acrimonious warfare

actively zealous

actualized ideals

acutely conscious

adamantine rigidity
[adamantine = unyielding;
inflexible]

adaptive wit

adduced facts [adduce =
cite as an example]

adequate execution

adhesive quality

administered rebuke

admirable reserve

admissible evidence

admittedly inferior

admonitory gesture

adolescent youth

adorable vanity

adroit flatterer

adulated stranger

adventitious way
[adventitious = not
inherent; added
extrinsically]

adventurous mind

adverse experience

affably accommodating

affected indifference

affectionate approval

affianced lady

affirmative attitude

affluent language

affrighted slave

aggravated faults

aggregate body

aggressive selfishness

agile mind

agitated imagination

agonizing appeal

agreeable frankness

aimless confusion

airy splendor

alarming rapidity

alert acceptance

algebraic brevity

alien splendor

alleged reluctance

allegorical vein

allied subjects

alliterative suggestion

all-pervading influence

alluring idleness

alternating opinion

altogether dissimilar

altruistic ideal

amatory effusions
[amatory = expressive of sexual love]

amazing artifice

ambidextrous assistant

ambiguous grimace

ambitious project

ambling pedestrian

ambrosial essence
[ambrosial = fragrant or delicious; worthy of the gods; divine.]

amiable solicitude

amicable arrangement

amorous youth

ample culture

amusing artlessness

analogous example

analytical survey

ancestral creed

ancient garb

angelic softness

angry protestations

anguished entreaty

angular features

animated eloquence

annoying complications

anomalous appearance

anonymous benefactor

answering response

antagonistic views

antecedent facts

anticipated attention

antiquated prudery

anxious misgiving

apathetic greeting

aphoristic wit [aphoristic = Tersely phrased statement]

apish agility

apocalyptic vision

apocryphal lodger
[apocryphal = questionable authenticity]

apologetic explanation

apostrophic dignity

appalling difficulties

apparent significance

appealing picture

appointed function

apposite illustration

appreciable relief

appreciative fervor

apprehensive dread

apprentice touch

appropriate designation

approving smile

approximately correct

aptly suggested

arbitrarily imposed

arch conspirator

arched embrasure
[embrasure = flared
opening for a gun in a wall
or parapet]

archeological pursuits

architectural grandeur

ardent protest

arduous quest

arid formula

aristocratic lineage

aromatic fragrance

arrant trifling

arrested development

arrogant imposition

artful adaptation

artificial suavity

artistic elegance

artless candor

ascending supremacy

ascetic devotion

ascribed productiveness

aspiring genius

assembled arguments

asserted activity

assiduously cultivated

assimilative power

assumed humiliation

assuredly enshrined

astonishing facility

astounding mistakes

astute observer

athletic prowess

atmospheric vagueness

atoning sacrifice

atrocious expression

atrophied view

attending circumstances

attentive deference

attenuated sound

attested loyalty

attractive exordium
[exordium = introduction
of a speech or treatise]

audacious mendicant
[mendicant = depending on
alms; beggar]

audible intimations

augmented force

august tribunal

auspicious moment

austere charm

authentic indications

authoritative critic

autobiographical pages

autocratic power

automatic termination

autumnal skies

auxiliary aids

available data

avaricious eyes

avenging fate

average excellence

averted calamity

avowed intention

awakened curiosity

awed devotion

awful dejection

awkward dilemma

axiomatic truth

azure sky

B

babbling gossip

bacchanalian desires

bachelor freedom

bad omen

baffled sagacity [sagacity = farsighted; wise]

balanced capacity

baldly described

baleful glances

balmy fragrance

bandying talk

baneful impression

banished silence

barbarous statecraft

barefaced appeal

barest commonplaces

barren opportunities

base intrigues

baseless assumptions

bashful modesty

basic principles

battered witticism

beaming countenance

bearish rudeness

beatific vision

beautiful modesty

beckoning horizon

becoming diffidence

bedraggled wretch

befitting honor

beggarly flimsiness

beguiling voice

belated acknowledgment

belittling fears

bellicose humanity

beneficent career

benevolent regard

benighted sense

benignant pity [benignant = favorable; beneficial; kind]

beseeching gesture

besetting heresy

besotted fanaticism

bestial ferocity

bewildering maze

bewitching airs

beyond peradventure [peradventure = perhaps]

bibulous diversions [bibulous = consumes alcoholic drink]

bigoted contempt

binding obligation

bitter recrimination

bizarre apparel

blackening west

blameless indolence

blanched desolation

bland confidence

blank misgivings

blasphemous hypocrisy

blatant discourse

blazing audacity

blazoned shield

bleak loneliness

blended impression

blessed condolence

blighted happiness

blind partisan

blissful consciousness

blistering satire

blithe disregard

bloated equivalent

bloodless creature

bloodthirsty malice

blundering discourtesy

blunt rusticity [rusticity = rustic; awkward or tactless]

blurred vision

blustering assertion

boastful positiveness

bodily activity

boisterous edification

bold generalization

bombastic prating [prating = idle talk]

bookish precision

boon companion

boorish abuse

bored demeanor

borrowed grace

bottomless abyss

boundless admiration

bountiful supply

boyish appreciation

braggart pretense

bravely vanquished

braying trumpet

brazen importunity [importunity = insistent request]

breathless eagerness

brief tenure

briefless barrister

bright interlude

brilliant embodiment

brisk energy

bristling temper

brittle sarcasm

broadening fame

broken murmurs

brooding peace

brutal composure

bubbling frivolities

bucolic cudgeling [bucolic = about shepherds or flocks; pastoral] [cudgeling = beat with a short heavy stick]

budding joy

bulky figure

buoyant pluck

burdensome business

burly strength

burning zeal

bursting laugh

busily engrossed

business acumen

bygone period

C

cabalistic phrase [cabalistic = secret or hidden meaning]

cadaverous appearance

calamitous course

calculating admiration

callous indifference

calm resignation

calumnious suspicions [calumnious = harmful and often untrue; discredit]

cantankerous enemy

canting hypocrite [canting = monotonous platitudes; hypocritically pious]

capacious mind

capricious allurements

captivating speech

cardinal merit

careless parrying

caressing grasp

carping critic

castellated towers [castellated = with turrets and battlements like a castle]

casual violation

cataclysmic elements

causelessly frightened

caustic remark

cautious skepticism

cavernous gloom

ceaseless vigilance

celebrated instance

celestial joy

censorious critic

centralized wealth

ceremonious courtesy

cerulean blue [cerulean = azure; sky-blue]

challenge admiration

chance reflections

changing exigencies [exigencies = pressing or urgent situation]

chaotic plans

characteristic audacity

charitable allowance

charming radiance

chary instincts [chary = cautious; wary]

chastened hope

chatty familiarity

cheap resentment

cheery response

chequered career

cherished objects

childlike ingenuousness [ingenuous = frank; candid.]

chilled cynicism

chirpy familiarities

chivalrous spirit

choicest refinements

choleric temperament [choleric = easily angered; bad-tempered]

choral chant

chronic frailties

churlish temper [churlish = boorish; vulgar; rude]

circling eddyings

circuitous information

circumscribed purpose

civic consciousness

civilizing influence

clammy death

clamorous vibration

clangorous industry

clarion tone

class demarcations

classical objurgation [objurgation = harsh rebuke]

clattering accents

clear insight

climactic revelation

clinching proof

cloaked nature

cloistered virtue

close condensation

cloudy magnificence

clownishly insensible

cloying sweetness [cloying = too filling, rich, or sweet]

clumsy talk

clustering trees

coarse necessity

coaxing eloquence

coercive enactment

cogent statement

coherent thinking

coined metaphor

cold formalities

collateral duties

collective wisdom

colloquial display

colonial character

colossal failure

comatose state

combative tone

comforting reassurance

comic infelicity

commanding attitude

commendable purpose

commercial opulence

commingled emotion

commodiously arranged

common substratum

commonplace allusions

compact fitness

comparative scantiness

compassionate love

compelling force

compendious abstract

compensatory character

competent authority

competitive enterprise

complacent platitudes

complaining sea

complaisant observation

complete aloofness

complex notions

complicated maze

complimentary glance

component aspects

composed zeal

composite growth

compound idea

comprehensive design

compressed view

compromising rashness

compulsory repetition

compunctious visitings [compunctious = feeling guilt]

concatenated pedantries [pedantries = attention to detail or rules]

concealed advantage

conceivable comparison

concentrated vigor

concerted action

conciliating air

concomitant events

concrete realities

concurrent testimony

condemnable rashness

condescending badinage [badinage = frivolous banter]

conditional approval

confessed ardor

confidently anticipated

confirmed misanthrope [misanthrope = one who dislikes people in general]

conflicting influences

confused mingling

conjectural estimate

conjugal felicity

connected series

connotative damage

connubial love

conquering intelligence

conscientious objection

conscious repugnance

consecrated endeavor

consequent retribution

conservative distrust

considerate hint

consistent friendliness

consoling consciousness

conspicuous ascendency

constant reiteration

constitutional reserve

constrained politeness

constructive idealists

consuming zeal

consummate mastery

contagious wit

contaminating influence

contemplative nature

contemporary fame

contemptuous disrespect

contented indolence

contingent reasons

continuous endeavor

contorted expression

contracted view

contradictory theories

contrary tendencies

contrasted types

controversial disputant

contumelious epithet [contumelious = Rudeness or contempt arising from arrogance]

convenient footing

conventional verbiage

conversational decorum

convincing forcefulness

convivial habits

convulsive agony

cool confidence

copious materials

coquettish advances

cordial approval

corporate selfishness

corporeal constituent

correct forecast

corresponding variation

corroborated truth

corrosive effect

corrupting tendency

cosmical changes

cosmopolitan position

costly advantages

counterbalancing power

countless barriers

courageous eagerness

courteous solicitude

courtly bearing

covert curiosity

coveted honors

cowardly concession

cowering agitation

coy reluctance

crackling laughter

crafty deception

craggy eminence

cramped energies

crass stolidity

craven determination

creative faculty

credibly informed

creditable performance

credulous superstition

creeping progress

criminal negligence

cringing smile

crisp dialogue

critical judgment

crouching culprit

crowning indiscretion

crucial instance

crucifying irony

crude affectation

cruel handicap

crumbling precipice

crunching jangle

crushing sorrow

cryptic saying

crystalline sky

crystallized conclusions

culinary myrmidons [myrmidon = one who carries out orders without question]

culminating fascination

culpable behavior

cultivated ferocity

cultured idleness

cumbrous fragments [cumbrous = cumbersome; difficult to handle or use]

cumulative tendency

cunningly contrived

curbed profligacy

curious coincidence

current gossip

curry favor

cursed inactivity

cursory acquaintance

curt formality

curtained embrasure

cutting directness

cycloramic sweep

cynical disregard

D

damaging admission

damask cheek [damask = rich patterned fabric; wavy pattern on Damascus steel]

dampened ardor

dancing sunshine

dangerous temerity

dappled shadows

daring candor

dark superstition

dashing gallantry

dastardly injustice

dauntless courage

dawning instinct

dazed brain

dazzling triumph

deadly virulence

deaf tribunal

deathless structure

debasing tendency

debatable point

debilitating features

decadent poets

deceiving mists

decided superiority

decisive manner

declamatory treatment [declamatory = pretentiously rhetorical; bombastic]

declared brotherhood

decorously adorned

deepening dusk

deep-seated curiosity

deep-toned lamentations

defective construction

defenseless innocence

defensive alliance

deferential regard

defiant coldness

deficient vitality

definite conception

deformed visage

deft evasion

degrading tendencies

delectable speculations

delegated power

deliberate abnegation [abnegation = self-denial]

delicate discrimination

delicious vagueness

delightful variation

delirious ecstasies

delusive charm

demagogic style

democratic institutions

demoniacal force

demonstrable conclusion

demoralizing luxury

demure composure

denunciatory terms

departed glories

deplorable decay

deprecatory shrug

depressing concomitants

depthless forest

derisive voice

derogatory denial

descriptive power

desecrated ideals

deserted desert

deserved approbation [approbation = warm approval; praise]

desirable distinction

desolating dread

despairing austerity

desperate defiance

despicable vices

despondent exaggeration

despotic rulers

destructive radicalism

desultory vacillation [desultory = disconnected; haphazard; random]

detailed portraiture

detected hypocrisies

determinate swing

detestable purpose

dethroned princes

detrimental result

devastating effect

devilish sophistries

deviously subtle

devitalized personality

devoted attachment

devouring ambition

devout thanksgiving

dewy coolness

dexterous impudence

diabolical passion

dialectic power

diametrically opposite

dictatorial manner

dictionary significance

didactic exposition [didactic = intended to be morally instructive]

different distortion

difficult portraiture

diffident civility [diffident = lacking self-confidence; shy; timid]

diffuse verbosity

dignified austerity

digressional adventure

dilettante mind [dilettante = dabbler in a field of knowledge]

diligently propagated

dim comprehension

diminished efficacy

diminutive stature

diplomatic skill

dire consummation

direct obligation

disappointing attitude

disarmed criticism

disastrous termination

discarded reminiscences

discerning critic

disciplined mind

disclosed insincerity

discomfited opponent

disconcerted conjecture

disconnected fancies

disconsolate opinions

discordant sounds

discredited statement

discretional opinion

discriminating homage

discursive staggerings

disdainful comment

diseased hallucinations

disembodied personality

disengaged air

disfiguring disguise

disgraceful plight

disgruntled pessimist

disguised contempt

disgusted protest

disheartening facts

dishonorable submission

disillusioned youth

disintegrating tendency

disinterested motive

disjoined reminiscences

dismal seclusion

dismantled appearance

disordered imagination

disparaging criticism

dispassionate judgment

dispelling fear

displeasing softness

disproportionate ideas

disputative philosopher

disquieting thrill

disreputable aspect

dissenting opinion

dissimilar laws

dissipated illusion

dissolute audacity

dissolving years

dissonant jargon

distant adherent

distasteful notion

distempered feeling

distinct desideratum

distorted vanity

distracting babble

distraught air

distressing laxity

disturbed equanimity

diurnal rotation

divergent calculations

diversified attributes

diverting interests

divine potentialities

dizzy precipice

documentary evidence

dogged determination

doggerel expressions
[doggerel = crude,
humorous verse]

dogmatic assurance

doleful forebodings

domestic endearment

dominating influence

domineering insolence

dormant capacities

doubly odious

doubtful authenticity

downright nonsense

downtrodden drudge

drab apology

dramatic liveliness

drastic action

dread presence

dreaming adventurer

dreamless rest

dreary disrelish

droll incongruity

droning world

drowsy tranquillity

dubious success

ductile language

dulcet tone

dull aversion

dumb surprise

dumbfounded amazement

durable impression

dusky obscurity

dutiful compliance

dynamic energy

dynastic insolence

E

eager animosity

early servitude

earnestly espoused

earthly splendor

easy garrulity [garrulity = excessive talkativeness]

eccentric casuists [casuistry = excessively subtle reasoning intended to mislead]

ecclesiastical rule

echoless silence

economic absurdity

ecstatically happy

edifying exhortation

educational enterprise

effective embellishment

effectual stimulus

effeminate grace

effervescent multitude

effete aristocracy

efficacious power

efficient education

efflorescent style [efflorescent = bursting into flower]

effulgent daybeams [effulgent = radiating light]

egoistic sentiment

egregious mistake [egregious = outrageously reprehensible]

ejaculatory prayer

elaborate composition

elastic ductility

electric effluvium [effluvium = invisible emanation; an aura]

elegant mediocrity

elemental emotions

elephantine footsteps

elevated enjoyment

elfish grace

eloquent refutation

elusive charm

emancipating labors

embarrassing variety

embellished truths

embittered gaze

emblazoned pinnacles

embryo enterprise

emerald scintillations

eminent nonentity

emotional warmth

emotive power

emphatic earnestness

empirical corroboration

empty phraseology

emulative zeal

enamored troubadour

enchanted garden

encircling embrace

endearing appellation [appellation = name, title; act of naming]

endless dissertation

enduring charm

energetic enthusiasm

enervating humility [enervating = weaken or destroy the strength]

enfeebled activity

enforced silence

engaging affability

engendered feelings

engrossing purpose

engulfing waters

enhanced reputation

enigmatical silence

enlightened solicitude

enlivened monotony

ennobling personality

enormously outbalanced

enraptured attention

enriched experience

entangled subject

enthralling charm

enthusiastic adherents

enticing odors

entire domain

entrancing sadness

enveloping presence

envenomed attacks

enviable superiority

environing conditions

ephemeral duration
[ephemeral = markedly
short-lived]

epicurean taste

epigrammatic sallies
[epigrammatic = terse and
witty]

equable composure

equally efficacious

equitably governed

equivocal compliment

erotic poem

errant thoughts

erratic flight

erroneous assumption

erudite labors [erudite =
having or showing
profound knowledge]

eruptive violence

esoteric doctrine

especial pleasure

essential prerequisite

estimable qualities

eternal hostility

ethereal azure

ethical wisdom

euphuistic affectations
[euphuistic = affected
elegance of language]

evanescent glances
[evanescent = vanishing
like vapor]

evangelic doctrine

evasive answer

eventful circumstance

eventual failure

everlasting mysteries

everyday reality

evident authority

evil necromancy
[necromancy =
communicating with the
dead to predict the future;
black magic; sorcery]

eviscerating shrieks

exact antithesis

exacting taskmaster

exaggerated estimate

exalted imagination

exasperating coolness

exceedingly acceptable

excellent discernment

exceptional magnitude

excessive zeal

excitable temperament

exclusive pursuit

excretory secretion

excruciating accents

excursive fancy

execrable villainy [execrable = hateful; extremely inferior; very bad]

executive efficiency

exemplary conduct

exhaustless energy

exhilarating charm

exoteric scorn [exoteric = easily comprehensible; popular; outside]

exotic appearance

expansive benevolence

expectant throng

expeditionary force

expeditiously secreted

experimental suggestion

expiatory sacrifices

explicit injunction

explosive violence

expressionless visage

expressive lineaments [lineaments = distinctive shape, especially of the face]

exquisite tact

extemporaneous effusion

extended magnitude

extenuating circumstance

external cheerfulness

extraneous ideas

extraordinary vivacity

extravagant caprice

extremely picturesque

exuberant mirth

exultant condition

F

facetious mood

facile criticism

factitious propensity

faded magnificence

faintly sinister

faithfully perpetuated

fallacious hopes

false illusions

faltering tongue

familiar sacredness

famished voracity

fanatical admiration

fanciful alliance

fantastic display

farcical expedient

far-reaching influence

fascinating illusiveness

fashioned symmetrically

fastidious taste

fatal disclosure

fatalistic belief

fathomless powers

fatiguing assertion

fattening servitude

fatuous pedantry [pedantry = attention to detail or rules]

faultless taste

favorable augury

fawning flatteries

fearful imprecations

fearless integrity

feasible mode

feeble dribble

feigned reluctance

felicitous expression

feminine capriciousness

ferocious foe

fertile fancy

fervent invocation

fervid enthusiasm

festive illuminations

fetid dampness

fettered tyranny

feverish bewilderment

fickle fancy

fictitious pretext

fidgety impatience

fierce resentment

fiery indignation

figurative eloquence

filial tenderness

final enthronement

fine sensibilities

finished artistry

fireside delights

fitful desire

fitting opportunity

fizzing flame

flaccid faith

flagging popularity

flagitious attack [flagitious = extremely brutal or cruel crimes; vicious; infamous]

flagrant boasting

flamboyant brilliancy

flaming zeal

flashing wit

flat denial

flattering aspect

flaunting insolence

flawless constitution

fleecy clouds

fleeting intimation

flickering conscience

flighty obstinacy

flimsy organization

flippant ease

floating blackness

florid oratory [florid = ornate; flowery]

flowery circumlocution

flowing imagery

fluctuating light

fluent sophist

fluffy indignation

fluid ideas

flushed embarrassment

fluttering laugh

focused attention

foggy notion

fond enthusiast

foolish frenzy

forbearing silence

forbidding air

forceful audacity

foregone conclusion

foremost opponent

forensic orator

forest stillness

forgotten graveyard

forlorn desolation

formal acquiescence

formidable barrier

formless jottings

formulated conclusions

fortified selfishness

fortuitous circumstance

foul calumny [calumny = maliciously lying to injure a reputation]

fragile form

fragmentary facts

fragrant reminiscence

frail craft

frank admiration

frantic ardor

fraternal pity

freakish humor

freeborn soul

freezing disdain

frenzied haste

frequent digression

fresh impetus

freshening breeze

fretful discontent

friendly familiarity

frightened sense

frightful apparition

frigid disdain

frisky lightness

frivolous expedient

frolicsome extravagance

frozen wonder

fructifying thought [fructifying = make fruitful or productive]

fruitful indignation

fruitless repining

fugitive thoughts

full plenitude

fulsome praise

fumbling endeavor

functional disparity

fundamental principles

funereal gloom

furious invective [invective = abusive language]

furrowed cheeks

furtive glance

fussy enthusiasms

futile babble

G

gabbling reminiscences [gabbling = speak rapidly or incoherently; jabber]

galling thought

galvanic jumpings

gaping chasm

garbled information

garish decorations

garnered experience

gathering gloom

gaudy embellishments

gaunt specter

gay defiance

general acclamation

generative influence

generic characteristics

generous abundance

genial tolerance

genteel parlance

gentle blandishments [blandishments = coax by flattery]

gentlemanly personage

genuine cynicism

geological enigma

geometrical progression

germinal idea

ghastly loneliness

ghostly apparitions

giant height

giddy pleasure

gifted intelligence

gigantic sagacity [sagacity = discerning, sound in judgment; wisdom.]

girlish sprightliness

gladdening influence

gladiatorial exercise

gladsome glow

glaring impropriety

glassy smoothness

gleaming escutcheon [escutcheon = shield-shaped emblem bearing a coat of arms]

gleeful spirit

glibly condoned

gliding measures

glimmering idea

glistening dewdrop

glittering epigram

gloomy musing

glorious freedom

glossed faults

glowering countenance

glowing anticipations

gnawing thoughts

godlike independence

golden opportunity

good-humored gibes

gorgeous splendor

gossiping opinion

governing impulse

graceful demeanor

gracious immunity

graduated sequence

grandiose nomenclature

graphic portrayal

grasping credulity

gratuitous rudeness

grave reticence

greedy grasp

gregarious humanity

grievously mistaken

grim swiftness

grinding despotism

grinning ghosts

griping fascination

grizzled warrior

gross exaggeration

grotesque perversion

groundless fear

groveling servility

growing tension

grudging thanks

grumbling monotone

guileless zeal

gullible humanity

gurgling brooks

gushing enthusiasm

gusty clamor

guttural incoherence

gymnastic agility

H

habitual deference

hackneyed statement

hairbreadth difference

halcyon innocence [halcyon = tranquil; prosperous; golden]

hallowed stillness

halting praise

hampered power

handsomely recompensed

haphazard ostentation

happy intuition

harassing anxiety

hardened indifference

harmless mirth

harmonious grace

harrowing details

harsh jarrings

hasty generalization

hateful malignity

haughty composure

haunting despair

hazardous enterprise

hazy recollection

headlong vehemence

healthful vitality

heartfelt amity

heartless perfidy [perfidy = breach of faith; treachery]

heartrending outcry

hearty contempt

heated discussion

heathen hordes

heavenly ecstasies

heavy handicap

hectic tittering

hectoring rant

heedless love

heightened charm

heinous enormity

helpless innocence

herculean monster

hereditary arrogance

heretical opinions

hermetically sealed

heroic fortitude

hesitating courage

heterogeneous mass

hidden pitfalls

hideous phantom

high-flying theories

highly meritorious

hilarious outburst

hillside mist

hissing murmur

historic edifice

hoarded vengeance

hoary antiquity

hollow joys

homebred virtues

homeless wind

homely pathos

homespun play

homicidal mania

homogeneous whole

honest admiration

honeyed eloquence

hooligan wind

hopelessly befogged

horrible swiftness

horrid significance

hortatory moonshine

hospitable courtesy

hostile partisan

hot frenzy

hovering presence

howling chaos

huddled faculties

huge aspiration

human derelict

humanitarian impulse

humbly propitiating
[propitiating = appeasing]

humdrum inconsistencies

humid luster

humiliating discomfiture

humorless variety

humorous urbanity

hungry satisfaction

hurrying years

hurtful indulgence

hushed laughter

husky shrillness

hybrid emotions

hypnotic fascination

hypochondriacal terrors

hypocritical pretense

hysterical agitation

I

iconoclastic attitude

icy smile

idealistic type

identical mode

idiomatic propriety

idiotic obstinacy

idle jesting

idolatrous fervor

idyllic nonsense

ignoble domination

ignominious retreat

ill-concealed impatience

illiberal superstition

illimitable progression

illiterate denizens

illogical interruption

illuminating insight

illusive touch

illustrative anecdote

illustrious era

imaginative warmth

imbittered controversy

immaterial connection

immature dissent

immeasurable scorn

immediate abjuration
[abjuration = renounce
under oath]

immemorial bulwark

immense complacency

imminent perplexities

immitigable contempt

immoderate grief

immortal creation

immovably silent

immutable law

impaired prestige

impalpable nothingness

impartial justice

impassable serenity

impassioned impulse

impatient yearning

impeccable felicity

impecunious exile

impelling movement

impending fate

impenetrable calmness

imperative necessity

imperceptible deviation

imperfect equipment

imperial authority

imperious mind [imperious = arrogantly domineering or overbearing]

imperishable renown

impersonal compliment

impertinent drollery

imperturbable gravity

impetuous zeal

impious defiance

impish humor

implacable resentment

implicit faith

implied concealment

implored pardon

imponderable air

important epoch

importunate questions [importunate = insistent request]

imposing mien [mien = manner revealing a state of mind; appearance or aspect]

impossible contingency

impotent desperation

impoverished age

impracticable obstinacy

impregnable fortress

impressionistic stroke

imprisoning limitations

improbable conjecture

impromptu utterance

improvising powers

imprudent indebtedness

impudent knowingness

impulsive gratitude

inaccessible dignity

inadequate appreciation

inadmissible expression

inadvertent remark

inalienable right

inanimate existence

inapposite blandness [inapposite = inappropriate or misapplied nature]

inaptly designated

inarticulate lisping

inaugural discourse

inborn refinement

inbred taste

incalculable mischief

incarnate hate

incendiary opinions

incessant volume

incidental duty

incipient fancy

incisive critic

incoherent loquacity [loquacity = very talkative]

incommunicable gift

incomparable excellence

incompletely apprehended

inconceivable absurdity

incongruous contrast

inconsiderable trifle

inconsistent conduct

inconsolable cares

incontestable inference

incontrovertible proof

incorrigible merriment

incorruptible constancy

increasing clamor

incredible swiftness

indecent saturnalia
[saturnalia = unrestrained
revelry; an orgy]

indecorously amused

indefatigable diligence
[indefatigable = tireless]

indefeasible title
[indefeasible = cannot be
annulled]

indefinable reluctance

indefinite yearning

indelible obligation

indelicate impetuosity

indented outline

independent research

indescribably lugubriou
[lugubriou = exaggerated
gloom]

indestructible atoms

indeterminable value

indifferent promise

indigenous growth

indignant denunciation

indirect interrogation

indiscriminate censure

indispensable requisites

indisputable chronicler

indissoluble compact

indistinct association

individual valor

indivisible aspects

indolent neglect

indomitable pride

indubitable signs

indulgent construction

indwelling delight

ineffable disdain

ineffaceable incongruity
[ineffaceable = indelible]

ineffectual blandishment

ineradicable coquetry

inestimable honor

inevitable corollary

inexcusable laughter

inexhaustible abundance

inexorable authority
[inexorable = incapable of
being persuaded]

inexplicable reluctance

inexpressible benignity

inextricable confusion

infallible judgment

infamous pretense

infantile simplicity

infectious hilarity

infelicitous arrangement

inferential method

infernal machinations

infinite deference

infinitesimal gradations

infirm purpose

inflamed curiosity

inflated optimism

inflexible integrity

influential voice

informing feature

infuriated demagogues

ingenious trick

inglorious victory

ingrained love

ingratiating exterior

inharmonious prelude

inherent dignity

inherited anxieties

inimitable felicity

iniquitous fortune

initiatory period

injudicious yielding

injured conceit

inky blackness

inmost recesses

innate forbearance

inner restlessness

innocent amenities

innocuous desuetude
[desuetude = state of
disuse or inactivity]

innovating spirit

inoffensive copiousness

inopportune condition

inordinate ambition

inquisitional rack

inquisitive observer

insatiable vanity

inscrutable austerity

insecure truce

insensate barbarism

insensibly flattered

inseparably associated

insidious tendency

insignificant blot

insincere profession

insinuatingly pursued

insipid tameness

insistent babel

insolent placidity

insoluble riddles

inspiring achievement

inspiriting spectacle

instant readiness

instantaneous cessations

instinctive disapproval

insufferably dull

insufficient appeal

insular strength

insulting invectives
[invective = abusive
language]

insuperable difficulty

insurmountable obstacles

intangible something

integral element

intellectual integrity

intelligent adaptation

intemperate scorn

intense perplexity

intensive cultivation

intentional garbling

interior spirit

interlocking directorate

intermediate link

interminable question

intermingled gloom

intermittent threats

internal dissension

interpolated speech

interpretative criticism

interwoven thread

intimately allied

intolerably tedious

intoxicating hum

intractable temper

intrenched privilege

intrepid dexterity

intricate interlacing

intriguing braggart

intrinsic fecundity [fecundity = productive or creative power]

intrusive brightness

intuitive perception

invaluable composition

invariable kindness

inveighing incessantly [inveighing = angry disapproval]

inventive jealousy

inveterate antipathy

invidious mention [invidious = rousing ill will or resentment]

invigorating discipline

invincible optimism

inviolable confidence

involuntary yearnings

involuted sentences [involuted = intricate; complex]

involved pomposity

invulnerable solemnity

inward disinclination

irascible doggedness

irate remonstrance

iridescent sheen

irksome task

iron resolution

ironic iciness

irradiating spirit

irrational awe

irreclaimable dead

irreconcilable parting

irrecoverably lost

irrefragable laws [irrefragable = indisputable]

irrefutable argument

irregular constellations

irrelevant suggestion

irremediable sorrow

irreparable injury

irrepressible excitement

irreproachable exterior

irresistible will

irresponsible gossip

irretrievable blunder

irreverent audacity

irreversible facts

irrevocable verdict

irritable impatience

isolated splendor

J

jaded sensibility

jagged outline

jarring discord

jaundiced opinion

jaunty confidence

jealous animosity

jesting allusion

jingling alliteration

jocular mirth

jocund host [jocund = sprightly; lighthearted]

jostling confusion

jovial fancy

joyful alacrity

joyous stagnation

jubilant antagonist

judicial impartiality

judicious candor

just rebuke

juvenile attempt

K

kaleidoscopic pictures

keen insight

kindled enthusiasm

kindly innocence

kindred sympathies

kingly generosity

knavish conduct

knightly achievement

known disingenuousness [ingenuous = frank; candid.]

L

labored levity

labyrinthian windings

lacerated feelings

lachrymose monotony

lackadaisical manner

laconic force

lagging footsteps

lamentable helplessness

languid impertinence

large receptivity

lashing scorn

latent conviction

laudable zeal

laughable absurdity

lavish liberality

lawless freedom

lazy acquiescence

leaden steps

leaping ambition

learned gravity

leering smile

legal perspicacity [perspicacity = perceptive, discerning]

legendary associations

legislative enactment

legitimate inference

leisurely composure

lengthening shadows

leonine powers

lethargic temperament

lettered coxcomb [coxcomb = conceited dandy; jester's cap]

liberal contemplations

lifeless imbecility

lifelong adherence

lightless eyes

lightly disregard

lightning glare

limpid twilight

lingering tenderness

linguistic attainments

liquid eloquence

lisping utterance

listening reverence

listless apathy

literal exactness

literary research

lithe contortions

little idiosyncrasies

lively susceptibility

livid lightning

living manifestation

loathsome oppression

local busybody

loftiest aspirations

logical precision

lone magnificence

longing fancy

looming probabilities

loquacious assurances [loquacious = very talkative]

lordly abhorrence

loud vociferation [vociferation = cry out loudly, especially in protest]

lounging gait

loutish rudeness

lovingly quizzical

lowering aspects

lowest degradation

loyal adhesion

lucid treatment

lucrative profession

ludicrous incongruity

lugubrious question [lugubrious = mournful, dismal, gloomy]

lukewarm repentance

lumbering gaiety

luminous interpretation

lurid picturesqueness

lurking suspicion

lustrous surface

luxuriant richness

lying equivocations

M

maddening monotony

magic fascination

magisterial emphasis

magnanimous concessions

magnetic fascination

magnificent florescence

magniloquent diction [magniloquent = extravagant in speech]

maidenly timidity

main ramifications

majestic dignity

maladjusted marriages

malevolent ingenuity

malicious aspersions

malign influence

malodorous gentility

manageable proportions

mangled arguments

manifest reluctance

manifold functions

manly reticence

mantling smile [mantling = cover with a mantle; concealing]

manual dexterity

manufactured melancholy

marked individuality

marketable commodity

marshaled hosts

martial footsteps

marvelous lucidity

masculine power

masked expression

massive strength

master achievement

matchless charm

material misconception

maternal solicitude

mathematical precision

matrimonial alliance

matured reflection

maudlin sentimentalism
[maudlin = tearfully
sentimental]

mawkish insipidity

maximum intensity

meager evidence

mean trickeries

meaningless confusion

measured cadence

mechanical handicraft

meditatively silent

meek ambition

melancholy musing

mellifluous eloquence
[mellifluous = flowing
with sweetness or honey]

mellow refinement

melodious platitudes

melodramatic resource

melting mood

memorable experience

menacing attitude

mendacious tongue
[mendacious = false;
untrue]

mendicant pilgrim
[mendicant = beggar]

mental metamorphosis

mercenary view

merchantable literature

merciful insensibility

merciless censor

mercurial temperament

mere generalization

meretricious allurements
[meretricious = plausible
but false]

meridian splendor

merited ridicule

merry jest

metallic immobility

metaphysical obscurity

meteoric splendors

methodical regularity

metrical exactness

microscopic minuteness

mighty animosity

mild rejoinder

militant struggles

military autocracy

millennial reign

mimic gestures

minatory shadow
[minatory = menacing or
threatening]

mincing precision

mingled decorousness

miniature imitations

minor impulses

minute consideration

miraculous profusion

mirroring lake

mirthful glance

mischievous effusion

miserable musings

misleading notion

misshapen oddities

misspent strength

mistaken assumption

mistrustful superiority

misty depression

mitigating circumstances

mobile countenance

mock seriousness

modest cheerfulness

modified sentiment

moldy doctrines

mollifying conditions
[mollifying = calming;
soothing]

momentary discomfiture

momentous pause

monarchial institutions

monastic austerity

monotonous sameness

monstrous absurdity

monumental structure

moody silence

moonlight witchery

moral obliquity [obliquity
= deviation or aberration]

morbid imagination

mordant wit

moribund mediocrities

mortal affront

mortified coldness

motley appearance

mountainous inequalities

mournful magnificence

mouthing amplitude

muddled opinion

muddy inefficiency

muffled detonations

mullioned windows
[mullioned = vertical
member dividing a
window]

multifarious activity

multiform truth

multiple needs

multitudinous details

mundane importance

mural decorations

murderous parody

murky recesses

musical diapason
[diapason = full, rich
outpouring of harmonious
sound]

mute insensibility

mutinous thoughts

muttered warning

mutual animosity

myriad lights

mysterious potency

mystic meaning

mythical kingdom

N

naive manner

naked eye

nameless fear

narcotic effect

narrowing axioms

nasal drone

nascent intercourse

national shortcomings

native incompetence

natural sluggishness

nauseous dose

nautical venture

neat refutation

nebulous uncertainty

necessary adjuncts

necromantic power
[necromancy =
communicating with the
dead to predict the future.
Black magic; sorcery.]

needless depression

nefarious scheme

negative approbation [approbation = warm approval; praise]

negligible quantity

neighboring mists

nerveless hand

nervous solicitude

nettled opponent

neutral eye

new perplexities

nice discrimination

niggardly allowance

nightmare fantasy

nimble faculty

noble condescension

nocturnal scene

nodding approval

noiseless reverie

noisy platitudes

nomadic life

nominal allegiance

nonchalant manner

non-committal way

nondescript garb

nonsense rhymes

noonday splendor

normal characteristics

notable circumstance

noteworthy friendship

noticeably begrimed

notoriously profligate

novel signification

nugatory cause [nugatory = little or no importance; trifling]

numbed stillness

numberless defeats

numerical majority

O

obdurate courage [obdurate = hardened in wrongdoing]

obedient compliance

objectionably apologetic

obligatory force

obligingly expressed

oblique tribute

obscure intimation

obsequious homage [obsequious = servile compliance; fawning]

observant eye

obsolete phraseology

obstinate defiance

obstreperous summons [obstreperous = noisily and stubbornly defiant]

obtrusive neatness

obvious boredom

occasional flights

occult sympathy

ocean depth

odd makeshifts

odious tyranny

odorous spring

offensive hostility

official asperity [asperity = harshness; ill temper or irritability]

olfactory sense

olive grayness

ominous rumors

omnipotent decree

omniscient affirmation

oncoming horde

onerous cares

onflaming volume

opalescent sea

opaque mass

openly disseminated

opinionated truculence
[truculence = ferociously
cruel behavior]

opportunely contrived

oppressive emptiness

opprobrious epithet
[opprobrious =
contemptuous reproach;
scornful]

oracular utterance
[oracular = solemnly
prophetic; enigmatic;
obscure]

oratorical display

ordinary delinquencies

organic assimilation

oriental spicery

originally promulgated

oscillatory movement

ostensible occupation

ostentatious display

outlandish fashion

outrageously vehement

outspoken encouragement

outstanding feature

outstretching sympathies

outward pomp

outworn creed

overbearing style

overestimated importance

overflowing sympathy

overhanging darkness

overmastering potency

overpowering argument

overshadowing dread

overstrained enthusiasm

overt act

overvaulting clouds

overweening sense
[overweening =
presumptuously arrogant;
overbearing]

overwhelming solicitude

overworked drudge

P

pacific disposition

painful obstinacy

painstaking reticence

palatable advice

pallidly illumined

palpable originality

palpitating emotion

paltry hypocrisies

pampered darling

panic fear

panting eagerness

parabolic obscureness

paradoxical talker

paralyzing sentimentalism

paramount authority

parasitical magnificence

parental permission

paroxysmal outburst

particularly notable

partizan prejudice

passing panorama

passionate insistence

passive obedience

patchwork manner

patent example

paternal tenderness

pathetic helplessness

patient endurance

patriarchal visage

patriotic enthusiasm

peacefully propagated

peculiar piquancy
[piquancy = appealingly
provocative; charming]

pecuniary privation

pedantic ineptitude
[pedantic = attention to
detail or rules]

pedestrian vigor

peerless raconteur
[raconteur = skilled
storyteller]

peevish ingratitude

pending determination

penetrating warmth

penitential cries

penniless wanderer

pensive reflections

perceptible difference

peremptory punishment
[peremptory = ending all
debate or action]

perennial charm

perfect embodiment

perfunctory inquiries

perilous expedient

permanent significance

pernicious doctrine

perpetual oscillation

perplexing problem

persecuting zeal

persistent adherence

personal predilection
[predilection = a
preference]

persuasive eloquence

pert prig

pertinacious solemnity
[pertinacious = stubbornly
persistent]

pertinent question

perusing earnestness

pervading tendencies

perverse quaintness

pessimistic skepticism

pestiferous career
[pestiferous = evil or
deadly; pernicious]

pet aversion

petrified smile

petticoat diplomacy

pettifogging business

petty pedantries
[pedantries = attention to
detail or rules]

phantom show

philanthropic zeal

philosophical acuteness

phlegmatic temperament
[phlegmatic = calm,
sluggish; unemotional]

phosphorescent shimmer

photographic exactitude

physical convulsion

pictorial embellishments

picturesque details

piercing clearness

pinchbeck dignity
[pinchbeck = cheap
imitation]

pining melancholy

pioneering spirit

pious platitudes

piquant allusions [piquant = attracting or delighting]

pitiable frenzy

pitiless precision

pivotal point

placid stupidity

plainly expedient

plainspoken rebuke

plaintive cadence

plastic mind

plausible commonplaces

playful wit

pleasing reveries

pleasurable excitement

plenary argument

plentiful harvest

plighted word [plighted = promised by a solemn pledge]

poignant clearness

pointless tale

poisonous counsels

polished ease

polite indifference

political malcontent

polluting taints

pompous platitudes

ponderous research

pontifical manner

popular resentment

populous fertility

portentous gulf

positively deteriorating

posthumous glory

potential energy

powerful stimulant

practical helpfulness

precarious path

precautionary measure

precipitous flight

precise purpose

precocious wisdom

preconceived view

predatory writers

predestined spinster

predominant habit

pregnant hint

preliminary assumption

premature ripening

premonitory symptoms

preoccupied attention

prepossessing appearance

preposterous assertion

prescient reflection [prescient = perceiving the significance of events before they occur]

prescribed conditions

presiding genius

pressing necessity

pretended surprise

pretentious dignity

preternatural sagacity [preternatural = extraordinary] [sagacity = farsighted; wise]

pretty plaintiveness

prevailing misconception

priestly austerity

primal energy

prime factor [no integer factors; irreducible; 1,2,3,5,7,11…]

primeval silence

primordial conditions

princely courtesy

prismatic blush

pristine dignity

private contempt

privileged caste

prized possession

problematic age

prodigally lavished

prodigious variety

productive discipline

profane denunciation

professedly imitated

professional garrulity [garrulity = excessive talkativeness]

proffered service

profitable adventure

profligate expenditure

profound conviction

profuse generosity

projected visit

prolegomenous babbler [prolegomenous = preliminary discussion]

prolific outpouring

prolix narrative [prolix = wordy]

prolonged happiness

promiscuous multitude

promising scions [scions = descendants]

prompt courage

propagandist literature

propelling impulse

proper punctilio [punctilio = fine point of etiquette]

prophetic vision

propitious moment [propitious = auspicious, favorable]

proportionately vigilant

proprietary sense

prosaic excellence [prosaic = dull and lacking excitement]

prospective success

prosperity revival

prostrate servility

protoplasmic ancestors

protracted agony

proud destiny

proverbial situation

provincial prejudice

provoked hostility

prudential wisdom

prurient desire

prying criticism

psychic processes

public derision

puerile fickleness [puerile = immature; childish]

pugnacious defiance

pulsating life

punctilious care [punctilious = precise; scrupulous]

pungent epigram

puny dimensions

purblind brutality [purblind = partly blind; slow to understanding]

pure coincidence

purgatorial fires

puritanical primness

purplish shadows

purposed attempt

purposeful drama

pursuing fancies

pusillanimous desertion [pusillanimous = cowardly]

pyrotechnic outburst

Q

quailing culprit

quaint peculiarities

qualifying service

quavering voice

queer tolerance

quenchless despair

querulous disposition [querulous = habitually complaining]

questionable data

questioning gaze

quibbling speech

quick sensibility

quiescent melancholy

quiet cynicism

quivering excitement

quixotic impulse

quizzical expression

quondam foe [quondam = former]

R

racial prejudice

racy humor

radiant happiness

radical distinction

raging billows

rambling looseness

rampant wickedness

rancorous animosities

random preconceptions

rank luxuriance

ranting optimism

rapacious speculation [rapacious = taking by force; plundering]

rapid transitions

rapturous adoration

rare endowment

rarefied humor

rashly overrated

rational discourse

ravenous eagerness

ravishing spectacle

raw composition

reactionary movement

ready sympathy

realistic portrayal

reanimating ideas

reasonably probable

rebellious thought

reciprocal influence

reckless lavishness

recognized authority

recondite description [recondite = not easily understood; abstruse]

reconstructive era

recovered composure

recumbent figure

recurring doubt

reddening dawn

redoubled activity

refining influence

reflective habits

refractory temper

refreshing novelty

regal countenance

regretful melancholy

regular recurrence

relatively mild

relaxed discipline

relentless justice

religious scruples

reluctant tolerance

remarkable sagacity [sagacity = wisdom]

remedial measure

remorseless logic

remote epoch

renowned achievement

repeated falsification

repelling vices

repentant sense

reprehensible action

repressed ardor

reproachful misgiving

repulsive spectacle

reputed disposition

requisite expertness

resentful flame

resilient spirit

resistless might

resolute daring

resonant gaiety

resounding blare

resourceful wickedness

respectful condescension

resplendent brightness

responsive throb

restless inquisitiveness

restorative influence

restricted meaning

resultant limitation

retaliating blows

retarding influence

retreating footsteps

revengeful scowl

reverent enthusiasm

revolting cynicism

revolutionary tradition

rhapsodical eulogy

rhetorical amplification

rhythmical movements

richly emblazoned

righteous indignation

rightful distinction

rigid propriety

rigorous reservation

riotous clamor

ripe reflection

rising misgivings

riveted attention

robust sense

rollicking mirth

romantic solitudes

rooted habits

roseate tints

rough brutality

roundabout approach

rousing chorus

royal exultations

rubicund tinge [rubicund = healthy rosiness]

rude awakening

rudimentary effort

rueful conclusion

ruffled feelings

rugged austerity

ruling motive

rumbling hoarseness

ruminating mood

rural imagery

rustic simplicity

rustling forest

ruthless commercialism

S

sacerdotal preeminence [sacerdotal = priestly]

sacred tenderness

sacrilegious violence

sacrosanct fetish

sadly disconcerted

sagacious mind [sagacious = keen discernment, sound judgment]

sage reflections

saintly serenity

salient feature

salutary amusement

sanctimonious hypocrite [sanctimonious = feigning piety]

sane observer

sanguinary measures [sanguinary = eager for bloodshed; bloodthirsty]

sanguine expectations [sanguine = cheerfully confident; optimistic]

sarcastic incredulity

sardonic taciturnity [sardonic = cynically mocking] [taciturnity = habitually untalkative]

satirical critic

satisfying equipoise [equipoise = equilibrium]

savage satirist

scalding jests

scandalous falsehood

scant recognition

scathing satire

scattered distractions

scholarly attainments

scientific curiosity

scintillating wit

scoffing defiance

scorching criticism

scornful negligence

scriptural exegesis [exegesis = Critical explanation or analysis]

scrubby foreland

scrupulous fidelity

sculptured sphinx

scurrilous blustering [scurrilous = foul-mouthed]

searching eye

secluded byways

secret dismay

sectarian sternness

secure anchorage

sedentary occupation

seditious speaking [seditious = arousing to action or rebellion]

seductive whisperings

sedulously fostered [sedulously = persevering]

seeming artlessness

seething hate

selective instinct

self-conscious activity

self-deprecating irony

selfish vindictiveness

selfsame strain

senile sensualist

senseless gibberish

sensibly abated

sensitively courteous

sensuous music

sententious wisdom [sententious = terse and energetic; pithy]

sentimental twaddle

sepulchral quiet

sequestered nook

seraphic promiscuousness

serene triumph

serious resentment

serpentine curves

servile obedience

sesquipedalian words [sesquipedalian = long]

settled dislike

severe censure

shabby imitation

shadowy abstraction

shady retirements

shallow sophistry

sham enthusiasm

shambling gait

shamed demeanor

shameless injustice

shapeless conformations

shaping impulses

sharp rebuke

shattered reason

sheepish look

sheer boredom

sheltering hypocrisy

shifting panorama

shimmering gaiety

shining virtues

shivering soul

shocking rudeness

shoreless sea

shortening days

shrewd suspicion

shrewish look

shrill dissonance

shrunken wisp

shuddering reluctance

shuffling preliminaries

shy obeisance

sibilant oath [sibilant = producing a hissing sound]

sickening jealousy

sidelong glance

significant symbol

silent agony

silken filaments

silly escapades

silvery sea

similar amplitude

simple rectitude

simulated rapture

simultaneous acclamation

sincere hospitality

singular sensitiveness

sinister forebodings

sinuous movements

skeptical contempt

skillfully maintained

skulking look

slackened tension

slavish imitation

sledge-hammer blows

sleepless soul

sleepy enchantment

slender resource

slight acceleration

slovenly deportment

slow stupefaction

sluggish resolution

slumbering stream

smacking breeze

small aptitude

smiling repose

smirking commonplace

smoldering resentment

smothered sob

smug hypocrisy

snappish impertinence

sneering jibes

snowy whiteness

snug retreat

soaring ambition

sobbing wail

sober melancholy

social banalities

sociological bearing

soft allurement

solemn emptiness

solid knowledge

solidifying substance

solitary grandeur

somber relations

somewhat scandalized

somnolent state

sonorous simplicity [sonorous = full, deep, rich sound; impressive in style of speech]

sophistical argument

soporific emanations [soporific = inducing sleep]

sordid selfishness

sorely beset

sorrowful resignation

soulless mechanism

sounding verbiage

sourly ascetic

sovereign panacea

spacious tracklessness

sparkling splendor

specialized skill

specific characteristics

specious artifice [specious = having the ring plausibility but actually fallacious]

spectral fears

speculative rubbish

speechless surprise

speedy extinction

spendthrift prodigality

spirited vindication

spiritual dazzlement

splendid irony

splenetic imagination [splenetic = ill humor or irritability]

spontaneous challenge

sporadic exception

sportive gaiety

spotless honor

sprightly talk

spurious enthusiasm

squalid distress [squalid = Dirty and wretched; morally repulsive; sordid]

squandered talent

squeamish taste

staggering surprise

stainless womanhood

stale sciolism [sciolism = superficial knowledge]

stalwart defiance

stammered apology

starched sterility

starlit eminence

startling eccentricity

starving proletariat

stately stride

statesmanlike person

statistical knowledge

statuesque immobility

staunch manhood

steadfast obedience

stentorian voice [stentorian = extremely loud]

stereotyped commonness

sterile hatred

sterling sense

stern defiance

stiff conceit

stifled convulsions

still solitudes

stilted bombast

stimulating impression

stinging reproach

stinted endowment

stipulated reward

stock pleasantries

stoic callousness

stolid obstinacy

stony stare

storied traditions

stormy passion

stout assertion

straggling association

straightforward logic

straightway vanished

strained interpretation

straitened circumstance

strange wistfulness

strenuous insistence

striking diversity

stringent statement

strong aversion

stubborn reality

studious reserve

stultified mind

stunning crash

stupendous magnitude

stupid bewilderment

sturdy genuineness

subaltern attitude [subaltern = secondary]

subconscious conviction

subduing influence

sublime anticipations

submissive behavior

subordinate pursuit

subsidiary advantage

substantial agreement

subterranean sunlessness

subtle sophistry

subversive accident

successfully dispelled

successive undulations

succinct phrase

sudden perturbation

sullen submission

summary vengeance

sumptuously decorated

superabundant energy

superannuated coquette
[superannuated = retired]
[coquette = flirt]

superb command

supercilious discontent
[supercilious = haughty
disdain]

superficial surliness

superfluous precaution

superhuman vigor

superior skill

superlative cleverness

supernatural incident

supine resignation

suppliant posture

suppressed excitement

supreme exaltation

surging multitude

surly tone

surpassing loveliness

surprising intimacy

surreptitious means
[surreptitious =
clandestine; stealthy]

sustained vigor

swaggering bully

swampy flatness

swarming population

sweeping assertion

sweet peaceableness

swelling magnitude

swift transition

swinging cadence

symmetrical brow

sympathetic insight

syncopated tune

synthetic judgment

systematic interaction

T

tacit assumption

taciturn magnanimity
[taciturn = habitually
untalkative]

tactical niceties

tameless energy

tangible realities

tangled network

tardy recognition

tarnished reputation

tart temper

tasteful gratification

tasteless insipidity

tattered mendicant
[mendicant = beggar]

taunting accusation

tawdry pretentiousness

tearful sensibilities

tearing gallop

teasing persistency

technical precision

tedious formality

teeming population

temerarious assertion
[temerarious =
presumptuous; reckless]

temperamental
complacency

tempered pathos

tempestuous breeze

temporary expedient

tenacious memory

tender solicitude

tense attention

tentative moment

tepid conviction

termagant wife [termagant = quarrelsome, scolding]

terrible sublimity

terrifying imprecations [imprecations = curses]

terse realism

testamentary document

thankless task

thawing laughter

theological complexities

thirsting ear

thorny pathway

thorough uprightness

thoughtful silence

thoughtless whim

threadbare sentiment

threatened wrath

thrilling eloquence

throbbing pride

throneless monarch

thronging images

thundering rage

thwarted impulse

tideless depth

tigerish stealth

tightened ominously

timid acquiescence

tingling expectation

tinkling cymbal

tipsy jocularity [jocularity = given to joking]

tip-toe curiosity

tireless egotism

tiresome braggadocio [braggadocio = pretentious bragging]

titanic force

toilsome pleasure

tolerably comprehensive

tolerant indifference

tormenting thought

torn asunder

torpid faculties

tortuous labyrinth

tortured innocence

totally engrossed

touching pathos

tousled head

towering pride

traceable consanguinity

trackless forest

traditional type

tragic intensity

trailing sweetness

tranquil grandeur

transcendent power

transfiguring tints

transient emotion

translucent cup

transmuting touch

transparent complement

treacherous intelligence

treasured possessions

trembling anxiety

tremendous domination

tremulous sense [tremulous = timid or fearful]

trenchant phrase [trenchant = forceful, effective, vigorous]

trifling superfluity

trite remark

triumphant boldness

trivial conventionality

tropical luxuriance

troubled inertness

trudging wayfarer

trustworthy source

tumultuous rapture

tuneful expression

turbulent times

turgid appeal [turgid = excessively ornate or complex]

twilight shadow

twittered sleepily

twofold bearing

typical excellence

tyrannical disposition

U

ubiquitous activity

ugly revelation

ulterior purpose

ultimate sanction

ultrafashionable world

unabashed insolence

unabated pleasure

unaccountable protervity [protervity = peevishness; petulance]

unaccustomed toil

unadorned style

unaffected pathos

unaffrighted innocence

unagitated abstraction

unalloyed satisfaction

unalterable determination

unanimous acclamation

unanswerable argument

unapologetic air

unappeasable resentment

unapproached supremacy

unassailable position

unassuming dignity

unattainable perfection

unavailing consolation

unavoidable propensities

unballasted eloquence [unballasted = unsteady; wavering]

unbeaten track

unbecoming behavior

unbending reserve

unbiased judgment

unblemished character

unblinking observation

unblushing iteration

unbounded hospitality

unbridgeable chasm

unbridled fancy

unbroken continuity

uncanny fears

unceasing variation

unceremonious talk

uncertain tenure

unchallenged supremacy

unchanging affection

uncharitable ambition

uncharted depths

unchastised offense

unclouded splendor

uncomfortable doubt

uncommonly attractive

uncommunicable quality

uncomplaining endurance

uncomprehending smile

uncompromising dogmatism

unconcealed aversion

unconditioned freedom

uncongenial task

unconquerable patience

unconscious serenity

uncontrollable delight

unconventional demeanor

uncounted generations

uncouth gambols

uncritical position

unctuously belaud [unctuously = exaggerated, insincere] [belaud = praise greatly]

undaunted defender

undazzled eyes

undefined anticipations

undeniable charm

underlying assumption

undeviating consistency

undignified peccadilloes [peccadilloes = small sin or fault]

undiluted skepticism

undiminished relish

undimmed luster

undisciplined genius

undisguised amusement

undismayed expression

undisputed ascendency

undistracted attention

undisturbed silence

undivided energies

undoubted authenticity

undue predilection [predilection = preference]

undulating hills

unduly troublesome

undying friendship

unearthly gladness

uneasy craving

unembarrassed scrutiny

unembittered sweetness

unending exactions

unenlightened zealot

unenvied insipidity

unequaled skill

unequivocally resented

unerring fidelity

unessential details

unexampled sweetness

unexhausted kindliness

unexpected confidence

unfailing courtesy

unfaltering glance

unfamiliar garb

unfathomable indifference

unfeigned assent

unfettered liberty

unflagging zest

unflattering truth

unflecked confidence

unfledged novice [unfledged = young bird

without feathers necessary to fly]

unflinching zeal

unfolding consciousness

unforced acquiescence

unforeseen vicissitudes [vicissitudes = sudden or unexpected changes]

unforgivable tragedy

unfounded conjecture

unfulfilled longing

ungainly figure

ungarnished reality

ungenerously resolved

ungenial temperament

ungovernable vehemence

ungracious temper

ungrudging tribute

unguessed riches

unhallowed threshold

unhampered expression

unhappy predecessor

unheeded beauties

unheroic measure

unhesitating faith

unhindered flight

unholy triumph

uniform blending

unimaginable bitterness

unimpassioned dignity

unimpeachable sentiment

unimpeded activity

uninstructed critic

uninterrupted process

unique personality

universal reprobation [reprobation = condemned to hell; severe disapproval]

unjust depreciation

unknown appellations [appellation = name, title, or designation]

unlettered laborer

unlikely contingency

unlimited opulence

unlucky dissembler

unmanly timidity

unmastered possibility.

unmeaning farce

unmeasured hostility

unmellowed dawn

unmelodious echoes

unmerciful plundering

unmingled consent

unmistakably fabulous

unmitigated gloom

unmixed astonishment

unmodified passion

unmurmuringly sea

unnecessary platitudes

unnumbered thousands

unobtrusive deference

unostentatious display

unpalatable truth

unparalleled atrocities

unpardonable error

unphilosophical dreamer

unpleasant excrescence [excrescence = abnormal enlargement]

unprecedented advance

unprejudiced intelligence

unpretentious character

unprincipled violence

unprofitable craft

unpurchasable luxury

unqualified submission

unquenchable tenderness

unquestionable genius

unquestioning fate

unreasonable pretense

unreasoning distrust

unredeemable forfeit

unrefreshing sameness

unrelaxing emphasis

unrelenting spirit

unremembered winter

unremitting toil

unrepining sadness

unreproved admiration

unrequited love

unresentful disposition

unreserved assent

unresisted authority

unresolved exceptions

unresponsive gloom

unresting speed

unrestrained anger

unrestricted ease

unrivaled distinction

unruffled concord

unsatisfied yearning

unscrupulous adventurer

unseasonable apology

unseemly mirth

unselfish fidelity

unsettled trait

unshakable foundation

unshrinking determination

unslackened volubility
[volubility = ready flow of
speech; fluent]

unsophisticated youth

unsparing abuse

unspeakable delight

unspiritual tone

unspoiled goodness

unstinted praise

unsullied virtue

unsurpassed purity

unswerving integrity

untamable energy

unthinkable hypothesis

untiring energy

untold calamity

untoward circumstances
[untoward = improper]

untrammeled expression

untrodden woodland

untroubled repose

untuneful phrase

untutored mind

unusual audacity

unutterable sadness

unvarnished feeling

unwarranted limitation

unwasting energies

unwavering allegiance

unwearied diligence

unwelcome alliance

unwieldy bulk

unwilling homage

unwittingly mingled

unwonted kindness
[unwonted = unusual]

unworldly foolishness

unworthy alliance

unyielding nature

uproarious laughter

upstart pretensions

useless fripperies [fripperies = pretentious, showy]

utmost scorn

V

vacant stupidity

vacillating obedience

vacuous ease

vagabond spirit

vagrant wandering

vaguely discursive

vain contemplation

vainglorious show

valid objection

valuable acquisition

valueless assertion

vampire tongue

vanished centuries

vantage ground

vapid generalities [vapid = lacking liveliness, interest; dull]

variable temperament

variegated career [variegated = varied]

vast advantage

veering purpose

vehement panting

veiled insolence

velvety lawn

venerable placidity

venomous passion

veracious journals [veracious = honest; truthful; accurate; precise]

verbal audacities

verbose manner

verdant hope

verifiable facts

veritable triumph

vernacular expression

vernal charm [vernal = resembling spring; fresh; youthful]

versatile grace

vexatious circumstances

vicarious virtue

vigilant sensibility

vigorous invective [invective = abusive language]

vile desecrater

villainous inconsistency

vindictive sentiment

violent agitation

virgin grace

virile leadership

virtual surrender

virtuous disdain

virulent prejudice

visible embarrassment

visionary dreamer

vital interpretation

vitiated taste [vitiated = reduce the value; corrupt morally]

vitriolic sneer

vivacious excitement

vivid portrayal

vociferous appeal

voiceless multitude

volatile fragrance

volcanic suddenness

voluble prose [voluble = ready flow of speech; fluent]

voluminous biography

voluntary relinquishment

voracious animosity

votive wreath

vulgar prosperity

vulnerable foe

W

wabbling enterprise [wabbling = wobbling]

waggishly sapient [sapient = wise]

wailing winds

wandering fancy

waning popularity

wanton butchery

warbling lute

warlike trappings

warning prophecy

warped purpose

warranted interference

wasteful prodigality

wavering courage

waxwork sex

wayward fancy

weakly imaginative

wearisome wordiness

wedded incompatibility

weighty argument

weird fascination

welcoming host

well-turned period

weltering current

whimsical touch

whirling confusion

whirring loom

whispering breeze

whistling winds

whited sepulcher

wholesome aspirations

wholly commendable

wicked ingratitude

wide signification

widespread acclaim

wild extravagance

willful waywardness

willing allegiance

willowy nothingness

wily antagonist

winding pilgrimage

windowless soul

winged fancies

winking stars

winning plaintiveness

winsome girlhood

wise dissertations

wistful entreaty

withering scorn

witnessing approval

witty expedient

wizard influence

woebegone countenance

woeful weariness

wolfish tendency

womanlike loveliness

wonderful affluence

wonted activity [wonted = usual]

wordy warfare

worthy achievement

wounded avarice

wrathful pugnacity

wretched effeminacy

wriggling disputant

writhing opponent

Y

yawning space

yearning tenderness

yielding disposition

youthful ambition

Z

zealous devotion

zigzag method

zoologically considered

SECTION II

SIGNIFICANT PHRASES

A

abashed and ashamed

abhorrence and repulsion

abilities and attainments

abject and hopeless

ably and vigorously

abrupt and perilous

absolute and eternal

absorbed and occupied

abstinence and self-denial

abstract and metaphysical

absurd and impertinent

abundant and sustained

abuse and slander

accentual and rhythmic

accidental and temporary

accomplished and popular

accurate and illuminating

achievement and character

acquisition and possession

active and aggressive

actual and immediate

acute and painful

admirable and accomplished

adorned and amplified

adroitness and judgment

adventurous and prodigal

advice and assistance

affable and courteous

affectation and coquetry

affectionate and warm-hearted

affluent and exuberant

affright and abhorrence

agencies and influences

ages and generations

aggrandizement and plunder

agreeable and ingenuous

aggressive and sullen

aghast and incredulous

agility and briskness

agitate and control

agony and despair

aids and auxiliaries

aim and purpose

airy and frivolous

alarm and uneasiness

alert and unsparing

all and sundry

allegiance and fidelity

alone and undistracted

alterations and additions

amazement and admiration

ambiguity and disagreement

ambition and determination

amiable and unpretending

ample and admirable

amusing and clever

analytical and critical

anarchy and chaos

ancient and venerable

anecdote and reminiscence

anger and fury

anguish and hopelessness

animated and effective

anomalies and absurdities

antagonism and opposition

antipathies and distastes

antiquated and obsolete

anxiety and trepidation

apathy and torpor

apologetic and uneasy

appalling and devastating

apparent and palpable

appearance and surroundings

apprehensive and anxious

appropriate and eloquent

approve and admire

apt and novel

archness and vivacity [archness = inappropriate playfulness]

ardent and aspiring

argument and inference

arid and unprofitable

arrangement and combination

arrogant and overbearing

artificial and elaborate

artistic and literary

artlessness and urbanity

ashamed and speechless

aspects and phases

aspiring and triumphal

assiduity and success

assimilated and combined

assuaged and pacified

astonished and curious

astound and perplex

athletic and nimble

atonement and forgiveness

atrocious and abominable

attacks and intrigues

attention and respect

attitudes and expressions

attractiveness and ability

audacity and skill

august and splendid

austere and icy

available and capable

avarice and cruelty

avidity and earnestness [avidity = desire; craving]

awake and active

awe and reverence

awkwardness and crudity

B

babel and confusion

backbone and sinew

baffled and disappointed

balanced and forceful

barbarity and wickedness

bards and sages

base and unworthy

beam and blaze

bearing and address

beautiful and majestic

bedraggled and disappointed

befogged and stupefied

beliefs and practices

bellowing and shouting

benevolence and candor

benign and hopeful

bent and disposition

benumbed and powerless

bewildered and stupefied

bigots and blockheads

billing and cooing

birth and breeding

bite and sting

bits and scraps

bitter and disdainful

black and solitary

bland and ingenious

blasphemous and profane

bleak and unrelenting

blend and harmonize

blessing and benediction

blind and unreasoning

blundering and plundering

blurred and confused

bluster and vulgarity

boast and assertion

bold and haughty

bombast and egotism

bone and sinew

boundless and unlimited

bourgeois and snobbish

brag and chatter

bravado and cowardice

brave and chivalrous

breathless and reverential

brevity and condensation

bribery and corruption

brief and pithy

bright and vivacious

brilliancy and grace

brisk and enlivening

broad and deep

brooding and solemn

brutal and degrading

bulks and masses

bungling and trifling

businesslike and practicable

bustle and business

C

cajoled and bullied

calamity and sorrow

callous and impervious

calmness and composure

calumny and exaggeration [calumny = maliciously lying to injure a reputation]

candor and kindness

cant and hypocrisy [cant = hypocritically pious language]

capable and efficient

capacity and ability

capricious and unreasonable

career and occupation

cares and anxieties

carping and ungenerous

casual and transient

causes and circumstances

cautious and reticent

celebrated and praised

celerity and violence [celerity = swiftness of action]

ceremony and splendor

certain and verifiable

chafe and exasperate

chagrin and despondency

chance and opportunity

change and variety

chaos and confusion

character and temperament

characteristic and complete

charges and insinuations

charm and perfection

chaste and refined

cheap and convenient

checked and thwarted

cheerfulness and gaiety

cherish and guard

chief and paramount

chilled and stiffened

choleric and sanguine [choleric = easily angered; bad-tempered] [sanguine = cheerfully confident; optimistic]

churlishness and violence [churlish = boorish or vulgar]

citation and allusion

civility and communicativeness

civilized and cultured

clamorous and wild

claptrap and platitude

clarity and straightforwardness

classical and perspicuous [perspicuous = easy to understand]

clatter and clang

clear and decisive

cleverness and acuteness

clogged and dulled

clumsy and smudgy

coarse and grotesque

coaxed and threatened

coexistent and correlative

cogent and conclusive

cohesion and sequence

cold and unemotional

comely and vivacious

comfort and security

command and threaten

common and familiar

commotion and annoyance

compact and complete

comparison and discrimination

compass and power

competent and experienced

complaints and imprecations [imprecation = a curse]

complaisance and readiness

complete and permanent

complex and various

composure and gracefulness

comprehensive and accurate

compression and pregnancy

conceal and deny

conceit and impertinence

conceived and consummated

concentrated and intensified

conception and treatment

concern and wonder

concise and emphatic

concrete and definite

condemned and upbraided

conditions and limitations

confession and doubt

confidence and loyalty

confusion and dismay

congratulations and welcomings

connection and interdependence

conquered and transformed

conquest and acquisition

consciously and purposely

consistent and harmonious

conspicuous and impressive

conspired and contrived

constant and intimate

constructive and vital

contemn and decry [contemn = despise]

contempt and indignation

contentment and serenity

continuous and undeviating

contorted and fantastic

contradictions and inconsistencies

contrast and comparison

contrivance and disguise

conventional and limited

cool and indifferent

copiousness and vivacity

cordial and cheerful

corruption and decay

costly and gorgeous

counselor and guide

countless and indescribable

courage and endurance

courted and feted

courteous and sympathetic

coveted and deserved

coy and furtive

cramped and distorted

creative and inventive

credulity and ignorance

creeds and dogmas

crime and misdemeanor

crippled and maimed

crises and struggles

crisp and sparkling

critical and skeptical

crowded and jostled

crowned and sceptered

crude and primitive

cruel and rapacious

crumbling and shapeless

crushed and bewildered

cultured and refined

cumbrous and diffuse [cumbrous = cumbersome]

cunning and cruelty

curious and inexpressible

curved and channeled

customs and manners

cynical and contemptuous

D

dangers and pitfalls

daring and resolute

dark and starless

dart and quiver

dashing and careless

dates and details

dazzled and confounded

debased and demoralized

debilitating and futile

decencies and restraints

deception and cruelty

decided and definite

declamation and delivery

decline and decay

deductions and inferences

deep and subtle

deface and injure

defame and tarnish

deference and concession

defiant and antagonistic

deficient and unskilled

definite and memorable

deft and offensive

degraded and dishonored

deliberate and effective

delicate and lambent
[lambent = effortlessly
brilliant]

delight and consolation

delusion and trickery

demands and expectations

demeanor and conduct

demoralizing and
enfeebling

denial and defense

dense and luminous

denunciations and censures

deplorable and baneful

depravity and frivolity

depressing and
discouraging

depth and richness

derision and skepticism

described and classified

desecration and decay

designs and activities

desires and motives

desolation and
wretchedness

despatch and resolution

desperation and defiance

despise and satirize

despoiled and destroyed

despondency and
melancholy

despotism and coercion

destitution and misery

desultory and slipshod
[desultory = haphazardly;
random]

detached and isolated

determined and courageous

detestable and intolerable

development and culture

devoted and unwavering

dictatorial and insolent

diction and pronunciation

differences and disputes

difficult and arduous

diffidence and constraint

diffuseness and warmth

dignified and austere

digressive and wanton

dilatory and hesitating
[dilatory = postpone or
delay]

diligent and sedulous
[sedulous = persevering]

dim and distant

din and traffic

directed and controlled

disagreeable and painful

disappointed and abashed

disapprobation and
condemnation
[approbation = warm
approval; praise]

disapproval and
apprehension

discipline and development

discomfiture and degradation

disconcerted and dismayed

discontent and disquiet

discords and differences

discouraging and distressing

discovery and invention

discretion and moderation

disdain and mockery

disfigured and shapeless

disgrace and ruin

disgust and dismay

dishonor and ruin

disillusioned and ironical

disintegration and decay

disinterested and gracious

disjointed and voluble
[voluble = fluent]

dislike and disdain

dislocation and chaos

dismay and apprehension

dispirit and discourage

disposition and power

disquietude and uneasiness

dissolute and hateful

dissolve and disappear

distant and diverse

distended and distorted

distinctive and appropriate

distinguishing and differentiating

distress and humiliation

distrust and aversion

disturbed and anxious

diverging and contracting

docile and obedient

dogma and ritual

dominant and permanent

dormant and subdued

doubt and trepidation

dramatic and sensational

drastic and revolutionary

dread and terror

dreams and ambitions

dreariness and desolation

dregs and sediments

drill and discipline

driveling and childish

drollery and ridicule

drooping and disconsolate

dubious and dangerous

dull and spiritless

dumb and nerveless

dupe and victim

duplicity and equivocation

dust and oblivion

duties and difficulties

dwarfed and obscured

dwindle and disappear

E

eagerness and ecstasy

earnestness and animation

ease and lightness

ebb and flow

eclectic and assimilated

edifying and enchanting

education and skill

effective and competent

efficiency and success

egotism and bigotry

elaboration and display

elation and delight

elegance and gentility

elementary and simple

elevate and ennoble

eligibility and suitableness

elongated and narrow

eloquent and expressive

elusive and exquisite

embarrassed and concerned

embittered and despairing

embodiment and actualization

emerged and flowered

eminent and remarkable

emoluments and honors [emoluments = compensation]

emotion and passion

emphasize and magnify

employment and profession

encouragement and stimulus

energy and activity

enfeebled and exhausted

enfold and enwrap

engulfed and buried

enjoyment and satisfaction

enlightenment and progress

enraptured and amazed

enriched and ennobled

enslave and dominate

enterprising and intelligent

entertaining and diverting

enthusiasm and zeal

enticing and alluring

entire and complete

environment and training

envy and despair

ephemeral and feeble [ephemeral = markedly short-lived]

episodes and interludes

epithet and description

equality and solidarity

equity and justice

erratic and confused

errors and infirmities

essential and predominating

estimable and agreeable

eternal and sublime

ethical and religious

ever and anon

evident and manifest

exactitude and completeness

exaggerate and distort

exaltation and enthusiasm

examination and comparison

examples and models

exasperations and paroxysms [paroxysms = outbursts of emotion or action]

excellent and worthy

exceptional and remarkable

excessive and unreasonable

excitable and irritable

exclusive and limited

excusable and justifiable

execration and defiance [execration = curse]

exertion and excitement

exhaustion and fatigue

exhibition and display

exhilarating and beneficial

exigency and requirement
[exigency = urgent situation]

expansive and digressive

expediency and utility

expensive and unprofitable

experience and skill

experiment and explorations

expert and vigorous

explanation and elucidation

explore and examine

expressions and exclamations

expressive and effective

exquisite and powerful

extent and importance

extraordinary and unexpected

extravagant and grotesque

extreme and morbid

exuberant and infectious

F

fabulous and fabricated

facile and brilliant

facts and traditions

faculties and powers

faded and withered

failures and misadventures

faint and obscure

fair and impartial

faith and reverence

fallacy and danger

false and fugitive

fame and fortune

familiar and gracious

famous and foremost

fancies and sentiments

fanciful and chimerical
[chimerical = highly improbable]

fantastic and meretricious
[meretricious = plausible but false]

fascination and awe

fashion and frivolity

fastidious and exacting

fatigued and careworn

faults and delusions

favors and kindnesses

fear and bewilderment

feasible and practical

feebleness and folly

feeling and passion

felicitous and exquisite

ferocious and mercenary

fertility and vigor

fervor and simplicity

feverishly and furiously

fickle and uncertain

fidelity and zeal

fierce and menacing

fiery and controversial

final and irreversible

finish and completeness

firm and decisive

first and foremost

fitful and capricious

fitting and appropriate

fixity and finality

flaming and mendacious [mendacious = lying; untruthful]

flare and flicker

flatness and insipidity

flattery and toadyism

flexible and spontaneous

flickering and ambiguous

flighty and impetuous

flippant and contemptuous

florid and healthy [florid = ornate; flowery]

flotsam and jetsam

flow and fullness

flowery and figurative

fluctuating and transitory

fluency and flippancy

fluttering and restless

focus and concentrate

fogs and complications

foibles and follies

foiled and defeated

folly and indecorum

fools and underlings

force and effectiveness

formal and cold

formidable and profound

formlessness and exaggeration

fortitude and perseverance

foul and ominous

fragile and pale

fragments and morsels

fragrance and beauty

frailties and absurdities

frank and genial

free and independent

frequent and poignant

freshness and fragrance

fretful and timorous

friend and benefactor

frigid and pompous

frivolous and empty

froth and effervescence

frustrated and confounded

fuddled and contradictory

full and sonorous

fumbling and blundering

fuming and bustling

fun and satire

function and aim

fundamental and necessary

furrowed and ragged

furtive and illusive

fury and madness

fussing and fuming

futile and untrustworthy

G

gaiety and grace

gallant and proud

galling and humiliating

gaunt and ghastly

gay and genial

general and universal

generosity and prodigality

generous and humane

genial and refreshing

genius and reputation

gentle and amiable

genuine and infectious

germ and root

gesticulation and emphasis [gesticulation = deliberate, vigorous motion or gesture]

ghastly and inconceivable

gifts and graces

gigantic and portentous

glamour and fascination

glare and pretension

glib and loquacious [loquacious = very talkative]

glitter and glamour

gloomy and morose

glorious and gorgeous

glowing and exaggerated

glum and grim

goodness and rectitude

goodwill and merriment

gorgeousness and splendor

gossiping and grumbling

govern and overrule

grace and dignity

gracious and generous

gradual and progressive

graft and dishonesty

grand and sublime

grandeur and massiveness

grandiose and oracular [oracular = solemnly prophetic; obscure]

graphic and gorgeous

gratification and enjoyment

gratitude and generosity

gratuitous and ungracious

grave and stately

graveyards and solitudes

greatness and stability

greed and covetousness

grief and remorse

grim and sullen

grimaces and gesticulations

grope and fumble

grossness and brutality

grotesque and monstrous

grouped and combined

growth and development

guesses and fancies

guidance and inspiration

gush and hysteria

gusto and effect

H

habits and humors

habitual and intuitive

hackneyed and tawdry

haggard and pale

handsome and amiable

haphazard and dangerous

happiness and pleasantness

harass and pursue

hard and unsparing

hardships and indignities

harmony and beauty

harsh and austere

hasty and unwarranted

hateful and loathsome

haughtiness and arrogance

hauteur and disdain [hauteur = arrogance]

hazard and peril

hazy and indefinite

headstrong and foolish

healthy and vigorous

hearth and shrine

heartless and hypocritical

heat and impatience

heaviness and weariness

hecklings and interruptions

hectic and pitiful

heretics and schismatics

heritage and privilege

heroism and wisdom

hesitation and irresolution

hideous and grotesque

high and conscientious

hilarity and mirth

hints and suggestions

history and tradition

hither and thither

hoarse and rumbling

hobbies and eccentricities

hollowness and unreality

holy and prayerful

homeliness and simplicity

honestly and confessedly

honors and emoluments
[emoluments =
compensation]

hooted and mobbed

hopes and prospects

horror and ghastliness

hospitality and
magnificence

hubbub and confusion

huge and unwieldy

humane and sympathetic

humility and devoutness

humors and singularities

hurry and bustle

hushed and still

husks and phantoms

hypocrisy and impudence

I

ideas and achievements

idle and presumptuous

ignoble and shabby

ignominy and misfortune

ignorance and superstition

illiterate and unfit

ill-tempered and unjust

illuminative and suggestive

illustrative and typical

images and impressions

imagination and memory

imbitter and exasperate

imitators and disciples

immature and unpromising

immediate and
instantaneous

immensity and intricacy

imminent and terrible

immovable and
unchangeable

impalpable and spiritual

impassioned and energetic

impatient and restless

imperfection and fallibility

imperil and destroy

imperious and ruthless
[imperious = arrogantly
domineering]

impertinent and personal

impinging and inexorable

implacable and destructive

important and formidable

imposed and enforced

impossibilities and absurdities

impressible and plastic

improvement and progress

imprudent and thoughtless

impulse and indignation

inaccessible and audacious

inactive and supine

inadequate and misleading

inapplicable and alien

inarticulate and confused

inborn and native

incensed and alarmed

inchoate and tentative [inchoate = imperfectly formed]

incoherent and inconclusive

incompetence and ignorance

incomplete and erroneous

incongruity and absurdity

inconvenient and troublesome

incorrigible and irrepressible

incredulous and mortified

indefatigable and irresistible

indefinite and vague

independent and democratic

indifference and brevity

indigence and obscurity

indignation and chagrin

indirectly and unconsciously

indispensable and irreplaceable

indistinct and misty

indolence and indifference

indomitable and dogged

indorsed and applauded

indulge and cherish

industrious and vigilant

ineffective and bungling

inert and uncertain

inevitable and assured

inexhaustible and indomitable

inexperienced and timid

infallible and disdainful

inference and suggestion

infinite and eternal

inflexible and unchanging

influence and authority

informed and competent

ingenious and eloquent

ingratitude and cruelty

inharmonious and irregular

injustice and inhumanity

innocence and fidelity

innuendo and suggestion

inopportune and futile

insanely and blindly

inscrutable and perplexing

insecurity and precariousness

insensibly and graciously

insignificant and transitory

insincere and worthless

insipid and silly

insistent and incongruous

insolence and absurdity

inspiring and animating

instant and momentous

instinctive and rational

insulted and thwarted

intangible and indefinable

integral and indestructible

integrity and honor

intelligence and insight

intense and overpowering

intentness and interest

interesting and engrossing

intimate and familiar

intolerant and bumptious [bumptious = loudly assertive; pushy]

intractable and untameable

intricate and endless

intrusive and unmannerly

intuitive and axiomatic

invasion and aggression

invective and innuendo [invective = abusive language]

investigation and research

invidious and painful [invidious = rousing ill will, animosity]

inviolate and unscathed

invisible and silent

involuntary and automatic

irksome and distasteful

irrational and excessive

irregular and intermittent

irreligious and immoral

irremediable and eternal

irrepressible and insistent

irreverence and ingratitude

irritable and churlish [churlish = boorish or vulgar]

isolated and detached

J

jabber and chatter

jagged and multifarious

jargon and absurdity

jaundiced and jealous

jeer and scoff

jeopardy and instability

jests and sarcasms

jocular and vivacious

jostle and stumble

joy and felicity

jubilant and boastful

judgment and discretion

judicious and acute

juggled and manipulated

jumble and confuse

juncture and circumstance

jurisdiction and authority

justice and virtue

juvenile and budding

K

keen and pertinacious [pertinacious = stubbornly persistent]

kind and forbearing

kindle and intensify

kindred and analogous

kingly and autocratic

knavish and tyrannical

knowledge and conviction

known and recognized

L

labor and drudgery

lame and impotent

lamentable and depressing

languid and indifferent

large and opulent

lassitude and languor
[languor = dreamy, lazy
mood]

latent and lifeless

latitude and scope

laudable and deserving

laughable and grotesque

lavish and wasteful

lawlessness and violence

laxity and forbearance

laziness and profligacy

leafage and fruitage

learning and austerity

legends and traditions

legitimate and logical

leisure and tranquillity

lengthy and diffuse

lenient and sympathetic

lethargy and sloth

levity and gaiety

liberal and ample

liberty and freedom

license and laxity

likely and plausible

limited and abbreviated

listless and inert

literal and exact

literary and artistic

lithe and sinewy

lively and poignant

loathsome and abject

lofty and sonorous
[sonorous = producing a
full, rich sound; impressive
speech]

logical and consistent

loquacity and exuberance
[loquacity = very
talkative.]

loss and deterioration

loud and passionate

loving and reverential

low and groveling

loyal and devoted

lucidity and vividness

lucky and propitious
[propitious = auspicious,
favorable; kindly]

lucrative and advantageous

ludicrous and detestable

lugubrious and unfortunate
[lugubrious = dismal,
gloomy]

lukewarm and indifferent

lull and silence

luminous and keen

lure and captivate

lurid and fiery

luscious and lasting

luster and resplendence

lusty and big-sounding

luxury and pomp

M

madness and folly

magical and secret

magnificent and luxurious

majestic and imposing

malice and revenge

malignity and spitefulness

manifold and complex

manly and powerful

manner and conduct

marvels and mysteries

massive and compact

masterly and convincing

materialistic and sordid

maternal and filial

maudlin and grotesque
[maudlin = tearfully
sentimental]

maxims and morals

meager and bare

mean and debasing

meaning and significance

means and materials

mechanical and
monotonous

meddling and muddling

meditative and sympathetic

meek and manageable

melody and softness

memorable and glorious

menace and
superciliousness
[superciliousness =
haughty disdain]

merciful and chivalrous

merciless and unpitying

merit and virtue

mighty and majestic

mild and virtuous

mince and temporize

minds and memories

minuteness and fidelity

mirth and joviality

misdemeanors and
improprieties

misery and degradation

misrepresented and reviled

misty and indefinite

mobile and expressive

mockery and imposture

moderate and cautious

modes and methods

modest and retiring

molding and upbuilding

momentary and languid
[languid = lacking energy;
weak]

momentous and appalling

monopoly and injustice

monotony and indecorum

monstrous and
insupportable

moody and brooding

moral and religious

morbid and irritable

motionless and
commanding

motives and aims

mud and mire

muddled and incoherent

murmurs and reproaches

muscularity and morality

mutable and fleeting

mute and insensate

mutilated and disfigured

muttering and murmuring

mutual and friendly

mysterious and
incomprehensible

mystic and wonderful

N

nagging and squabbling

nameless and obscure

narrow and timorous

natural and spontaneous

nauseous and disgusting

neatness and propriety

necessarily and essentially

needs and demands

nefarious and malevolent

negations and contradictions

neglect and evade

negotiate and bargain

nerve and fiber

neutral and colorless

nicety and precision

nimble and airy

noble and powerful

nodding and blinking

noisy and scurrilous [scurrilous = vulgar, coarse, abusive language]

nonsense and absurdity

nooks and corners

notable and conspicuous

noted and distinguished

noteworthy and intelligible

notoriety and prominence

nourish and foster

novelty and freshness

novice and ignoramus

nucleus and beginning

nugatory and ineffectual [nugatory = no importance; trifling]

nullify and destroy

number and variety

numerous and important

O

oaths and revilings

obdurate and impenitent [obdurate = hardened in wrongdoing] [impenitent = without remorse for sins]

obedient and dutious

obeisance and submission

objectionable and inexpedient

obligation and dependence

obliquity and hypocrisy

oblivious and insensible

obloquy and detraction [obloquy = abusive language]

obnoxious and odious

obscure and enigmatical

obsequies and panegyrics [obsequies = funeral rite] [panegyrics = elaborate praise]

obsequious and conciliating [obsequious = servile compliance; fawning]

observations and reflections

obstacles and disasters

obstinate and stupid

obstreperous and noisy [obstreperous = stubbornly defiant]

obtrusive and vulgar

obtuse and imbecile

obvious and palpable

occasional and contingent

occult and hidden

occupations and habits

odd and dismal

odious and oppressive

offensive and aggressive

official and authoritative

oily and servile

old and decrepit

ominous and untrustworthy

omnivorous and sordid

oneness and unity

onerous and perplexing

open and inviting

opinions and hypotheses

opportunism and inconsistency

opposite and discordant

oppressed and sullen

optimistic and reassuring

opulence and magnitude

oracular and occult [oracular = solemnly prophetic; obscure]

order and uniformity

organic and rational

organization and system

origin and discovery

original and attractive

ornate and variegated

ostensible and explicit

ostentatiousness and gaiety

outlines and appearances

outrageous and scandalous

overburdened and confused

overcome and vanquish

overstep and contravene

overt and unmistakable

overwearied and outworn

overworked and fagged [fagged = worked to exhaustion]

P

pains and penalties

painstaking and cumbersome

pale and anxious

palpable and plain

paltry and inglorious

pampered and petted

parade and display

parched and dry

partial and provisional

particularly and individually

parties and sects

passion and prejudice

passive and indifferent

pastimes and diversions

patent and pertinent

pathos and terror

patience and perseverance

patriotism and reverence

pattern and exemplar [exemplar = worthy of imitation]

peaks and pinnacles

pedagogue and pedant [pedant = exhibits learning or scholarship ostentatiously]

pedantries and affectations

pedigree and genealogy

peevishness and spleen

pellucid and crystal [pellucid = transparently clear]

penetrating and insidious

penned and planned

peppery and impetuous

perception and recognition

peremptorily and irrevocably [peremptorily = not allowing contradiction] perilous and shifting

permanent and unchangeable

permeate and purify

pernicious and malign

perplexity and confusion

persistent and reiterated

personal and specific

perspicuous and flowing [perspicuous = clearly expressed]

perturbed and restless

perverted and prejudicial

pessimistic and disenchanted

pestilence and famine

petted and indulged

pettiness and prudence

petulance and acrimony

pharisaical and bitter [pharisaical = hypocritically self-righteous and condemnatory]

pictorial and dramatic

picturesque and illustrative

pilgrim and crusader

pillage and demolish

piquant and palatable [piquant = agreeable pungent taste]

pith and brevity

pitiful and destitute

place and power

plagued and persecuted

plainness and severity

plaintive and mournful

plans and projects

plastic and ductile

plausibility and humbug

pleasant and pungent

pleasurable and wholesome

pliant and submissive

plot and verisimilitude

plunder and sacrilege

poetical and pastoral

pointless and ineffective

polite and elegant

political and sociological

pomp and pageantry

ponderous and unwieldy

poor and barren

possession and dominion

potent and prevailing

power and luxury

praise and commend

precedence and usage

precision and efficiency

preference and prejudice

pregnant and suggestive

prejudice and predilection [predilection = preference]

presence and address

present and tangible

prestige and authority

presumptuous and futile

pretentious and inept

pretty and enchanting

pride and indignation

primary and essential

priority and predominance

probity and candor [probity = integrity; uprightness]

prodigal and careless

profile and outline

profound and philosophical

profuse and tearful

prolix and tedious [prolix = prolonged; wordy]

prominence and importance

promise and performance

promptitude and dispatch

proneness and readiness

pronounced and diversified

proof and illustration

propensity and desire

proportion and consistency

propriety and delicacy

prostration and loss

protection and safety

protesting and repelling

protracted and fruitless

provincialism and vulgarity

prudent and sagacious [sagacious = keenly discerning]

puerile and sickly [puerile = immature; childish]

puffy and dissipated

puissant and vigorous [puissant = with power, might]

punctilious and severe [punctilious = precise; scrupulous]

purity and simplicity

purpose and intention

pusillanimous and petty [pusillanimous = cowardly]

puzzled and affected

Q

quackery and incompetence

quaintness and oddity

qualities and gifts

quarrel and wrangle

queer and affected

querulous and plaintive [querulous = complaining; peevish]

quibble and fabricate

quickness and agility

quiet and unobtrusive

quintessential and nuclear [quintessential = perfect example]

quips and cranks

quirks and graces

quivering and fearful

quizzical and whimsical

R

racked and oppressed

racy and incisive

rage and apprehension

rank and learning

rant and gush

rapacity and villainy [rapacity = plundering]

rapidity and precision

rapt and silent

rapture and enthusiasm

rare and exquisite

rashness and heedlessness

ready and spontaneous

real and positive

realistic and effective

reasonable and practical

rebellion and disloyalty

rebuffs and anxieties

receptive and responsive

recognized and honored

recoil and reaction

reconciliation and peace

recondite and abstruse [recondite = concealed; hidden] [abstruse = difficult to understand]

reconnoiter and explore

recreation and amusement

rectitude and delicacy

redeeming and transforming

refined and dignified

refreshing and invigorating

regard and esteem

regret and remorse

regular and symmetrical

rejection and scorn

reliable and trustworthy

relief and redress [redress = set right; remedy]

remarkable and interesting

remorseful and sullen

remote and distant

rend and devastate

repellent and ungracious

repetition and reiteration

repress and silence

repugnance and aversion

repulsive and loathsome

resentment and indignation

reserve and coyness

resistless and implacable

resolution and effort

resonant and tuneful

resourceful and unscrupulous

respected and obeyed

responsibilities and burdens

restive and bored

restless and impatient

retaliation and revenge

reticence and repose

revered and cherished

reverses and disasters

revised and corrected

revolution and sedition [sedition = insurrection; rebellion]

rhapsodies and panegyrics [panegyrics = elaborate praise]

richness and fertility

ridicule and censure

right and praiseworthy

rigid and inexpressive

ripeness and plenitude

rivals and antagonists

roar and ring

robust and rugged

rococo and affected [rococo = elaborate ornamentation]

romantic and pathetic

rough and barren

roundabout and complicated

roused and stimulated

rude and fiery

rugged and inaccessible

rumors and impressions

rushing and gurgling

rust and disuse

S

sad and melancholy

sagacity and virtue [sagacity = farsighted; wise]

sane and simple

sarcastic and cruel

sayings and quibbles

scant and incidental

scattered and desultory [desultory = haphazard; random]

scenes and associations

scholastic and erudite [erudite = learned]

scientific and exact

scintillating and brilliant

scoffing and unbelief

scope and significance

scorched and shriveled

scorn and loathing

scrupulous and anxious

scrutiny and investigation

searching and irresistible

seared and scorched

secondary and subsidiary

secretive and furtive

sedate and serious

selfish and overbearing

sensational and trivial

senseless and unreasoning

sensibilities and emotions

sensitive and capricious

sententious and tiresome [sententious = pompous moralizing; terse and energetic]

sentiment and passion

serene and quiet

serious and studious

severe and saturnine [saturnine = melancholy or sullen]

shabbiness and vulgarity

shadowy and confused

shame and mortification

shams and hypocrisies

shaped and sculptured

sharp and vigorous

shelter and safeguard

shifts and compromises

shivering and chattering

shocked and astonished

short and precarious

shreds and tatters

shrewd and diligent

shrill and piercing

shrinking and nervous

shy and subdued

significant and sinister

signs and tokens

silence and obscurity

similarities and resemblances

simple and straightforward

simpletons and nincompoops

sincerity and frankness

sinewy and active

skill and coolness

skulk and shirk

sleek and languid [languid = lacking energy or vitality; weak]

slight and precarious

slipshod and untidy

slothfulness and perversity

slow and sluggish

slumbering and unsuspected

small and hampered

smirched and tarnished

smoothness and artifice

sneering and sentimental

soberly and truthfully

softness and effeminacy

solemn and dramatic

solitary and idle

solitude and depression

sonorous and musical

sons and scions [scions = descendant or heir]

soporific and sodden [soporific = inducing sleep]

sordid and stupid

sorrow and lamentation

soulless and mindless

sovereign and independent

spacious and lofty

sparkling and spontaneous

spasmodic and hysterical

speedy and inevitable

spicy and pungent

spiritual and invisible

spiteful and sordid

splash and dash

splendor and glory

spontaneity and intensity

sportive and playful

sprightly and vigorous

spur and impulse

spurious and misleading

squalid and dismal [squalid = wretched, dirty, repulsive]

stare and gasp

stately and ponderous

statesmanship and character

staunch and influential

stay and solace

steadfast and resolute

steadily and patiently

stealthy and hostile

stern and unbending

stiff and cumbersome

stifling and venomous

still and translucent

stimulating and wholesome

stings and stimulants

stir and tumult

stolid and soulless

strain and struggle

strange and incomprehensible

stratagems and plots

strenuous and energetic

strictly and absolutely

strife and contention

striking and picturesque

strong and youthful

structure and organization

struggles and misgivings

studied and artificial

stunned and insensible

stupor and despair

sturdy and manly

style and temperament

suave and winning

sublime and aspiring

submission and patience

subordinate and dependent

substance and basis

subtle and elusive

suddenness and vehemence

suffering and desperation

suffused and transfigured

suggestions and stimulations

sullen and fierce

summarize and epitomize

sumptuous and aromatic

sunshine and smiles

superb and showy

supercilious and obstinate [supercilious = haughty disdain]

superficial and obvious

superfluous and impertinent

suppressed and restrained

surmises and suggestions

surprise and wonder

susceptibility and vulnerability

suspense and excitement

suspicion and innuendo [innuendo = indirect derogatory implication]

sustained and measured

sweet and wholesome

swelled and bloated

swift and stealthy

swoop and range

symbolism and imagery

sympathetic and consoling

T

taciturn and laconic [taciturn = untalkative] [laconic = terse]

tactful and conciliatory

talkative and effusive

tame and insipid

tangible and sufficient

tangled and shapeless

tardy and belated

tartness and contradiction

taste and elegance

tattle and babble

taunt and reproach

tawdry and penurious [tawdry = gaudy, cheap] [penurious = stingy]

tears and lamentations

tedious and trivial

temperament and taste

temperately and judiciously

tempest and violence

temporal and evanescent [evanescent = vanishing like vapor]

tenacity and coherence

tender and emotional

tense and straining

tentative and experimental

terrible and satanical

testiness and crabbedness

thankfulness and acknowledgment

theories and speculations

thorough and effective

threatening and formidable

thriftless and unenterprising

thrilling and vitalizing

ties and associations

time and opportunity

timid and vacillating

tiresome and laborious

tolerant and kindly

tone and treatment

topics and instances

tormented and tantalized

tortuous and twisted

tottering and hopeless

touched and thrilled

tractable and gracious

traditions and practices

training and temperament

tranquility and benevolence

transfuse and irradiate

transitory and temporary

transparent and comprehensible

treacherous and cowardly

tremble and oscillate

trenchant and straightforward [trenchant = effective, and vigorous]

trials and tribulations

tricks and stratagems

trifling and doubtful

trite and commonplace

trivial and ridiculous

troublous and menacing

truisms and trivialities

trust and confidence

truth and righteousness

turbid and noise some

turgid and bombastic [turgid = excessively complex] [bombastic = pompous]

turmoil and shouting

twisted and perverted

type and forerunner

tyrant and oppressor

U

unaccountable and grotesque

unaffected and undaunted

unapproached and unapproachable

unassuming and unpretending

unchangeable and enduring

unconsciously and innocently

uncouth and barbarous

unctuous and irresistible [trenchant = insincere earnestness]

undeveloped and ignorant

undignified and futile

uneasiness and apprehension

uneducated and inexperienced

unfamiliar and distant

unfettered and vigorous

unforced and unchecked

unfortunate and unparalleled

unfounded and incredible

ungracious and reluctant

unhappiness and discomfort

unique and original

unity and completeness

unjust and ungrateful

unlimited and absolute

unnatural and harmful

unobserved and unsuspected

unobtrusive and tactful

unparalleled and inexhaustible

unpleasant and bewildering

unpopular and unimpressive

unprecedented and objectionable

unpremeditated and heartfelt

unpromising and scanty

unprotected and friendless

unreal and unsubstantial

unreasoning and uncompromising

unrecognized and unrewarded

unseemly and insufferable

unseen and unsuspected

unsmiling and critical

unswerving and unfaltering

unthinking and careless

untutored and infantine

unusual and unexpected

unuttered and unutterable

unwholesome and vile

upright and credible

uproar and confusion

upstart and braggart

urbanity and unction [unction = exaggerated earnestness]

utter and disastrous

V

vacillation and uncertainty

vague and indistinct

vain and profitless

validity and value

vanities and vices

vapory and chaotic

varied and animated

varnish and falsehood

vassals and inferiors

vast and superlative

vehement and clamorous

veiled and unreadable

venality and corruption

venerable and interesting

veracity and fidelity

verbally and literally

versatility and sympathy

vexation and anxiety

vibrating and sonorous

views and experiences

vigilant and inflexible

vigorous and graphic

violent and ill-balanced

virtuous and wise

virulence and invective [invective = abusive language]

visible and apparent

visionary and obscure

vistas and backgrounds

vital and vigorous

vitiate and poison [vitiate = reduce the value]

vituperation and abuse [vituperation = abusive language]

vivacious and agreeable

vivid and varied

void and nothingness

volatile and fiery

volubly and exuberantly [volubly = ready flow of speech]

volume and impetus

voluminous and varied

voluntarily and habitually

vulgar and artificial

W

wandering and erratic

wanton and unnecessary

war and revelry

warp and woof [warp = lengthwise threads]   [woof = crosswise threads]

wasteful and circuitous

waxing and waning

weak and perfidious

wealth and distinction

wearisome and dull

weighed and winnowed

weighty and dominant

weird and fantastic

wheezing and puffing

whims and inconsistencies

wholesome and beautiful

wholly and solely

wicked and malicious

widened and amplified

wild and irregular

wily and observant

winking and blinking

winning and unforced

wise and beneficent

wistful and dreamy

wit and jocularity [jocularity = given to joking]

withered and wan

woe and lamentation

wonder and delight

work and utility

worldly and ambitious

worth and excellence

wrath and menace

wretched and suppliant

Y

yearning and eagerness

yielding and obedience

yoke and bondage

young and fragile

youthful and callow [callow = immature]

Z

zeal and vehemence

zenith and climax

zest and freshness

zigzag and deviating

SECTION III

FELICITOUS PHRASES

A

ability, humor, and perspicacity [perspicacity = perceptive]

abrupt, rough, and immoderate

abstruse, metaphysical, and idealistic

abundant, varied, and vigorous

accessible, knowable, and demonstrable

accomplished, inventive, and deft-fingered

accuracy, ease, and grace

acquire, classify, and arrange

action, incident, and interest

active, learned, and liberal

acts, activities, and aims

actual, stern, and pathetic

acuteness, honesty, and, fearlessness

addition, correction, and amplification

adventurous, eager, and afraid

affected, pedantic, and vain [pedantic = attention to detail or rules]

affluent, genial, and frank

aggressive, envious, and arrogant

agreeable, engaging, and delightful

air, woodland, and water

alarmed, anxious, and uneasy

alert, hopeful, and practical

amazement, resentment, and indignation

ambiguous, strange, and sinister

amiable, genial, and charitable

amusing, sympathetic, and interesting

ancient, subtle, and treacherous

annoyances, shifts, and inconveniences

anxious, fearful, and anticipative

appearance, conversation, and bearing

approbation, wealth, and power [approbation = warm approval; praise]

apt, explicit, and communicative

ardent, undisciplined, and undirected

arrogance, conceit, and disdain

artificial, rhetorical, and mundane

artistic, progressive, and popular

aspirations, dreams, and devotions

assured, stern, and judicial

astonishment, apprehension, and horror

attainments, possessions, and character

attention, forbearance, and patience

attract, interest, and persuade

augmenting, furthering, and reinforcing

austere, calm, and somber

authority, leadership, and command

avarice, pride, and revenge

awakened, girded, and active

awe, reverence, and adoration

awkwardness, narrowness, and self-consciousness

B

barbarous, shapeless, and irregular

beautiful, graceful, and accomplished

beggar, thief, and impostor

belittling, personal, and selfish

birth, rank, and fortune

bitter, baleful, and venomous

bland, patient, and methodical

blessing, bestowing, and welcoming

blind, partial, and prejudiced

blithe, innocent, and free

bluster, swagger, and might

body, soul, and mind

boisterous, undignified, and vulgar

bold, original, and ingenious

bombastic, incongruous, and unsymmetrical

bountiful, exuberant, and luxurious

brain, energy, and enterprise

brave, authoritative, and confident

breadth, richness, and freshness

breathless, confused, and exhilarated

brief, isolated, and fragmentary

brilliancy, energy, and zeal

broad, spare, and athletic

broken, apologetic, and confused

brotherhood, humanity, and chivalry

brusqueness, rudeness, and self-assertion

brutish, repulsive, and terrible

busy, active, and toiling

C

calculated, logical, and dispassionate

calm, earnest, and genial

candor, integrity, and straightforwardness

capricious, perverse, and prejudiced

careful, reasoned, and courteous

cautious, prudent, and decisive

caviling, petulance, and discontent [caviling = finding trivial objections]

censured, slighted, and despised

certain, swift, and final

chance, doubt, and mutability

character, life, and aims

charitable, just, and true

charm, grace, and glory

cheerful, modest, and delicate

childish, discordant, and superfluous

chill, harden, and repel

circumstances, properties, and characteristics

civilized, mild, and humane

clear, cloudless, and serene

cleverness, independence, and originality

coarseness, violence, and cunning

coherent, interdependent, and logical

cold, cynical, and relentless

color, intensity, and vivacity

comfort, virtue, and happiness

comments, criticisms, and judgments

common, dull, and threadbare

compact, determinate, and engaging

conceited, commonplace, and uninspiring

conception, direction, and organization

confident, inflexible, and uncontrollable

conflict, confusion, and disintegration

confused, broken, and fragmentary

conscience, heart, and life

conscientious, clear-headed, and accurate

consistent, thoughtful, and steadfast

consoling, pacifying, and benign

constant, wise, and sympathetic

constitution, temperament, and habits

convince, convert, and reconstruct

copious, redundant, and involved

corroding, venomous, and malignant

corrupt, self-seeking, and dishonest

countenance, voice, and manner

country, lake, and mountain

courage, patience, and honesty

courteous, patient, and indefatigable

covetousness, selfishness, and ignorance

credulous, weak, and superstitious

crimes, follies, and misfortunes

crisp, emphatic, and powerful

crude, warped, and barren

cruelty, violence, and injustice

culture, growth, and progress

cunning, cruelty, and treachery

curious, fantastic, and charming

D

danger, difficulty, and hardship

darkness, doubt, and difficulty

dazzle, amaze, and overpower

deadly, silent, and inaccessible

deceitful, lazy, and dishonest

decent, respectable, and sensible

decisions, affirmations, and denials

deep, flexible, and melodious

defeated, discredited, and despised

deferential, conciliatory, and courteous

definite, tangible, and practicable

deftness, delicacy, and veracity

degraded, defeated, and emasculated

dejected, discouraged, and disappointed

deliberately, coolly, and methodically

delicate, mobile, and complex

delightful, witty, and sensible

denounced, persecuted, and reviled

dependent, subsidiary, and allied

depth, tenderness, and sublimity

desolated, impoverished, and embittered

despair, finality, and hopelessness

detailed, described, and explained

devastating, horrible, and irremediable

devout, gentle, and kindly

difficult, painful, and slow

digestion, circulation, and assimilation

dignity, solemnity, and responsibility

diligent, cautious, and painstaking

dingy, cumbersome, and depressing

directness, spontaneity, and simplicity

disciplined, drilled, and trained

discontent, revolt, and despair

discordant, coarse, and unpleasing

discourses, lectures, and harangues

disheveled, wild, and distracted

disinterested, patient, and exact

dislikes, jealousies, and ambitions

dismal, cold, and dead

dismay, remorse, and anguish

disordered, wild, and incoherent

dispassionate, wise, and intelligent

disposition, taste, and temperament

dissension, discord, and rebellion

distracted, hopeless, and bankrupt

disturbed, shaken, and distressed

diversified, animated, and rapid

division, prejudice, and antagonism

doctrine, life, and destiny

dogmatic, scientific, and philosophic

doubt, cynicism, and indifference

draggled, dirty, and slouching

dramatic, picturesque, and vigorous

dream, speculate, and philosophize

drunkenness, licentiousness, and profanity

dry, inane, and droll

dull, hideous, and arid

dullards, hypocrites, and cowards

dust, turmoil, and smoke

duties, labors, and anxieties

dwarfed, scant, and wretched

E

eagerness, heartiness, and vehemence

earnestness, zeal, and intelligence

ease, power, and self-confidence

easy, natural, and unembarrassed

effluent, radiating, and fructifying [fructifying = Make fruitful or productive]

egotistic, disdainful, and proud

elegant, convincing, and irresistible

emotion, affection, and desire

empty, noisy, and blundering

end, aim, and purpose

energies, capacities, and opportunities

enlighten, uplift, and strengthen

enmity, suspicion, and hatred

enrich, discipline, and embellish

enthusiasm, vehemence, and spirit

envy, jealousy, and malice

equable, animated, and alert

erect, elastic, and graceful

error, ignorance, and strife

essence, existence, and identity

esteem, confidence, and affection

evil, disease, and death

exact, logical, and convincing

examine, compare, and decide

excessive, inaccurate, and unliterary

excitements, interests, and responsibilities

experience, knowledge, and conduct

exposure, ruin, and flight

exterior, formal, and imposing

F

faded, dusty, and unread

failures, experiences, and ambitions

fair, proud, and handsome

fairies, sprites, and angels

faith, hope, and love

false, wicked, and disloyal

fantastic, absurd, and impossible

fear, dread, and apprehension

features, form, and height

feeble, illogical, and vicious

feelings, motives, and desires

fertility, ingenuity, and resource

fervently, patiently, and persistently

fibs, myths, and fables

fierce, dogmatic, and bigoted

figure, face, and attitude

fire, force, and passion

flit, change, and vary

flushed, trembling, and unstrung

foibles, tricks, and fads

foliage, color, and symmetry

follies, fashions, and infatuations

foolish, ignorant, and unscrupulous

force, grace, and symmetry

forcible, extraordinary, and sublime

foremost, preeminent, and incomparable

foresight, prudence, and economy

form, color, and distance

formless, silent, and awful

forward, onward, and upward

frank, kindly, and unfaltering

free, equal, and just

freedom, honor, and dignity

fresh, vigorous, and telling

fretfulness, irritability, and petulance

friendly, amiable, and sincere

frigid, austere, and splendid

fruitful, luminous, and progressive

full, animated, and varied

fullness, force, and precision

furious, sanguinary, and disorganizing
[sanguinary = Accompanied by bloodshed]

fustian, padding, and irrelevancy
[fustian = pompous, bombastic, and ranting]

G

gaunt, desolate, and despoiled

gay, easy, and cordial

generous, large-hearted, and magnanimous

genial, frank, and confiding

genius, learning, and virtue

gentle, firm, and loving

genuineness, disinterestedness, and strength

germinate, develop, and radiate

gesture, accent, and attitude

ghastly, hateful, and ugly

gibes, sneers, and anger

gifts, graces, and accomplishments

gladness, exaltation, and triumph

glean, gather, and digest

gloomy, silent, and tranquil

glow, grace, and pleasantness

good, gentle, and affectionate

gorgeous, still, and warm

grace, simplicity, and sweetness

gracious, mild, and good

gradual, cautious, and well-reasoned

gratitude, happiness, and affection

grave, disastrous, and wanton

gravity, sweetness, and patience

gray, monotonous, and uninteresting

great, grand, and mighty

greed, lust, and cruelty

grim, lean, and hungry

gross, ignorant, and impudent

growth, progress, and extension

guide, philosopher, and friend

H

habits, tastes, and opinions

hard, stern, and inexorable

harmony, peace, and happiness

harsh, intolerant, and austere

health, character, and efficiency

helpful, suggestive, and inspiring

helpless, hopeless, and downtrodden

high, lofty, and noble

high-spirited, confident, and genial

history, philosophy, and eloquence

homage, ability, and culture

honesty, probity, and justice [probity = integrity; uprightness]

honors, riches, and power

hopes, aspirations, and longings

hot, swift, and impatient

humanity, freedom, and justice

humble, submissive, and serviceable

humor, fancy, and susceptibility

I

idle, profuse, and profligate

ignorance, fear, and selfishness

illuminating, chastening, and transforming

images, events, and incidents

imagination, judgment, and reason

immediate, sure, and easy

immethodical, irregular, and inconsecutive

impatient, inconsiderate, and self-willed

impetuous, fierce, and irresistible

impracticable, chimerical, and contemptible

impulse, energy, and activity

inclinations, habits, and interests

incoherent, loud, and confusing

incomparable, matchless, and immortal

inconsiderate, irritable, and insolent

indignation, surprise, and reproach

indirect, obscure, and ambiguous

indolent, dreamy, and frolicsome

inert, torpid, and lethargic

ingenuity, force, and originality

innocence, intelligence, and youth

inordinate, excessive, and extravagant

insight, knowledge, and capacity

insincere, partial, and arbitrary

insipid, commonplace, and chattering

insolence, injustice, and imposture

intelligence, taste, and manners

intense, weighty, and philosophical

inventions, sciences, and discoveries

irksome, painful, and depressing

irresolute, procrastinating, and unenterprising

irritable, sulky, and furious

issues, hopes, and interests

J

jealousy, exclusiveness, and taciturnity [taciturnity = habitually untalkative]

jovial, ready-witted, and broad-gaged

joyous, delightful, and gay

justice, mercy, and peace

K

keen, clear, and accurate

knowing, feeling, and willing

knowledge, skill, and foresight

L

labors, anxieties, and trials

large, rhythmical, and pleasing

laughter, ridicule, and sneers

lead, attack, and conquer

learning, profundity, and imagination

legislation, education, and religion

levity, indolence, and procrastination

libelers, reviewers, and rivals

liberating, vitalizing, and cheering

liberty, justice, and humanity

light, easy, and playful

literature, history, and legend

lively, careless, and joyous

lofty, serene, and impregnable

logical, clear, and consistent

loitering, heart-sick, and reluctant

lonely, sad, and enslaved

long, wailing, and passionate

lost, ruined, and deserted

loud, deep, and distinct

love, veneration, and gratitude

lucid, lively, and effective

luxurious, whimsical, and selfish

M

magnificent, sumptuous, and stately

magnitude, duration, and scope

majesty, beauty, and truth

malevolence, vanity, and falsehood

manly, refined, and unaffected

mean, pitiful, and sordid

meek, humane, and temperate

melancholy, grave, and serious

mercy, truth, and righteousness

methodical, sensible, and conscientious

might, majesty, and power

mild, sweet, and peaceable

mischief, cruelty, and futility

moans, shrieks, and curses

mobile, quick, and sensitive

modest, sympathetic, and kind

molding, controlling, and conforming

monstrous, incredible, and inhuman

moral, material, and social

motionless, staring, and appalled

motives, purposes, and intentions

mountains, seas, and vineyards

moved, swayed, and ruled

murder, destruction, and agony

mystery, vagueness, and jargon

N

narrow, precise, and formal

natural, innocent, and laudable

neatness, order, and comfort

necessary, just, and logical

neglect, rashness, and incompetence

new, strange, and unusual

niggardly, sordid, and parsimonious [grudging, wretched and frugal]

noble, laudable, and good

noise, clatter, and clamor

null, void, and useless

O

obscure, difficult, and subtle

observation, discrimination, and comparison

obsolete, artificial, and inadequate

obstinacy, stupidity, and willfulness

officious, fidgety, and talkative

old, absurd, and meaningless

one, individual, and integral

openly, frankly, and legitimately

opposition, bitterness, and defiance

oppressive, grasping, and slanderous

opulent, powerful, and prosperous

organization, monopoly, and pressure

origin, character, and aim

original, terse, and vigorous

overriding, arrogant, and quarrelsome

P

pain, toil, and privation

pale, ugly, and sinister

parable, precept, and practice

partial, false, and disastrous

passion, tenderness, and reverence

patient, gentle, and kind

peace, order, and civilization

pellucid, animated, and varied [pellucid = transparently clear]

permanent, true, and real

perplexed, tedious, and obscure

personal, sharp, and pointed

perspicuity, vivacity, and grace [perspicuity = clearness and lucidity]

pert, smirking, and conceited

pervading, searching, and saturating

petty, unsuccessful, and unamiable

philosophy, morals, and discoveries

picturesque, daring, and potent

piety, charity, and humility

pillage, arson, and bloodshed

pious, patient, and trustful

pity, sympathy, and compassion

placable, reasonable, and willing [placable = easily calmed; tolerant]

place, fame, and fortune

placid, clear, and mellow

plague, pestilence, and famine

plan, purpose, and work

pleasant, friendly, and amiable

pleased, interested, and delighted

pleasure, enjoyment, and satisfaction

plenty, content, and tranquility

plodding, sedentary, and laborious

poise, dignity, and reserve

polished, elegant, and sumptuous

politics, business, and religion

pompous, affected, and unreal

poor, miserable, and helpless

pose, gesture, and expression

powerful, dazzling, and daring

practical, visible, and tangible

precious, massive, and splendid

precise, formal, and cynical

prejudice, dulness, and spite

prepossessions, opinions, and prejudices

presiding, directing, and controlling

pride, passion, and conceit

princely, picturesque, and pathetic

principles, conduct, and habits

progress, order, and happiness

prolonged, obstinate, and continued

prompt, fiery, and resolute

propriety, perspicacity, and accuracy [perspicacity = perceptive]

prosaic, dull, and unattractive

protective, propitiatory, and accommodating [propitiatory = conciliatory]

protests, criticisms, and rebukes

proud, reserved, and disagreeable

prudence, mildness, and firmness

puckered, winking, and doddering

pure, honorable, and just

purge, brace, and strengthen

purpose, intention, and meaning

puzzles, tangles, and questionings

Q

quarrels, misunderstandings, and enmities

questions, disputes, and controversies

quicken, sharpen, and intensify

quiet, unaffected, and unostentatious

R

raise, refine, and elevate

rapid, robust, and effective

rapt, emotional, and mystic

raptures, transports, and fancies

rash, violent, and indefinite

readiness, skill, and accuracy

reading, reflection, and observation

reaffirmed, amplified, and maintained

real, earnest, and energetic

regard, esteem, and affection

relaxation, recreation, and pleasure

religion, politics, and literature

reminiscences, associations, and impressions

remote, careless, and indifferent

reparations, restitutions, and guarantees

repress, curb, and correct

reproach, shame, and remorse

reproof, correction, and instruction

resentment, hatred, and despair

resolute, patient, and fervent

resourceful, steadfast, and skillful

respect, admiration, and homage

rest, respite, and peace

restless, discontented, and rebellious

restraint, self-denial, and austerity

reticent, restrained, and reserved

reverie, contemplation, and loneliness

rich, thoughtful, and glowing

ridicule, sarcasm, and invective [invective = abusive language]

rights, powers, and privileges

rise, flourish, and decay

robustness, elasticity, and firmness

romance, adventure, and passion

rough, barren, and unsightly

rude, sulky, and overbearing

rush, roar, and shriek

S

sacredness, dignity, and loveliness

sad, gloomy, and suspicious

safe, sensible, and sane

sanguine, impulsive, and irrepressible [sanguine = cheerfully confident; optimistic]

sarcasm, satire, and ridicule

satiety, surfeit, and tedium

savage, fierce, and intractable

scheming, contriving, and dishonesty

self-absorbed, conceited, and contemptuous

self-conscious, artificial, and affected

self-exacting, laborious, and inexhaustible

selfishness, coarseness, and mendacity [mendacity = untruthfulness]

sense, grace, and good-will

sensibility, harmony, and energy

sensitive, ardent, and conscientious

serene, ineffable, and flawless [ineffable = indescribable]

serious, calm, and searching

settled, adjusted, and balanced

shallow, false, and petty

shapes, forms, and artifices

sharpness, bitterness, and sarcasm

shivering, moaning, and weeping

shrewd, artful, and designing

shy, wild, and provocative

sick, ashamed, and disillusioned

silent, cold, and motionless

simple, full, and impressive

sin, selfishness, and luxury

sincere, placable, and generous [placable = easily calmed; tolerant]

skill, sagacity, and firmness [sagacity = farsighted; wise]

sleekness, stealth, and savagery

slovenly, base, and untrue

slow, reluctant, and unwelcome

smirking, garrulous, and pretentious [garrulous = excessive and trivial talk]

smooth, sentimental, and harmonious

smug, fat, and complacent

sneers, innuendoes, and insinuations

social, esthetic, and intellectual

solitary, sedentary, and lifeless

sound, human, and healthy

sour, malignant, and envious

spacious, clean, and comfortable

speechless, motionless, and amazed

spirit, vigor, and variety

spitefulness, dishonesty, and cruelty

splendid, powerful, and enduring

startling, alarming, and vehement

statesmen, philosophers, and divines

steadiness, self-control, and serenity

stern, forbidding, and unfeeling

stiff, decorous, and formal

strained, worn, and haggard

strange, dark, and mysterious

strengthen, invigorate, and discipline

strenuous, intelligent, and alive

striking, bold, and magnificent

stripped, swept, and bare

strong, cool, and inflexible

studied, discussed, and debated

sturdy, energetic, and high-minded

style, manner, and disposition

subtle, delicate, and refined

successful, energetic, and ingenious

sudden, vehement, and unfamed

suggestive, stimulating, and inspiring

sullen, silent, and disconsolate

suppliant, gentle, and submissive [suppliant = asking humbly]

surprise, admiration, and wonder

suspicious, restive, and untractable

swiftness, mobility, and penetrativeness

sympathy, service, and compassion

T

talent, scholarship, and refinement

tameness, monotony, and reserve

taste, feeling, and sentiment

tedious, painful, and distressing

temper, pride, and sensuality

temperament, character, and circumstance

temperate, sweet, and venerable

tenderness, loyalty, and devotion

terror, remorse, and shame

terseness, simplicity, and quaintness

theatrical, sensational, and demonstrative

thought, utterance, and action

threats, cries, and prayers

thrilling, dramatic, and picturesque

thwart, criticize, and embarrass

time, thought, and consideration

touched, strengthened, and transformed

tradition, prejudice, and stupidity

tragic, tremendous, and horrible

transparent, theatric, and insincere

treachery, envy, and selfishness

tremulous, soft, and bright [tremulous = trembling, quivering, shaking]

trial, discipline, and temptation

tricks, shufflings, and frauds

trivial, labored, and wearisome

true, lasting, and beneficial

tyranny, injustice, and extortion

U

ugly, scowling, and offensive

unbending, contemptuous, and scornful

unclean, shameful, and degrading

undecided, wavering, and cautious

unearthly, horrible, and obnoxious

uneasy, overstrained, and melancholy

unity, emphasis, and coherence

unmodulated, cold, and expressionless

unphilosophical, unsystematic, and discursive

unscrupulous, heartless, and hypocritical

unwholesome, bewildering, and unprofitable

unworldly, peaceable, and philosophical

upright, kind-hearted, and blameless

urgent, tumultuous, and incomprehensible

V

vague, impalpable, and incongruous

vanities, stupidities, and falsehoods

venerable, patriotic, and virtuous

verities, certainties, and realities

vigilant, inveterate, and unresting [inveterate = long established]

vigorous, subtle, and comprehensive

violent, sinister, and rebellious

virtue, genius, and charm

visionary, fraudulent, and empirical

vital, formidable, and dominant

vivid, comprehensible, and striking

vulgarity, ignorance, and misapprehension

W

waddling, perspiring, and breathless

want, worry, and woe

wasteful, indolent, and evasive

watchful, suspicious, and timid

wealth, position, and influence

wearied, despondent, and bewildered

weight, size, and solidity

well-proportioned, logical, and sane

whimsical, fantastic, and impracticable

wholesome, beautiful, and righteous

wicked, pernicious, and degrading

wild, confused, and dizzy

wilful, wanton, and
deliberate

will, energy, and self-
control

wisdom, patriotism, and
justice

wit, fancy, and imagination

worthless, broken, and
defeated

wretchedness, deformity,
and malice

wrinkled, careworn, and
pale

SECTION IV

IMPRESSIVE PHRASES

A

able, skillful, thorough, and genuine

absolute, complete, unqualified, and final

accurate, precise, exact, and truthful

active, alert, vigorous, and industrious

actual, positive, certain, and genuine

adequate, uniform, proportionate, and equitable

adventurous, fine, active, and gossipy

adverse, antagonistic, unfriendly, and hostile

advisable, advantageous, acceptable, and expedient

affable, diffident, humble, and mild

affectionate, tender, loving, and attached

affluent, opulent, abundant, and ample

allurements, pits, snares, and torments

anger, indignation, resentment, and rage

animate, impel, instigate, and embolden

animosity, malice, enmity, and hatred

annul, frustrate, reverse, and destroy

anxiety, caution, watchfulness, and solicitude

apparent, ostensible, plausible, and specious

appropriate, use, arrogate, and usurp [arrogate = claim without right; appropriate]

approval, enthusiasm, sympathy, and applause

aptitude, capacity, efficiency, and power

arbitrary, dictatorial, domineering, and imperious [imperious = arrogantly domineering or overbearing]

architecture, sculpture, painting, and poetry

ardent, impatient, keen, and vehement

argue, discuss, dispute, and prove

arrangement, place, time, and circumstance

art, science, knowledge, and culture

artful, wily, insincere, and disingenuous

artificial, soulless, hectic, and unreal

assemble, amass, accumulate, and acquire

assiduity, tenderness, industry, and vigilance [assiduity = persistent application]

assurance, persuasion, fidelity, and loyalty

attention, effort, diligence, and assiduity [assiduity = persistent application]

august, magnanimous, important, and distinguished

authoritative, independent, arbitrary, and supreme

avaricious, grasping, miserly, and parsimonious [parsimonious = excessively frugal]

aversion, dislike, hatred, and repugnance

B

bad, vicious, unwholesome, and distressing

babble, prate, chatter, and prattle

barbarous, brutal, inhuman, and cruel

base, cowardly, abject, and hideous

battle, defeat, frustrate, and ruin

bearing, deportment, manner, and behavior

beg, entreat, implore, and supplicate

beliefs, doctrines, ceremonies, and practices

boorish, clownish, rude, and uncultivated

boundless, immeasurable, unlimited, and infinite

bravery, courage, fearlessness, and confidence

breadth, knowledge, vision, and power

brilliant, beautiful, elegant, and faithful

broaden, enlarge, extend, and augment

business, profession, occupation, and vocation

C

candid, sincere, familiar, and ingenuous

captious, petulant, peevish, and splenetic [captious = point out trivial faults]

cautious, discreet, considerate, and provident

certain, confident, positive, and unquestionable

chagrin, vexation, irritation, and mortification

character, disposition, temperament, and reputation

charm, fascinate, bewitch, and captivate

cheap, inexpensive, inferior, and common

cheer, animate, vivify, and exhilarate [vivify = bring life to]

chiefly, particularly, principally, and especially

childhood, youth, manhood, and age

circumstance, condition, environment, and surroundings

claim, grab, trick, and compel

clean, fastidious, frugal, and refined

clear, distinct, obvious, and intelligible

clumsy, crawling, snobbish, and comfort-loving

coarse, gross, offensive, and nauseous

coax, flatter, wheedle, and persuade

cogitate, contemplate, meditate, and ponder

cold, frigid, unfeeling, and stoical

commanding, authoritative, imperative, and peremptory [peremptory = ending all debate or action]

compassion, goodwill, admiration, and enthusiasm

confirm, establish, sustain, and strengthen

conform, submit, obey, and satisfy

confuse, distort, involve, and misinterpret

consistent, congruous, firm, and harmonious

cool, collected, calm, and self-possessed

copious, commanding, sonorous, and emotional

cowardly, timid, shrinking, and timorous

crazy, absurd, nonsensical, and preposterous

crude, rough, jagged, and pitiless

D

daring, cordial, discerning, and optimistic

darkness, dimness, dulness, and blackness

deadly, destructive, fatal, and implacable

deceit, delusion, treachery, and sham

deep, abstruse, learned, and profound

deficient, inadequate, scanty, and incomplete

define, explain, determine, and circumscribe

degrade, defame, humble, and debase

delicacy, daintiness, tact, and refinement

delicious, sweet, palatable, and delightful

democracy, equality, justice, and freedom

deny, dismiss, exclude, and repudiate

deprive, dispossess, divest, and despoil

describe, delineate, depict, and characterize

designed, contrived, planned, and executed

desperate, extreme, reckless, and irremediable

despicable, abject, servile, and worthless

destructive, detrimental, deleterious, and subversive

desultory, discursive, loose, and unmethodical [desultory = disconnected: haphazard]

detestable, abominable, horrible, and hideous

developed, revealed, measured, and tested

difference, disagreement, discord, and estrangement

difficult, arduous, intricate, and perplexing

diffuse, discursive, rambling, and wordy

diligence, attention, industry, and assiduity [assiduity = persistent application]

disagreement, discrepancy, difference, and divergence

disconsolate, desolate, pessimistic, and impossible

discrimination, acuteness, insight, and judgment

disgust, distaste, loathing, and abhorrence

dissatisfied, rebellious, unsettled, and satirical

distinct, definite, clear, and obvious

distinguished, glorious, illustrious, and eminent

disturbed, shaken, distressed, and bewildered

docile, tractable, compliant, and teachable

dogmatic, bigoted, libelous, and unsympathizing

doubt, indecision, suspense, and perplexity

dread, disgust, repugnance, and dreariness

dreary, dispirited, unhappy, and peevish

dry, lifeless, tiresome, and uninteresting

dubious, equivocal, fluctuating, and uncertain

dull, heavy, painstaking, and conscientious

E

earth, air, stars, and sea

efficient, forcible, adequate, and potent

emaciated, scraggy, meager, and attenuated

endless, ceaseless, immutable, and imperishable

energy, eagerness, earnestness, and enthusiasm

enhance, exalt, elevate, and intensify

enormous, base, prodigious, and colossal

enrage, incense, infuriate, and exasperate

enthusiasm, devotion, intensity, and zeal

envy, discontent, deception, and ignorance

equitable, reasonable, just, and honest

equivocal, uncertain, cloudy, and ambiguous

eradicate, extirpate, exterminate, and annihilate [extirpate = pull up by the roots]

erroneous, faulty, inaccurate, and inexact

eternal, unchangeable, unerring, and intelligent

evil, misfortune, corruption, and disaster

exacting, suspicious, irritable, and wayward

exalt, dignify, elevate, and extol

examination, inquiry, scrutiny, and research

exceed, outdo, surpass, and transcend

exceptional, uncommon, abnormal, and extraordinary

excitement, distraction, diversion, and stimulation

exhaustive, thorough, radical, and complete

expend, dissipate, waste, and squander

F

facile, showy, cheap, and superficial

faithful, truthful, loyal, and trustworthy

fame, distinction, dignity, and honor

fanatic, enthusiast, visionary, and zealot

fanciful, unreal, fantastic, and grotesque

fancy, humor, vagary, and caprice [vagary = extravagant or erratic notion or action]

fashion, practice, habit, and usage

fastidious, proud, gracious, and poised

fate, fortune, contingency, and opportunity

fatuous, dreamy, moony, and impracticable

fear, timidity, cowardice, and pusillanimity

feeble, languid, timid, and irresolute

ferocious, restive, savage, and uncultivated

fervent, enthusiastic, anxious, and zealous

fiction, fancy, falsehood, and fabrication

fine, fragile, delicate, and dainty

firmness, steadfastness, stability, and tenacity

flash, flame, flare, and glare

flat, insipid, tame, and monotonous

fluctuating, hesitating, vacillating, and oscillating

folly, foolishness, imbecility, and fatuity

foolhardy, hasty, adventurous, and reckless

fop, coxcomb, puppy, and jackanapes [jackanapes = conceited person]

force, vigor, power, and energy

formal, precise, stiff, and methodical

fortunate, happy, prosperous, and successful

fragile, frail, brittle, and delicate

freedom, familiarity, liberty, and independence

frightful, fearful, direful, and dreadful

frivolous, trifling, petty, and childish

fruitful, fertile, prolific, and productive

fruitless, vain, trivial, and foolish

frustrate, defeat, disappoint, and thwart

fully, completely, abundantly, and perfectly

furious, impetuous, boisterous, and vehement

G

gaiety, merriment, joy, and hilarity

gallant, ardent, fearless, and self-sacrificing

garnish, embellish, beautify, and decorate

generous, candid, easy, and independent

genius, intellect, aptitude, and capacity

genteel, refined, polished, and well-bred

gentle, persuasive, affective, and simple

genuine, true, unaffected, and sincere

ghastly, grim, shocking, and hideous

gibe, mock, taunt, and jeer

giddy, fickle, flighty, and thoughtless

gleam, glimmer, glance, and glitter

gloomy, dismal, dark, and dejected

glorious, noble, exalted, and resplendent

glut, gorge, cloy, and satiate [cloy = too filling, rich, or sweet]

good, safe, venerable, and solid

government, law, order, and organization

grand, stately, dignified, and pompous

grave, contemplative, reserved, and profound

great, joyous, strong, and triumphant

greed, avarice, covetousness, and cupidity

gross, academic, vulgar, and indiscriminate

H

habit, custom, method, and fashion

handsome, exquisite, brilliant, and accomplished

harmless, innocent, innocuous, and inoffensive

harmony, order, sublimity, and beauty

harsh, discordant, disagreeable, and ungracious

hasty, superficial, impatient, and desultory

[desultory = disconnected: haphazard]

healed, soothed, consoled, and assuaged

healthy, hale, sound, and wholesome

heavy, sluggish, dejected, and crushing

high-minded, truthful, honest, and courageous

holy, hallowed, sacred, and consecrated

homely, hideous, horrid, and unsightly

honor, obedience, virtue, and loyalty

hopefulness, peace, sweetness, and strength

hopes, dreams, programs, and ideals

hospitable, generous, tolerant, and kindly

hot, hasty, fervent, and fiery

humane, gentle, kind, and generous

humble, simple, submissive, and unostentatious

I

idea, imagination, conception, and ideal

idleness, recreation, repose, and rest

ignominious, infamous, despicable, and contemptible

illumine, instruct, enlighten, and inform

imaginative, sensitive, nervous, and highly-strung

impatience, indolence, wastefulness, and inconclusiveness

impel, stimulate, animate, and inspirit

imperious, wayward, empirical, and impatient [imperious = arrogantly domineering or overbearing]

improvident, incautious, prodigal, and thriftless

impudent, insolent, irrelevant, and officious

inadvertency, carelessness, negligence, and oversight

indecision, doubt, fear, and lassitude

indifference, caution, coldness, and weariness

indolent, passive, sluggish, and slothful

ineffectual, powerless, useless, and unavailing

infamy, shame, dishonor, and disgrace

infantile, childish, boyish, and dutiful

informal, natural, unconventional, and careless

insolent, impudent, impertinent, and flippant

integrity, frankness, sincerity, and truthfulness

intellectual, moral, emotional, and esthetic

intense, earnest, violent, and extreme

invent, discover, design, and contrive

inveterate, confirmed, chronic, and obstinate

invidious, envious, odious, and offensive

invincible, unconquerable, insurmountable, and insuperable

irksome, tiresome, tedious, and annoying

irregular, uncertain, devious, and unsystematic

irritable, choleric, petulant, and susceptible

J

jangle, wrangle, squabble, and quarrel

jealousy, suspicion, envy, and watchfulness

joyful, lively, happy, and hilarious

judgment, discrimination, penetration, and sagacity [sagacity = farsighted; wise]

just, impartial, equitable, and unbiased

juvenile, childish, trifling, and puerile [puerile = immature; childish]

K

keen, intelligent, penetrating, and severe

keep, protect, support, and sustain

kind, sympathetic, ready, and appreciative

kingly, noble, imperial, and august

knowledge, learning, enlightenment, and understanding

L

lapses, makeshifts, delays, and irregularities

lawful, legitimate, allowable, and just

lazy, listless, drowsy, and indifferent

lightly, freely, unscrupulously, and irresponsibly

lively, vivacious, vigorous, and forcible

loss, deprivation, forfeiture, and waste

loud, noisy, showy, and clamorous

loutish, prankish, selfish, and cunning

love, depth, loyalty, and faithfulness

lucidity, impressiveness, incisiveness, and pungency [pungency = to the point]

M

malice, anger, charitableness, and indignation

malignity, brutality, malevolence, and inhumanity

manners, morals, habits, and behavior

marvelous, wonderful, extraordinary, and incredible

massive, ponderous, solid, and substantial

mastery, proficiency, dexterity, and superiority

matchless, unrivaled, inimitable, and incomparable

maxim, proverb, truism, and apothegm [apothegm = terse, witty, instructive saying]

medley, mixture, jumble, and hodge-podge

meekness, inwardness, patience, and self-denial

merciless, remorseless, relentless, and ruthless

mild, gentle, humble, and submissive

mismanagement, indecision, obstinacy, and hardihood

mixture, medley, variety, and diversification

modesty, fineness, sensitiveness, and fastidiousness

money, position, power, and consequence

mood, temper, humor, and caprice

motive, impulse, incentive, and intimation

mysterious, dark, secret, and enigmatical

N

narrow, limited, selfish, and bigoted

necessary, expedient, indispensable, and unavoidable

necessity, emergency, exigency, and crisis [exigency = urgent situation]

neglect, overlook, disregard, and contemn [contemn = despise]

nice, finical, effeminate, and silly [finical = Finicky]

niggardly, close, miserly, and parsimonious [parsimonious = Excessively frugal]

noble, pure, exalted, and worthy

nonsense, trash, twaddle, and rubbish

novel, recent, rare, and unusual

noxious, unwholesome, mischievous, and destructive

O

obdurate, unfeeling, callous, and obstinate

obedient, respectful, dutiful, and submissive

object, propose, protest, and decline

obliging, kind, helpful, and courteous

obscure, shadowy, intricate, and mysterious

obsequious, cringing, fawning, and servile [obsequious = fawning.]

observations, sentiments, ideas, and theories

obstinacy, pertinacity, stubbornness, and inflexibility [pertinacity = persistent]

offensive, disagreeable, distasteful, and obnoxious

officious, impertinent, insolent, and meddlesome

P

particular, precise, formal, and punctilious [punctilious = scrupulous]

passions, weaknesses, uglinesses, and deformities

patient, loyal, hard-working, and true

peace, quiet, tranquility, and harmony

peculiar, individual, specific, and appropriate

perplex, embarrass, confuse, and mystify

phrases, figures, metaphors, and quotations

piteous, woebegone, dismal, and dolorous

placid, meek, gentle, and moderate

plain, transparent, simple, and obvious

play, diversion, pastime, and amusement

pleasant, jocular, witty, and facetious

pliable, ductile, supple, and yielding

poetry, sentiment, morality, and religion

polished, deft, superficial, and conventional

polite, polished, cultured, and refined

positive, direct, explicit, and dogmatic

powerful, efficient, vivid, and forcible

precise, delicate, discriminating, and fastidious

prejudicial, injurious, noxious, and pernicious

preposterous, irrational, unreasonable, and nonsensical

pretense, subterfuge, simulation, and disguise

prevent, restrain, dissuade, and dishearten

primary, foremost, leading, and principal

probity, directness, simplicity, and sincerity [probity = integrity]

profession, business, trade, and vocation

profit, advantage, benefit, and emolument [emolument = compensation]

profuse, excessive, copious, and extravagant

progress, prosperity, peace, and happiness

prolix, prosaic, prolonged, and wordy [prolix = excessive length]

property, comforts, habits, and conveniences

prudence, judgment, wisdom, and discretion

pulsing, coursing, throbbing, and beating

pure, kind, sweet-tempered, and unselfish

purified, exalted, fortified, and illumined

purpose, meaning, scope, and tendency

Q

quack, imposture, charlatan, and mountebank [mountebank = flamboyant charlatan]

qualified, powerful, vigorous, and effective

quality, property, attribute, and character

quarrels, misunderstandings, enmities, and disapprovals

queries, echoes, reactions, and after-thoughts

quick, impetuous, sweeping, and expeditious

quiet, peaceful, sane, and normal

R

racy, smart, spicy, and pungent

rational, sane, sound, and sensible

ravenous, greedy, voracious, and grasping

recreation, sport, pastime, and amusement

relation, work, duty, and pleasure

reliable, accurate, truthful, and duty-loving

reports, stories, rumors, and suspicions

reproach, dishonor, disgrace, and ignominy

restrained, calm, quiet, and placid

reverential, disciplined, self-controlling, and devoted

rigid, inelastic, stiff, and unbending

rough, rude, gruff, and surly

rude, curt, insolent, and unpleasant

S

sad, despondent, melancholy, and depressed

sane, sober, sound, and rational

scandalize, vilify, traduce, and offend [traduce = humiliate with false statements]

scanty, pinched, slender, and insufficient

science, art, religion, and philosophy

scope, design, purpose, and judgment

sensual, cruel, selfish, and unscrupulous

sentence, judgment, verdict, and doom

serene, composed, conservative, and orderly

several, sundry, many, and various

severe, stern, stiff, and stringent

shameless, corrupt, depraved, and vicious

shock, surprise, terror, and forlornness

simple, hearty, joyous, and affectionate

sin, injustice, grievance, and crime

skill, courage, prowess, and attractiveness

sleepy, soporific, sluggish, and dull [soporific = induces sleep]

slim, slender, slight, and scraggy

slow, dilatory, slack, and procrastinating [dilatory = postpone]

solemn, profound, serious, and difficult

solicit, urge, implore, and importune [importune = insistent requests]

sorrow, disaster, unhappiness, and bereavement

spontaneity, freedom, ease, and adequacy

stately, stern, august, and implacable

steady, reliable, dependable, and well-balanced

stern, severe, abrupt, and unreasonable

stories, pictures, shows and representations

strength, agility, violence, and activity

strong, inventive, daring, and resourceful

sublime, consoling, inspiring, and beautiful

substantial, solid, strong, and durable

suffering, regret, bitterness, and fatigue

superficial, shallow, flimsy, and untrustworthy

superfluous, excessive, unnecessary, and redundant

suspicious, cynical, crafty, and timid

symmetry, proportion, harmony, and regularity

T

tact, courtesy, adroitness, and skill

talents, opportunities, influence, and power

talkative, selfish, superstitious, and inquisitive

tastes, appetites, passions, and desires

tease, tantalize, worry, and provoke

tenacious, stubborn, pertinacious, and obstinate [pertinacious = perversely persistent]

tendency, drift, scope, and disposition

tests, trials, temptations, and toils

theatrical, ceremonious, meretricious, and ostentatious [meretricious = plausible but insincere]

theory, assumption, speculation, and conjecture

think, reflect, weigh, and ponder

tortuous, twisted, sinuous, and circuitous

tractable, gentle, pliant, and submissive

traditional, uncertain, legendary, and unverified

traffic, trade, commerce, and intercourse

tricky, insincere, wily, and shifty

trite, ordinary, commonplace, and hackneyed

trivial, petty, frivolous, and insignificant

true, upright, real, and authentic

tumultuous, riotous, disorderly, and turbulent

U

ugly, evil, hateful, and base

uncertain, questionable, erroneous, and mistaken

unctuous, shrill, brisk, and demonstrative [unctuous = exaggerated, insincere]

unhappy, unfortunate, distressed, and disastrous

uninteresting, lifeless, obscure, and commonplace

unity, aggressiveness, efficiency, and force

unkind, severe, oppressive, and callous

unpractical, childish, slipshod, and silly

unreasonable, foolish, excessive, and absurd

unrivaled, unequaled, incomparable, and matchless

upright, high-minded, brave, and liberal

urgent, important, immediate, and imperative

usage, custom, habit, and practise

V

vain, useless, unproductive, and unavailing

vanities, envies, devices, and jealousies

vast, scattered, various, and incalculable

versatile, eloquent, sagacious, and talented [sagacious = wise]

vigorous, upright, dignified, and imperative

vile, mean, debased, and sordid

violent, impetuous, intense, and ungovernable

virtuous, upright, honest, and moral

visionary, dreamy, pensive, and sensitive

vulgar, heavy, narrow, and obtuse

W

want, lack, poverty, and paucity

warm, soft, clear, and serene

waste, devastate, pillage, and destroy

watched, tendered, fostered, and pruned

weak, inefficient, stupid, and futile

wealth, position, influence, and reputation

well-being, happiness,
prosperity, and distress

wild, restless, aimless, and
erring

wisdom, judgment,
understanding, and far-
sightedness

wit, purity, energy, and
simplicity

wonderful, interesting,
active, and delightful

works, sorrows, visions,
and experiences

worry, annoyance,
awkwardness, and
difficulty

SECTION V

PREPOSITIONAL PHRASES

Preposition "of"

A

abandon of spontaneity

abatement of misery

aberrations of judgment

abhorrence of meanness

absence of vainglory

abyss of ignominy

accent of conviction

accretions of time

accumulation of ages

accuracy of aim

acquisition of knowledge

activity of attention

acuteness of sensibility

admixture of fear

affectation of content

affinity of events

age of ignorance

agility of brain

agony of despair

air of assumption

ambitious of success

amiability of disposition

amplitude of space

anachronisms of thought

anchor of moderation

angle of vision

annulment of influence

aping of manners

apostle of culture

ardor of life

arrogance of opinion

aspect of grandeur

assumption of sternness

atmosphere of obscurity

attitude of mind

attribute of weakness

austerities of fanaticism

authority of manner

avalanche of scorn

avenues of dissemination

B

babel of tongues

ban of exclusion

barren of enthusiasm

barriers of reticence

bars of sunlight

basis of fact

beam of moonlight

beast of prey

beauty of imagery

beggared of faith

bent of mind

betrayal of trust

bevy of maidens

bewilderment of feeling

birds of prey

bit of portraiture

bitterness of anguish

blackness of spirit

blandishments of society

blast of adversity

blaze of fury

blend of dignity

bliss of solitude

bloom of earth

blow of fate

boldness of conception

bond of alliance

bone of contention

bouts of civility

breach of law

breath of life

breeze of anxiety

brilliancy of wit

brimful of fun

broil of politics

brood of emotions

brow of expectation

brunt of disgrace

bulk of mankind

bundle of conceptions

buoyancy of youth

burden of proof

burst of confidence

business of life

C

cadences of delirium

calmness of manner

calumny of passion
[calumny = maliciously
lying to injure a reputation]

caprice of inclination

careless of opinion

catholicity of spirit
[catholicity = universality]

cause of solicitude

celerity of movement
[celerity = swiftness;
speed]

chain of evidence

change of habitude

chaos of confusion

chill of indifference

chimera of superstition
[chimera = fanciful
illusion]

chorus of approbation
[approbation = warm
approval; praise]

circle of hills

clamor of envy

clap of thunder

clarity of thinking

clash of arms

cloak of ecclesiasticism

code of morals

cogency of argument

combination of calamities

command of wit

community of interest

compass of imagination

complexity of life

confidence of genius

conflict of will

conquest of difficulty

consciousness of peril

constellation of luminaries

contagion of conflict

continuity of life

contradiction of terms

contrariety of opinion

convulsion of laughter

copiousness of diction

cord of sympathy

countenance of authority

courage of conviction

course of existence

courtliness of manner

cover of hospitality

crash of thunder

creature of circumstance

criteria of feeling

crown of civilization

crudity of thought

cry of despair

curl of contempt

current of thought

D

darkness of calamity

dash of eccentricity

dawning of recognition

day of reckoning

daylight of faith

decay of authority

declaration of indifference

deeds of prowess

defects of temper

degree of hostility

delicacy of thought

delirium of wonder

depth of despair

dereliction of duty

derogation of character

despoiled of riches

destitute of power

desultoriness of detail
[desultoriness =
haphazard; random]

device of secrecy

devoid of merit

devoutness of faith

dexterity of phrase

diapason of motives
[diapason = full, rich,
harmonious sound]

dictates of conscience

difference of opinion

difficult of attainment

dignity of thought

dilapidations of time

diminution of brutality

disabilities of age

display of prowess

distinctness of vision

distortion of symmetry

diversity of aspect

divinity of tradition

domain of imagination

drama of action

dream of vengeance

drop of comfort

ductility of expression

dull of comprehension

duplicities of might

dust of defeat

E

earnestness of enthusiasm

easy of access

ebullitions of anger
[ebullitions = sudden,
violent outpouring;
boiling]

eccentricity of judgment

ecstasy of despair

effect of loveliness

efficacy of change

effusion of sentiment

elasticity of mind

element of compulsion

elevation of sentiment

eloquence of passion

emotions of joy

emulous of truth [emulous
= prompted by a spirit of
rivalry]

encroachments of time

encumbrance of mystery

energy of youth

enigma of life

equanimity of mind

era of fads

error of judgment

essence of eloquence

excellence of vision

excess of candor

excitation of purpose

excursiveness of thought

exhibition of joy

exhilaration of spirits

expenditure of energy

explosion of rage

expression of sternness

extension of experience

extravagance of eulogy

extremity of fortune

exuberance of wit

F

fabric of fact

facility of expression

faculty of perception

failure of coordination

feast of reason

feats of strength

feebleness of purpose

feeling of uneasiness

felicities of expression

fertility of invention

fervor of devotion

fickleness of fortune

field of activity

fierceness of jealousy

fineness of vision

fire of imagination

firmament of literature

firmness of purpose

fit of laughter

fitness of circumstance

fixity of purpose

flag of truce

flash of humor

flashlight of introspection

fleetness of foot

flexibility of spirit

flicker of recognition

flight of fancy

flood of hatred

flourish of manner

flower of life

fluctuation of fortune

flush of youth

flutter of expectation

fog of sentimentalism

force of conviction

forest of faces

form of captiousness
[captiousness = point out
trivial faults]

fountain of learning

fragment of conversation

frame of mind

frankness of manner

freak of fancy

freedom of enterprise

frenzy of pursuit

freshness of feeling

frigidity of address

frivolity of tone

frown of meditation

fulfilment of purpose

fullness of time

fury of resentment

futility of pride

G

gaiety of spirit

gales of laughter

garb of thought

garlands of roses

gateway of fancy

gem of truth

genuineness of sentiment

gesture of despair

gift of repartee

glamor of sensationalism

glare of scrutiny

gleam of light

glib of speech

glimmer of suspicion

glory of salvation

glow of enthusiasm

gorgeousness of coloring

grace of simplicity

gradations of outrage

grandeur of outline

grasp of comprehension

gravity of manner

greatness of nature

greed of office

grimace of disappointment

grimness of spirit

grip of attention

groundwork of melancholy

growth of experience

guide of aspiration

gulf of incongruity

gust of laughter

H

harbor of refuge

harvest of regrets

haven of rest

haze of distance

heat of enthusiasm

height of absurdity

hint of bitterness

hopeful of success

horizon of life

horror of solitude

hubbub of talk

hue of divinity

hum of pleasure

hush of suspense

I

ideals of excellence

idol of society

illusion of youth

immensity of extent

immolation of genius

impatient of restraint

impetuosity of youth

implacability of resentment

impotent of ideas

impress of individuality

impulse of enthusiasm

imputation of eccentricity

incapable of veracity

independence of mind

index of character

indolence of temperament

indulgence of vanity

inequality of treatment

infinity of height

infirmity of temper

infusion of hatred

inheritance of honor

insensibility of danger

insolence of office

inspiration of genius

instability of purpose

instrument of expression

integrity of mind

intensity of faith

interchange of ideas

interval of leisure

intoxication of vanity

intrepidity of youth

intuition of immortality

invasion of thought

irony of life

J

jangle of sounds

jargon of philosophy

jumble of facts

justness of decision

K

keenness of intellect

kernel of truth

key of knowledge

keynote of success

king of finance

kinship of humanity

L

lack of restraint

languor of nature [languor = dreamy, lazy mood]

lapse of time

laws of decorum

laxity of mind

legacy of thought

liberty of conscience

light of experience

limit of endurance

link of sequence

loftiness of spirit

look of dominance

loophole of escape

love of approbation [approbation = warm approval; praise]

lust of conquest

lustihood of youth

luxuriance of expression

M

magnanimity of mind

majesty of despair

man of iron

mantle of verdure [verdure = lush greenness of flourishing vegetation]

martyrdom of ambition

marvel of competency

mask of flippancy

mass of mediocrity

master of phrasing

maze of words

measure of absurdity

minister of vengeance

minuteness of description

miracle of miracles

mists of criticism

modesty of reserve

moment of lassitude

monster of ingratitude

monstrosities of character

mood of tranquillity

muddle of motives

multitude of details

mummery of words
[mummery = meaningless
ceremonies and flattery]

murmur of satisfaction

mutations of time

myriads of stars

mysteries of taste

N

narrowness of range

nebulae of romance

nectar of enjoyment

neglect of duty

niceties of difference

nightingale of affection

nobility of purpose

note of triumph

O

obduracy of mind
[obduracy = intractable;
hardened]

object of contempt

obligation of loyalty

obliquity of vision
[obliquity = mental
deviation or aberration]

obscurity of twilight

ocean of eloquence

omission of fact

onrush of life

onsets of temptation

openness of mind

opulence of detail

orgy of lying

ornaments of eloquence

outbreak of hostilities

outburst of tears

outflow of sympathy

outposts of morality

overflow of vitality

P

page of desolation

pageant of life

pang of regret

parade of erudition
[erudition = extensive
learning]

passion of patriotism

passivity of mind

pattern of virtue

peals of laughter

pendulum of opinion

pensiveness of feeling

perils of fortune

period of lassitude

perturbation of mind

perversity of chance

pests of society

petrifaction of egoism
[petrifaction =
fossilization; paralyzed
with fear]

phantom of delight

phase of belief

physiognomy of nature

piece of pedantry [pedantry = attention to detail]

pinions of eloquence [pinions = primary feather of a bird]

pinnacle of favor

pit of oblivion

plainness of speech

play of fancy

plea of urgency

plenitude of power

point of view

poise of mind

policy of severity

portent of danger

power of imagination

precipice of stupefaction

precision of phrase

prerogative of age

presence of mind

pressure of expediency

presumption of doubt

prey of fancy

pride of life

process of effacement

profundity of thought

profusion of argument

progress of events

promptings of reason

propriety of action

provocative of scorn

puff of applause

pulse of life

purity of diction

pursuit of knowledge

puzzledom of life

Q

quagmire of distrust

qualities of leadership

qualm of conscience

question of honor

quickness of apprehension

quivering of pain

R

radiance of morning

range of experience

rashness of intention

ravages of time

ray of hope

reaches of achievement

realities of life

realm of peace

rebound of fascination

rectitude of soul

redress of grievances

redundancy of words

refinement of style

reins of life

relish of beauty

remorse of guilt

residue of truth

resoluteness of conviction

resource of expression

restraint of speech

revel of imagination

revulsion of feeling

richness of outline

riddle of existence

ridicule of ignorance

riot of words

ripeness of wisdom

roars of exultation

robe of humility

robustness of mind

root of individuality

round of platitudes

rush of agony

rust of neglect

ruts of conventionality

S

sadness of soul

sanguine of success [sanguine = cheerfully confident; optimistic]

sanity of judgment

savoring of quackery

scantiness of resources

scarves of smoke

school of adversity

scrap of knowledge

scruple of conscience

searchlight of truth

semblance of composure

sensation of pity

sense of urgency

sentiment of disapprobation [approbation = warm approval; praise]

sequence of events

serenity of mind

severity of style

shackles of civilization

shade of doubt

shadow of truth

shallowness of thought

shock of apprehension

shouts of approval

shower of abuse

shriek of wrath

shuttle of life

sigh of wind

singleness of purpose

slave of malice

slough of ignorance

slumber of death

smile of raillery [raillery = good-natured teasing; banter]

solace of adversity

soul of generosity

source of renown

spark of perception

species of despotism

spell of emotion

sphere of influence

spice of caricature

splendor of imagination

spur of necessity

start of uneasiness

stateliness of movement

sting of satire

stolidity of sensation

storehouse of facts

storm of criticism

stream of humanity

stress of life

string of episodes

stroke of fate

substratum of belief

subtlety of intellect

succession of events

suggestion of fancy

sum of happiness

summit of misery

sunshine of life

supremacy of good

surface of events

surfeit of verbiage [surfeit = supply to excess]

surge of pathos

suspense of judgment

suspicion of flattery

sweep of landscape

symbol of admiration

system of aspersion

T

taint of megalomania

tardiness of speech

task of conciliation

tempest of passion

tenacity of execution

tenderness of sentiment

term of reproach

threshold of consciousness

thrift of time

thrill of delight

throb of compunction

throng of sensations

tide of humanitarianism

timid of innovation

tincture of depreciation

tinge of mockery

tissue of misrepresentations

tolerant of folly

tone of severity

top of ambition

torrent of fervor

totality of effect

touch of severity

touchstone of genius

trace of bitterness

tradition of mankind

train of disasters

trait of cynicism

trance of delight

transport of enthusiasm

trappings of wisdom

trend of consciousness

tribute of admiration

trick of fancy

tumult of applause

turmoil of controversy

turn of events

twilight of elderliness

twinge of envy

U

unity of purpose

universality of experience

V

vagrancy of thought

valley of misfortune

vanguard of progress

vehemence of manner

vehicle of intercourse

veil of futurity

vein of snobbishness

velocity of movement

vestige of regard

vicissitudes of life [vicissitudes = sudden or unexpected changes]

vision of splendor

vividness of memory

voice of ambition

void of authority

volume of trade

vow of allegiance

W

warmth of temperament

waste of opportunity

wave of depression

wealth of meaning

weariness of sorrow

web of villainy

weight of argument

whiff of irritation

whirl of delight

whirligig of life

whirlwind of words

wilderness of perplexities

wiles of innocence

word of opprobrium
[opprobrium = disgrace
from shameful conduct]

work of supererogation
[supererogation = to do
more than is required]

world of fantasy

worthy of mention

y

yoke of convention

Z

zest of enjoyment

zone of delusion

Preposition "by"

A

affected by externals

allayed by sympathy

animated by victory

appraised by fashion

assailed by conscience

attained by effort

avert by prayer

B

ballasted by brains

beset by difficulties

bound by opinion

branded by defeat

C

characterized by discretion

chastened by sorrow

cheek by jowl

circulated by malice

clogged by insincerity

colored by environment

condemned by posterity

confirmed by habit

consoled by prayer

convinced by argument

convulsed by divisions

D

darkened by shadows

dazzled by fame

depraved by pain

devoured by curiosity

disgusted by servility

driven by remorse

E

embarrassed by timidity

encouraged by success

enfeebled by age

enforced by action

enjoined by religion

enriched by gifts

established by convention

evoked by shame

F

fascinated, by mystery

favored by fortune

fettered by systems

fired by wrath

forbid by authority

fortified by faith

G

governed by precedent

guided by instinct

H

haunted by visions

hushed by denial

I

impelled by duty

inculcated by practice

induced by misrepresentation

influenced by caution

inspired by love

L

learned by rote

M

marked by acuteness

measured by years

N

narrowed by custom

O

occasioned by irritation

oppressed by destiny

p

parched by disuse

persuaded by appeal

portray by words

prescribed by custom

prevented by chance

prompted by coquetry

purged by sorrow

R

racked by suffering

refuted by reason

repelled by censure

restrained by violence

rising by industry

S

sanctioned by experience

shaped by tradition

soured by misfortune

stung by derision

supplanted by others

supported by evidence

T

thwarted by fortune

tempered by charity

tormented by jealousy

tortured by doubt

U

unadorned by artifice

undaunted by failure

undetermined by sorrow

undone by treachery

unfettered by fear

urged by curiosity

V

vitalized by thought

W

won by aggression

worn by time

wrenched by emotions

Preposition "in"

A

absorbed in meditation

affable in manner [affable = gentle and gracious]

atone in measure

B

barren in intellect

basking in sunshine

buried in solitude

C

call in question

clothed in truth

cloying in sweetness [cloying = too filling, rich, or sweet]

confident in opinion

confute in argument

contemplative in aspect

cumbrous in style [cumbrous = cumbersome; difficult to use]

D

deficient in insight

delight in learning

deterioration in quality

difference in detail

diligent in application

diminish in respect

dwarfed in numbers

E

end in smoke

enumerate in detail

experienced in duplicity

F

feeble in influence

fertile in consequence

flourish in luxuriance

founded in truth

G

gaze in astonishment

go in pursuit

graceful in proportion

grievously in error

H

hold in bondage

I

immersed in thought

indulge in reverie

inferior in character

influential in society

ingenuity in planning

instance in point

involved in obscurity

K

kept in abeyance

L

landmarks in memory

languish in obscurity

lie in wait

limited in scope

linger in expectation

listen in amazement

lost in awe

lower in estimation

luxuriant in fancy

M

monstrous in dullness

mysterious in origin

N

noble in amplitude

nursed in luxury

O

organized in thought

P

petulant in expression

plead in vain

pleasing in outline

plunged in darkness

positive in judgment

practical in application

pride in success

protest in vain

pursued in leisure

Q

quick in suggestion

R

ready in resource

recoiling in terror

remote in character

revel in danger

rich in variety

rooted in prejudice

S

schooled in self-restraint

scrupulous in conduct

set in motion

skilled in controversy

sound in theory

stammer in confusion

stricken in years

strides in civilization

striking in character

stunted in growth

T

tender in sentiment

U

unique in literature

unity in diversity

unprecedented in kind

V

versed in knowledge

W

wallow in idolatry

wanting in dignity

waver in purpose

weak in conception

Preposition "into"

A

abashed into silence

B

beguile into reading

betray into speech

blending into harmony

bring into disrepute

bullied into silence

burn into memory

burst into view

C

call into question

carry into conflict

chill into apathy

coming into vogue

cringe into favor

crumbled into dust

crystallized into action

D

dash into fragments

deepen into confusion

degenerate into monotony

deluded into believing

descent into death

dissolve into nothingness

dragged into pursuit

drawn into controversy

dribbling into words

driven into servitude

dulled into acquiescence

E

electrify into activity

elevated into importance

enquire into precedents

enter into controversy

expand into weakness

F

fade into insignificance

fall into decay

fashion into festoons

flame into war

flower into sympathy

forced into action

frozen into form

fuse into unity

G

galvanize into life

go into raptures

goaded into action

H

hushed into silence

I

incursions into controversy

insight into truth

inveigled into dispute
[inveigled = convince by
coaxing, flattery]

K

kindle into action

L

lapse into pedantry
[pedantries = attention to
detail or rules]

lash into silence

launch into disapproval

lead into captivity

leap into currency

lulled into indifference

M

melt into space

merge into character

p

pass into oblivion

plunge into despair

pour into print

Q

quicken into life

R

relapse into savagery

rendered into music

resolve into nothingness

retreat into silence

ripened into love

rush into print

S

shocked into attention

sink into insignificance

smitten into ice

snubbed into quiescence

stricken into silence

summoned into being

swollen into torrents

T

take into account

thrown into disorder

transform into beauty

translated into fact

U

usher into society

V

vanish into mystery

W

wander into digression

wheedled into acquiescence

withdraw into solitude

Preposition "to"

A

addicted to flattery

adherence to principle

affect to believe

akin to truth

alive to opportunity

allied to virtue

amenable to reason

aspire to rule

attempt to suppress

aversion to publicity

B

blind to demonstration

brought to repentance

C

claim to perpetuity

come to nothing

committed to righteousness

common to humanity

conducive to happiness

conformable to fact

consigned to oblivion

constrained to speak

contribution to knowledge

D

deaf to entreaty

dedicated to friendship

deference to custom

devoted to ideals

disposed to cavil [cavil = raise trivial objections]

doomed to destruction

driven to despair

dwarf to unimportance

E

empowered to act

endeared to all

excite to pity

exposed to derision

F

fly to platitudes

foredoomed to failure

G

given to extravagance

ground to atoms

H

harassed to death

hostile to progress

I

impervious to suggestion

impossible to reconcile

impotent to save

incentive to devotion

incitement to anger

inclined to vacillate

indifference to truth

intent to deceive

intolerable to society

inured to fatigue [inured = habituate to something undesirable]

invocation to sleep

L

laugh to scorn

left to conjecture

lost to remembrance

O

obedience to conscience

oblivious to criticism

offensive to modesty

open to reason

opposed to innovation

p

pander to prejudice

pertaining to fashion

prone to melancholy

propose to undertake

provoke to laughter

put to confusion

R

recourse to falsehood

reduced to impotence

related to eternity

repeat to satiety

repugnant to justice

requisite to success

resort to violence

run to seed

S

seek to overawe

serve to embitter

spur to action

stimulus to ambition

stirred to remonstrance

subject to scrutiny

succumb to fascination

superior to circumstances

susceptible to argument

T

temptation to doubt

tend to frustrate

trust to chance

U

utilize to advantage

V

venture to say

vital to success

W

wedded to antiquity

Y

yield to reason

Preposition "with"

A

abounding with plenty

accord with nature

act with deliberation

adorn with beauty

afflict with ugliness

aflame with life

allied with economy

anticipate with delight

ascertain with exactness

attended with danger

B

beam with self-approval

behave with servility

big with fate

blinded with tears

blush with shame

branded with cowardice

bubbling with laughter

burn with indignation

C

cling with tenacity

clothe with authority

compatible with freedom

comply with tradition

conceal with difficulty

consistent with facts

covered with ignominy

crush with sorrow

D

deny with emphasis

depressed with fear

dispense with formality

distort with passion

E

echo with merriment

endow with intelligence

endued with faith [endued
= provide with a quality;
put on]

endure with fortitude

examine with curiosity

F

face with indifference

flushed with pride

fraught with peril

furious with indignation

G

glowing with delight

I

imbued with courage

incompatible with reason

inconsistent with beauty

inflamed with rage

inspired with patriotism

intoxicated with joy

K

kindle with enthusiasm

L

laugh with glee

M

meet with rebuke

mingled with curiosity

move with alacrity

O

oppressed with hardship

overcome with shyness

overflowing with love

overhung with gloom

P

performed with regularity

pervaded with grandeur

proceed with alertness

punish with severity

Q

quicken with pride

quiver with anxiety

R

radiant with victory

regard with loathing

relate with zest

repel with indignation

S

saddle with responsibility

scream with terror

scrutinize with care

seething with sedition [sedition = conduct or language inciting rebellion]

sick with dread

sob with anguish

squirm with delight

suffuse with spirituality

T

tainted with fraud

teeming with life

tense with expectancy

thrill with excitement

throb with vitality

tinged with romance

touched with feeling

treat with contempt

tremble with fear

U

unmixed with emotion

utter with sarcasm

V

vibrant with feeling

view with awe

W

wield with power

work with zeal

SECTION VI

BUSINESS PHRASES

A

A request for further particulars will not involve any obligation

A telegram is enclosed for your use, as this matter is urgent

Accept our thanks for your recent remittance

Acknowledging the receipt of your recent inquiry

After examination we can confidently say

After very carefully considering

Again thanking you for the inquiry

Agreeable to our conversation

An addressed envelope is enclosed for your convenience

An early reply will greatly oblige

Answering your recent inquiry

Any information you may give us will be appreciated

Any time that may suit your convenience

As a matter of convenience and economy

As a special favor we ask

As directed in your letter, we are shipping to you

As explained in our previous letter

As it will give us an opportunity to demonstrate our ability

As stated in our previous letter

As we have received no response from you

As you, doubtless, are aware

As you probably have been told

As your experience has probably shown you

Assuring you of every courtesy

Assuring you of our entire willingness to comply with your request

Assuring you of prompt and careful cooperation

At the present writing

At the suggestion of one of our patrons

At your earliest opportunity

Awaiting the favor of your prompt attention

Awaiting the pleasure of serving you

Awaiting your early communication

Awaiting your further commands

Awaiting your pleasure

B

Believing you will answer this promptly

C

Complying with your request

Conditions make it obligatory for us

D

Do not hesitate to let us know

Do not overlook this opportunity

Do you realize that you can

E

Enclosed please find a memorandum

Enclosed we beg to hand you

Enclosed you will find a circular which will fully explain

F

For some years past

For your convenience we enclose a stamped envelope

For your further information we take pleasure in sending to you

Frankly, we believe it is extremely worth while for you

From the standpoint of serviceability

H

Here is a complete answer to

Here is your opportunity

Hoping for a continuance of your interest

Hoping for a definite reply

Hoping that our relations may prove mutually satisfactory

Hoping to be favored with your order

How may we serve you further?

However, because of the special circumstances attached

I

I am compelled to inform you

I am confident that you will be thoroughly satisfied

I am directed to say to you

I am, gentlemen, yours faithfully

I am giving the matter my personal attention

I am, my dear sir, yours faithfully

I am still holding this offer open to you

I ask that you be good enough

I beg to request that you give me some information

I believe I understand perfectly just how you feel about

I have been favorably impressed by your

I have now much pleasure in confirming

I have pleasure in acknowledging

I have the honor to acknowledge the receipt

I have the honor to remain

I herewith submit my application

I highly appreciate this mark of confidence

I look forward to pleasant personal relations in the future

I regret exceedingly to inform you

I remain, my dear sir, yours faithfully

I shall be pleased to forward descriptive circulars

I shall esteem it a personal favor

I should welcome an interview at your convenience

I sincerely hope that you will give the subject your earnest consideration

I take pleasure in replying to your inquiry concerning

I trust I shall hear from you soon

I want to express the hope that our pleasant business relations will continue

I want to interest you

I want to thank you for your reply

I wish to confirm my letter

If I can be of further service, please address me

If it is not convenient for you

If there is any valid reason why you are unable

If we can be of service to you

If we can help you in any way

If we have not made everything perfectly clear, please let us know

If you accommodate us, the favor will be greatly appreciated

If you are interested, please let us hear from you

If you are thinking about ordering

If you desire, our representative will call

If you have any cause for dissatisfaction

If you give this matter your prompt attention

In accordance with the terms of our offer

In accordance with your request

In answering your inquiry regarding

In any event, a reply to this will be very much appreciated

In closing we can only assure you

In compliance with your favor

In compliance with your request, we are pleased to send to you

In conclusion, we can assure you

In order to facilitate our future transactions

In reference to your application

In regard to your proposition

In reply thereto, we wish to inform you

In reply to your valued favor

In response to your recent request

In spite of our best efforts it is not probable

In thanking you for the patronage with which you have favored us

In view of all these facts, we feel justified in claiming

Information has just reached me

It gives us pleasure to recommend

It has consistently been our aim to help our customers

It is a matter of great regret to us

It is a pleasure for me to answer your inquiry

It is a well-known fact

It is interesting to note

It is our very great pleasure to advise you

It is the policy of our house

It seems clear that our letter must have miscarried

It was purely an oversight on our part

It will be entirely satisfactory to us

It will be our aim to interest you

It will be readily
appreciated

It will be to your
advantage

It will doubtless be more
convenient for you

It will interest you to know

It will receive the same
careful attention

J

Just mail the enclosed card

K

Kindly endorse your reply
on the enclosed sheet

Kindly let us have your
confirmation at your
earliest convenience

Kindly let us know your
pleasure concerning

Kindly read the enclosed
list

L

Let me thank you for the
opportunity to give this
matter my personal
attention

Let us assure you of our
desire to cooperate with
you

Let us assure you that we
are very much pleased

Let us know if there is any
further attention

Let us thank you again for
opening an account with us

Looking forward to the
early receipt of some of
your orders

M

May I ask you to do us a
great favor by

May we be favored with a
reply

Meantime soliciting your
forbearance

Meanwhile permit me to
thank you for your kind
attention

O

On referring to your
account we notice

Our letter must have gone
astray

Our relations with your
house must have hitherto
been very pleasant

Our services are at your
command

Our stock has been
temporarily exhausted

Owing to our inability to
collect out-standing debts

P

Permit me to add

Permit us to express our
sincere appreciation

Please accept the thanks of
the writer

Please consider this letter
an acknowledgment

Please favor us with a
personal communication

Please feel assured that we
shall use every endeavor

Possibly the enclosure may
suggest to you

Promptly on receipt of
your telegram

Pursuant to your letter

R

Recently we had occasion

Referring to your esteemed
favor

Regretting our inability to
serve you in the present
instance

Reluctant as we are to
believe

Requesting your kind attention to this matter

S

Should you decide to act upon this latter suggestion

So many requests of a similar nature come to us

Soliciting a continuance of your patronage

T

Thank you for your expression of confidence

Thanking you for your inquiry

Thanking you for your past patronage

Thanking you for your promptness.

Thanking you in advance for an early reply

Thanking you in anticipation

The causes for the delay were beyond our control

The margin of profit which we allow ourselves

The proof is in this fact

The proposition appeals to us as a good one

Therefore we are able to make you this offer

Therefore we trust you will write to us promptly

These points should be most carefully considered

This arrangement will help us over the present difficulty

This is according to our discussion

This matter has been considered very seriously

This personal guarantee I look upon as a service to you

This privileged communication is for the exclusive use

This will amply repay you

Trusting that we may have the pleasure of serving you

Trusting to receive your best consideration

U

Under no circumstances can we entertain such an arrangement

Under separate cover we are mailing to you

Under these circumstances

we are willing to extend the terms

Unfortunately we are compelled at certain times

Unless you can give us reasonable assurance

Upon being advised that these terms are satisfactory

Upon receiving your letter of

W

We acknowledge with pleasure the receipt of your order

We admit that you are justified in your complaint

We again solicit an opportunity

We again thank you for your inquiry

We always endeavor to please

We appreciate the order you were kind enough to send to us

We appreciate your patronage very much

We are always glad to furnish information

We are anxious to make satisfactory adjustment

We are at a loss to
understand why

We are at your service at
all times

We are confident that you
will have no further trouble

We are extremely desirous
of pleasing our patrons

We are in a position to
give you considerable help

We are in receipt of your
communication regarding

We are indeed sorry to
learn

We are perfectly willing to
make concessions

We are pleased to receive
your request for
information

We are pleased to send you
descriptive circulars

We are reluctant to adopt
such severe measures

We are satisfied regarding
your statement

We are sending to you by
mail

We are sorry to learn from
your letter

We are thoroughly
convinced of the need

We are totally at a loss to
understand

We are very anxious to
have you try

We are very glad to testify
to the merit of

We ask for a continuance
of your confidence

We ask that you kindly let
us hear from you

We assume that you are
considering

We assure you of our
confidence in the
reliability

We assure you of our
desire to be of service

We await an early, and we
trust, a favorable reply

We await the courtesy of
an early answer

We beg a moment of your
attention and serious
consideration

We believe that if you will
carefully consider the
matter

We believe you will
readily understand our
position

We can assure you that any
order with which you favor
us

We desire information
pertaining to your financial
condition

We desire to effect a
settlement

We desire to express our
appreciation of your
patronage

We desire to impress upon
you

We expect to be in the
market soon

We feel assured that you
will appreciate

We feel sure that you will
approve of our action in
this matter

We frankly apologize to
you

We hasten to acknowledge
the receipt

We have anticipated a
heavy demand

We have, as yet, no
definite understanding

We have come to the
conclusion

We have endeavored to
serve the needs of your
organization

We have found it
impossible

We have much pleasure in answering your inquiry

We have no desire to adopt harsh measures

We have not had the pleasure of placing your name on our ledgers

We have not, however, had the pleasure of hearing from you

We have not yet had time to sift the matter thoroughly

We have the honor to be, gentlemen

We have the honor to inform you

We have thought it best to forward

We have your request for information regarding

We hesitated for a while to pursue the matter

We hope that an understanding can be reached

We hope that we shall have many opportunities to demonstrate our ability

We hope that you will find the enclosed booklet very interesting

We hope to hear favorably from you

We hope you will appreciate

We hope you will excuse the unavoidable delay

We invite your attention to

We must insist upon a prompt settlement

We must, therefore, insist on the terms of the agreement

We note that the time is at hand

We offer you the services of an expert

We particularly want to interest you

We realize that this matter has escaped your attention

We realize that this is simply an oversight on your part

We regret exceedingly that you have been inconvenienced

We regret our inability to meet your wishes

We regret that owing to the press of business

We regret that this

misunderstanding has occurred

We regret that we are not in a position

We regret that we are unable to grant your request

We regret the necessity of calling your attention

We regret to be compelled for this reason to withdraw the privilege

We regret to learn that you are disappointed

We remain, dear sir, yours faithfully

We remain, gentlemen, with thanks

We shall await your early commands with interest

We shall await your reply with interest

We shall be glad to fill your order

We shall be glad to have you tell us frankly

We shall be glad to render you any assistance in our power

We shall be happy to meet your requirements

We shall be indebted to you for your courtesy

We shall be pleased to receive the remittance

We shall be pleased to take the matter up further

We shall do everything in our power

We shall do our best to correct the mistake

We shall feel compelled

We shall heartily appreciate any information

We shall use every endeavor

We suggest that this is an opportune time

We suggest that you consider

We take pleasure in enclosing herewith

We take pleasure in explaining the matter you asked about

We take the liberty of deviating from your instructions

We take the liberty of writing to you.

We thank you for calling our attention

We thank you for your courteous letter

We thank you for your kind inquiry of recent date

We thank you very gratefully for your polite and friendly letter

We thank you very much for the frank statement of your affairs

We thank you very sincerely for your assistance

We think you will agree

We trust our explanation will meet with your approval

We trust that we may hear favorably from you

We trust that you will give this matter your immediate attention

We trust you may secure some of the exceptional values

We trust you will find it correct

We trust you will not consider us unduly strict

We trust you will promptly comply with our previous suggestions

We understand your position

We urge that you write to us by early mail

We venture to enclose herewith

We very much wish you to examine

We want every opportunity to demonstrate our willingness

We want particularly to impress upon you this fact

We want to please you in every respect

We want to remind you again

We want you to read the booklet carefully

We will at once enter your order

We will be compelled to take the necessary steps

We will be glad to lay before you the fullest details

We will be pleased to give it careful consideration

We will gladly accommodate you

We will gladly extend to

you similar courtesies whenever we can do so

We will make it a point to give your correspondence close attention

We would appreciate a remittance

We would consider it a great favor

We would draw your attention to the fact

We would request, as a special favor

We write to suggest to you

We write to urge upon you the necessity

We wrote to you at length

While we appreciate the peculiar circumstances

While we feel that we are in no way responsible

Why not allow us this opportunity to satisfy you

Will you give us, in confidence, your opinion

Will you give us the benefit of your experience

Will you kindly advise us in order that we may adjust our records

Will you please give us your immediate attention

With our best respects and hoping to hear from you

With reference to your favor of yesterday

With regard to your inquiry

With the fullest assurance that we are considering

With the greatest esteem and respect

Y

You are certainly justified in complaining

You are evidently aware that there is a growing demand

You are quite right in your statement

You cannot regret more than I the necessity

You undoubtedly are aware

You will find interest, we believe, in this advance announcement

You will get the benefit of this liberal offer

You will have particular interest in the new and attractive policy

Your early attention to this matter will oblige

Your further orders will be esteemed

Your inquiry has just been received, and we are glad to send to you

Your orders and commands will always have our prompt and best attention

Your satisfaction will dictate our course

Your trial order is respectfully solicited

Your usual attention will oblige

SECTION VII

LITERARY EXPRESSIONS

A

A bitterness crept into her face

A blazing blue sky poured down torrents of light

A book to beguile the tedious hours

A brave but turbulent aristocracy

A broad, complacent, admiring imbecility breathed from his nose and lips

A burlesque feint of evading a blow

A callous and conscienceless brute

A calm and premeditated prudence

A calmness settled on his spirit

A campaign of unbridled ferocity

A carefully appraising eye

A ceaselessly fleeting sky

A certain implication of admiring confidence

A charming air of vigor and vitality

A childish belief in his own impeccability

A cold, hard, frosty penuriousness was his prevalent characteristic [penuriousness = stingy; barren; poverty-stricken]

A compassion perfectly angelic

A constant stream of rhythmic memories

A covertly triumphant voice

A creature of the most delicate and rapid responses

A crop of disappointments

A cunning intellect patiently diverting every circumstance to its design

A curious and inexplicable uneasiness

A curious vexation fretted her

A daily avalanche of vituperation [vituperation = harshly abusive language]

A dandified, pretty-boy-looking sort of figure

A dark and relentless fate

A day monotonous and colorless

A dazzling completeness of beauty

A deep and brooding resentment

A delicious throng of sensations

A deliciously tantalizing sense

A detached segment of life

A dire monotony of bookish idiom

A disheveled and distraught figure

A face singularly acute and intelligent

A faint accent of reproach

A faint sense of compunction moved her

A faint, transient, wistful smile lightened her brooding face

A faint tremor of amusement was on his lips

A faintly quizzical look came into his incisive stare

A fawn-colored sea streaked here and there with tints of deepest orange

A fever of enthusiasm

A few tears came to soften her seared vision

A fiery exclamation of wrath and disdain

A figure full of decision and dignity

A firm and balanced manhood

A first faint trace of irritation

A fitful boy full of dreams and hopes

A flame of scarlet crept in a swift diagonal across his cheeks

A fleeting and furtive air of triumph

A flood of pride rose in him

A foreboding of some destined change

A fortuitous series of happy thoughts

A frigid touch of the hand

A fugitive intangible charm

A gay exuberance of ambition

A generation of men lavishly endowed with genius

A gentle sarcasm ruffled her anger

A ghastly whiteness overspread the cheek

A glance of extraordinary meaning

A glassy expression of inattention

A glassy stare of deprecating horror

A glittering infectious smile

A gloom overcame him

A golden haze of pensive light

A golden summer of marvelous fertility

A graceful readiness and vigor

A grave man of pretending exterior

A great pang gripped her heart

A great process of searching and shifting

A great sickness of heart smote him

A great soul smitten and scourged, but still invested with the dignity of immortality

A grim and shuddering fascination

A gush of entrancing melody

A gusty breeze blew her hair about unheeded

A half-breathless murmur of amazement and incredulity

A half-uneasy, half-laughing compunction

A harassing anxiety of sorrow

A harvest of barren regrets

A haunting and horrible sense of insecurity

A heavy oppression seemed to brood upon the air

A helpless anger simmered in him

A hint of death in the icy breath of the gale

A hot and virulent skirmish

A hot uprush of hatred and loathing

A kind of ineffable splendor crowns the day

A lapse from the well-ordered decencies of civilization

A large, rich, copious human endowment

A late star lingered, remotely burning

A laugh of jovial significance

A light of unwonted pleasure in her eyes [unwonted = unusual]

A little jaded by gastronomical exertions

A lukewarm and selfish love

A man of imperious will [imperious = arrogantly domineering]

A man of matchless modesty and refinement

A manner bright with interest and interrogation

A manner nervously anxious to please

A melancholy monotone beat on one's heart

A mere exhibition of fussy diffuseness

A mere figment of a poet's fancy

A mien and aspect singularly majestic [mien = bearing or manner]

A mild and deprecating air

A mind singularly practical and sagacious [sagacious = wise]

A mouth of inflexible decision

A murmur of complacency

A mystery everlastingly impenetrable

A nameless sadness which is always born of moonlight

A new and overmastering impulse

A new doubt assailed her

A new marvel of the sky

A new trouble was dawning on his thickening mental horizon

A nimble-witted opponent

A painful thought was flooding his mind

A pang of jealousy not unmingled with scorn

A patience worthy of admiration

A perfect carnival of fun

A perfect crime of clumsiness

A piteous aspect of woe

A portent full of possible danger

A potion to be delicately supped at leisure

A powerful agitation oppressed him

A prevailing sentiment of uneasy discontent

A prey to listless uneasiness

A profound and absorbing interest

A profound and eager hopefulness

A profound and rather irritating egotist by nature

A prop for my faint heart

A propitious sky, marbled with pearly white [propitious = favorable; kindly; gracious]

A protest wavered on her lip

A puissant and brilliant family [puissant = powerful; mighty]

A queer, uncomfortable perplexity began to invade her

A quick flame leaped in his eyes

A quick shiver ruffled the brooding stillness of the water

A quiver of resistance ran through her

A remarkable fusion of morality and art

A random gleam of light

A rare and dazzling order of beauty

A rhythmical torrent of eloquent prophecy

A river of shame swept over him

A sad inquiry seemed to dwell in her gaze

A satisfied sense of completeness

A secret sweeter than the sea or sky can whisper

A sensation of golden sweetness and delight

A sense of desolation and disillusionment overwhelmed me

A sense of infinite peace brooded over the place

A sense of meditative content

A sense of repression was upon her

A sentiment of distrust in its worth had crept into her thoughts

A sheaf of letters

A shimmer of golden sun shaking through the trees

A shiver of apprehension crisped her skin

A shuffling compromise between defiance and prostration

A sigh of large contentment

A sight for the angels to weep over

A skepticism which prompted rebellion

A slight movement of incredulous dissent

A smile full of subtle charm

A smile of exquisite urbanity

A soft insidious plea

A soft intonation of profound sorrow

A soft suspicion of ulterior motives

A solemn glee possessed my mind

A solemn gray expanse that lost itself far away in the gray of the sea

A solemn utterance of destiny

A somber and breathless calm hung over the deepening eve

A somewhat melancholy indolence

A somewhat sharp and incisive voice

A sonorous voice bade me enter

A soothing and quieting touch was gently laid upon her soul

A sort of eager, almost appealing amiability

A sort of stolid despairing acquiescence

A sort of stunned incredulity

A soundless breeze that was little more than a whisper

A spacious sense of the amplitude of life's possibilities

A staccato cough interrupted the flow of speech

A state of sullen self-absorption

A steady babble of talk and laughter

A step was at her heels

A stifling sensation of pain and suspense

A stinging wind swept the woods

A strange compound of contradictory elements

A stream of easy talk

A strong convulsion shook the vague indefinite form

A strong susceptibility to the ridiculous

A subtle emphasis of scorn

A sudden and stinging delight

A sudden gleam of insight

A sudden uncontrollable outburst of feeling

A super-abundance of boisterous animal spirits

A supercilious scorn and pity [supercilious = haughty disdain]

A super-refinement of taste

A swaggering air of braggadocio [braggadocio = pretentious bragging]

A sweet bewilderment of tremulous apprehension [tremulous = fearful]

A sweet, quiet, sacred, stately seclusion

A swift knowledge came to her

A swift unformulated fear

A swiftly unrolling panorama of dreams

A tangle of ugly words

A thousand evanescent memories of happy days [evanescent = vanishing like vapor]

A thousand unutterable fears bore irresistible despotism over her thoughts

A time of disillusion followed

A tiny stream meandering amiably

A tone of arduous admiration

A torn and tumultuous sky

A total impression ineffable and indescribable

A tragic futility

A treacherous throb of her voice

A true similitude of what befalls many men and women

A tumult of vehement feeling

A tumultuous rush of sensations

A twinge of embarrassment

A vague and wistful melancholy

A vast sweet silence crept through the trees

A veritable spring-cleaning of the soul

A very practiced and somewhat fastidious critic

A violent and mendacious tongue [mendacious = false; untrue]

A vivid and arresting presentation

A waking dream overshadowed her

A weird world of morbid horrors

A well-bred mixture of boldness and courtesy

A wild vivacity was in her face and manner

A wile of the devil's [wile = trick intended to deceive or ensnare]

A wind strayed through the gardens

A withering sensation of ineffable boredom

A wordless farewell

Absolutely vulgarized by too perpetual a parroting

Absorbed in a stream of thoughts and reminiscences

Absorbed in the scent and murmur of the night

Accidents which perpetually deflect our vagrant attention

Across the gulf of years

Administering a little deft though veiled castigation

Affected an ironic incredulity

Affecting a tone of gayety

After a first moment of reluctance

After an eternity of resolutions, doubts, and indecisions

Aghast at his own helplessness

Agitated and enthralled by day-dreams

Agitated with violent and contending emotions

Alien paths and irrelevant junketing's

All embrowned and mossed with age

All her gift of serene immobility brought into play

All hope of discreet reticence was ripped to shreds

All the lesser lights paled into insignificance

All the magic of youth and joy of life was there

All the place is peopled with sweet airs

All the sky was mother-of-pearl and tender

All the unknown of the night and of the universe was pressing upon him

All the world was flooded with a soft golden light

All was a vague jumble of chaotic impressions

All was incomprehensible

All was instinctive and spontaneous

Aloof from the motley throng

Ambition shivered into fragments

Amid distress and humiliation

Amid the direful calamities of the time

An acute note of distress in her voice

An agreeably grave vacuity

An air half quizzical and half deferential

An air of affected civility

An air of being meticulously explicit

An air of inimitable, scrutinizing, superb impertinence

An air of stern, deep, and irredeemable gloom hung over and pervaded all

An air of uncanny familiarity

An air which was distinctly critical

An almost pathetic appearance of ephemeral fragility [ephemeral = markedly short-lived]

An almost riotous prodigality of energy

An answering glow of gratitude

An antagonist worth her steel

An artful stroke of policy

An assumption of hostile intent

An assurance of good-nature that forestalled hostility

An atmosphere of extraordinary languor [languor = dreamy, lazy mood]

An atmosphere thick with flattery and toadyism

An attack of peculiar virulence and malevolence

An audacious challenge of ridicule

An avidity that bespoke at once the restlessness, [avidity = eagerness] and the genius of her mind

An awe crept over me

An eager and thirsty ear

An easy prey to the powers of folly

An effusive air of welcome

An equal degree of well-bred worldly cynicism

An erect, martial, majestic, and imposing personage

An eternity of silence oppressed him

An expression of mildly humorous surprise

An expression of rare and inexplicable personal energy

An exquisite perception of things beautiful and rare

An iciness, a sinking, a sickening of the heart

An ignoring eye

An impenetrable screen of foliage

An impersonal and slightly ironic interest

An impervious beckoning motion

An inarticulate echo of his longing

An increased gentleness of aspect

An incursion of the loud, the vulgar and meretricious [meretricious = plausible but false]

An inexplicable and

uselessly cruel caprice of fate

An inexpressible fervor of serenity

An ingratiating, awkward and, wistful grace

An inspired ray was in his eyes

An instant she stared unbelievingly

An intense and insatiable hunger for light and truth

An intense travail of mind

An obscure thrill of alarm

An odd little air of penitent self-depreciation

An open wit and recklessness of bearing

An oppressive sense of strange sweet odor

An optimistic after-dinner mood

An overburdening sense of the inexpressible

An uncomfortable premonition of fear

An unfailing sweetness and unerring perception

An unpleasant and heavy sensation sat at his heart

An unredeemed dreariness of thought

An unsuspected moral obtuseness

An utter depression of soul

And day peers forth with her blank eyes

And what is all this pother about? [pother = commotion; disturbance]

Animated by noble pride

Anticipation painted the world in rose

Appalled in speechless disgust

Appealing to the urgent temper of youth

Apprehensive solicitude about the future

Ardent words of admiration

Armed all over with subtle antagonisms

Artless and unquestioning devotion

As if smitten by a sudden spasm

As the long train sweeps away into the golden distance

August and imperial names in the kingdom of thought

Awaiting his summons to the eternal silence

B

Bandied about from mouth to mouth

Barricade the road to truth

Bartering the higher aspirations of life

Beaming with pleasurable anticipation

Before was the open malignant sea

Beguiled the weary soul of man

Beneath the cold glare of the desolate night

Bent on the lofty ends of her destiny

Beset by agreeable hallucinations

Beset with smiling hills

Beside himself in an ecstasy of pleasure

Betokening an impulsive character

Beyond the farthest edge of night

Birds were fluting in the tulip-trees

Biting sentences flew about

Black inky night

Blithe with the bliss of the morning

Blown about by every wind of doctrine

Bookish precision and professional peculiarity

Borne from lip to lip

Borne onward by slow-footed time

Borne with a faculty of willing compromise

Bowed with a certain frigid and deferential surprise

Broke in a stupendous roar upon the shuddering air

Browsing at will on all the uplands of knowledge and thought

Buffeted by all the winds of passion

Buried hopes rose from their sepulchers

Buried in the quicksands of ignorance

But none the less peremptorily [peremptorily

= ending all debate or action]

By a curious irony of fate

By a happy turn of thinking

By virtue of his impassioned curiosity

C

Carried the holiday in his eye

Chafed at the restraints imposed on him

Cheeks furrowed by strong purpose and feeling

Childlike contour of the body

Cleansed of prejudice and self-interest

Cloaked in prim pretense

Clothed with the witchery of fiction

Clutch at the very heart of the usurping mediocrity

Cold gaze of curiosity

Collapse into a dreary and hysterical depression

Comment of rare and delightful flavor

Conjuring up scenes of incredible beauty and terror

Conscious of unchallenged supremacy

Constant indulgence of wily stratagem and ambitious craft

Contemptuously indifferent to the tyranny of public opinion

Covered with vegetation in wild luxuriance

Crisp sparkle of the sea

Crystallize about a common nucleus

Cultivated with a commensurate zeal

Current play of light gossip

Curtains of opaque rain

D

Dallying in maudlin regret over the past [maudlin = tearfully sentimental]

Dark with unutterable sorrows

Darkness oozed out from between the trees

Dawn had broken

Day stood distinct in the sky

Days of vague and fantastic melancholy

Days that are brief and shadowed

Deep shame and rankling remorse

Deficient in affectionate or tender impulses

Delicately emerging stars

Delicious throng of sensations

Despite her pretty insolence

Dignity and sweet patience were in her look

Dim opalescence of the moon

Dimly foreshadowed on the horizon

Dimmed by the cold touch of unjust suspicion

Disfigured by passages of solemn and pompous monotony.

Disguised itself as chill critical impartiality

Dismal march of death

Distinguished by hereditary rank or social position

Distract and beguile the soul

Distressing in their fatuous ugliness

Diverted into alien channels

Diverting her eyes, she pondered

Dogs the footsteps

Doled out in miserly measure

Doubt tortured him

Doubts beset her lonely and daring soul

Down the steep of disenchantment

Dreams and visions were surpassed

Dreams that fade and die in the dim west

Drear twilight of realities

Drift along the stream of fancy

Drowned in the deep reticence of the sea

Drowsiness coiled insidiously about him

Dull black eyes under their precipice of brows

E

Earth danced under a heat haze

Easily moved to gaiety and pleasure

Either way her fate was cruel

Embrace with ardor the prospect of serene leisure

Endearing sweetness and manner

Endeavoring to smile away his chagrin

Endlessly shifting moods

Endowed with all those faculties that can make the world a garden of enchantment

Endowed with life and emphasis

Enduring with smiling composure the near presence of people who are distasteful

Enjoyed with astonishing unscrupulousness

Enticed irresistibly by the freedom of an open horizon

Essay a flight of folly

Evanescent shades of feeling [evanescent = vanishing like vapor]

Events took an unexpected sinister turn

Every curve of her features seemed to express a fine arrogant acrimony and harsh truculence

Everywhere the fragrance of a bountiful earth

Exasperated by what seemed a wilful pretense of ignorance

Exhibits itself in fastidious crotchets

Expectation darkened into anxiety

Experience and instinct warred within her

Exquisite graciousness of manner

Exquisitely stung by the thought

F

Familiar and endearing intimacy

Fatally and indissolubly united

Fathomless depths of suffering

Fear held him in a vice

Feeding his scholarly curiosity

Feeling humiliated by the avowal

Felicitousness in the choice and exquisiteness in the collocation of words

Fettered by poverty and toil

Feverish tide of life

Fine precision of intent

Fitful tumults of noble passion

Fleeting touches of something alien and intrusive

Floating in the clouds of reverie

Fluctuations of prosperity and adversity

Flushed with a suffusion that crimsoned her whole countenance

Forebodings possessed her

Foreshadowing summer's end

Forever echo in the heart

Forever sings itself in memory

Formless verbosity and a passionate rhetoric

Fragments of most touching melody

Free from rigid or traditional fetters

Freedom and integrity of soul

Freighted with strange, vague longings

Frosty thraldom of winter [thraldom = servitude; bondage]

Fugitive felicities of thought and sensation

Full of dreams and refinements and intense abstractions

Full of majestic tenderness

G

Gathering all her scattered impulses into a passionate act of courage

Gaze dimly through a maze of traditions

Generosity pushed to prudence

Gleams of sunlight, bewildered like ourselves, struggled, surprised, through the mist and disappeared

Glowing with haste and happiness

Go straight, as if by magic, to the inner meaning

Goaded on by his sense of strange importance

Graceful length of limb and fall of shoulders

Great shuddering seized on her

Green hills pile themselves upon each other's shoulders

Grim and sullen after the flush of the morning

Guilty of girlish sentimentality

H

Half choked by a rising paroxysm of rage

Half-suffocated by his triumph

Hardened into convictions and resolves

Haughtiness and arrogance were largely attributed to him

Haunt the recesses of the memory

Haunted with a chill and unearthly foreboding

He accosted me with trepidation

He adroitly shifted his ground

He airily lampooned their most cherished prejudices

He bowed submission

He braced himself to the exquisite burden of life

He condescended to intimate speech with her

He conversed with a colorless fluency

He could detect the hollow ring of fundamental nothingness

He could do absolutely naught

He drank of the spirit of the universe

He drew near to a desperate resolve

He evinced his displeasure by a contemptuous sneer or a grim scowl

He felt an unaccountable loathing

He felt the ironic rebound of her words

He flung diffidence to the winds

He flushed crimson

He found the silence intolerably irksome

He frowned perplexedly

He gave her a baffled stare

He gave himself to a sudden day-dream

He gave his ear to this demon of false glory

He grew wanton with success

He had acted with chivalrous delicacy of honor

He had the eye of an eagle in his trade

He had the gift of deep, dark silences

He held his breath in admiring silence

He laughed away my protestations

He lent no countenance to the insensate prattle

He listened greedily and gazed intent

He made a loathsome object

He made the politest of monosyllabic replies

He murmured a civil rejoinder

He murmured a vague acceptance

He mused a little while in grave thought

He never wears an argument to tatters

He only smiled with fatuous superiority

He paused, stunned and comprehending

He perceived the iron hand within the velvet glove

He raised a silencing hand

He ruled autocratically

He sacrificed the vulgar prizes of life

He sat on thorns

He set his imagination adrift

He shambled away with speed

He sighed deeply, from a kind of mental depletion

He smote her quickening sensibilities

He submitted in brooding silence

He suppressed every sign of surprise

He surrendered himself to gloomy thought

He threaded a labyrinth of obscure streets

He threw a ton's weight of resolve upon his muscles

He threw out phrases of ill-humor

He threw round a measuring eye

He treads the primrose path of dalliance

He used an unguarded adjective

He was a tall, dark, saturnine youth, sparing of speech [saturnine = melancholy; sullen]

He was aware of emotion

He was born to a lively and intelligent patriotism

He was dimly mistrustful of it

He was discreetly silent

He was empty of thought

He was entangled in a paradox

He was giving his youth away by handfuls

He was haunted and begirt by presences

He was measured and urbane

He was most profoundly skeptical

He was nothing if not grandiloquent

He was quaking on the precipice of a bad bilious attack

He was utterly detached from life

He went hot and cold

He would fall into the blackest melancholies

He writhed in the grip of a definite apprehension

He writhed with impotent humiliation

Her blank gaze chilled you

Her bright eyes were triumphant

Her eyes danced with malice

Her eyes dilated with pain and fear

Her eyes were full of wondering interest

Her eyes were limpid and her beauty was softened by an air of indolence and languor [languor = dreamy, lazy mood]

Her face stiffened anew into a gray obstinacy

Her face was lit up by a glow of inspiration and resolve

Her haughty step waxed timorous and vigilant

Her head throbbed dangerously

Her heart appeared to abdicate its duties

Her heart fluttered with a vague terror

Her heart pounded in her throat

Her heart was full of speechless sorrow

Her hurrying thoughts clamored for utterance

Her imagination recoiled

Her interest flagged

Her life had dwarfed her ambitions

Her limbs ran to marble

Her lips hardened

Her lips parted in a keen expectancy

Her mind was a store-house of innocuous anecdote

Her mind was beaten to the ground by the catastrophe

Her mood was unaccountably chilled

Her musings took a sudden and arbitrary twist

Her scarlet lip curled cruelly

Her smile was faintly depreciatory

Her smile was linked with a sigh

Her solicitude thrilled him

Her stare dissolved

Her step seemed to pity the grass it prest

Her strength was scattered in fits of agitation

Her stumbling ignorance which sought the road of wisdom

Her thoughts outstripped her erring feet

Her tone was gathering remonstrance

Her tongue on the subject was sharpness itself

Her tongue stumbled and was silent

Her voice had the coaxing inflections of a child

Her voice trailed off vaguely

Her voice was full of temper, hard-held

Her voice, with a tentative question in it, rested in air

Her wariness seemed put to rout

His accents breathed profound relief

His agitation increased

His brow grew knit and gloomy

His brow was in his hand

His conscience leapt to the light

His constraint was excruciating

His curiosity is quenched

His dignity counseled him to be silent

His ears sang with the vibrating intensity of his secret existence

His eyes had a twinkle of reminiscent pleasantry

His eyes literally blazed with savage fire

His eyes shone with the pure fire of a great purpose

His eyes stared unseeingly

His face caught the full strength of the rising wind

His face dismissed its shadow

His face fell abruptly into stern lines

His face lit with a fire of decision

His face showed a pleased bewilderment

His face torn with conflict

His face was gravely authoritative

His gaze faltered and fell

His gaze searched her face

His gaze seemed full of unconquerable hopefulness

His hand supported his chin

His hands were small and prehensible [prehensible = capable of being seized]

His heart asserted itself again, thunderously beating

His heart rebuked him

His heart was full of enterprise

His impatient scorn expired

His last illusions crumbled

His lips loosened in a furtively exultant smile

His lips seemed to be permanently parted in a good-humored smile

His mind echoed with words

His mind leaped gladly to meet new issues and fresh tides of thought

His mind was dazed and wandering in a mist of memories

His mood yielded

His mouth quivered with pleasure

His passions vented themselves with sneers

His pulses leaped anew

His reputation had withered

His sensibilities were offended

His shrewd gaze fixed appraisingly upon her

His soul full of fire and eagle-winged

His soul was compressed into a single agony of prayer

His soul was wrung with a sudden wild homesickness

His speech faltered

His swift and caustic satire

His temper was dark and explosive

His thoughts galloped

His thoughts were in clamoring confusion

His tone assumed a certain asperity [asperity = roughness; harshness]

His torpid ideas awoke again

His troubled spirit shifted its load

His vagrant thoughts were in full career

His voice insensibly grew inquisitorial

His voice was thick with resentment and futile protest

His whole face was lighted with a fierce enthusiasm

His whole frame seemed collapsed and shrinking

His whole tone was flippant and bumptious

His words trailed off brokenly

His youthful zeal was contagious

Hope was far and dim

How sweet and reasonable the pale shadows of those who smile from some dim corner of our memories

Humiliating paltriness of revenge

I

I capitulated by inadvertence

I cut my reflections adrift

I felt a qualm of apprehension

I suffered agonies of shyness

I took the good day from the hands of God as a perfect gift

I was in a somber mood

I was overshadowed by a deep boding

I was piqued [piqued = resentment; indignation]

I yielded to the ingratiating mood of the day

Ill-bred insolence was his only weapon

Ill-dissimulated fits of ambition

Imbued with a vernal freshness [vernal = resembling spring; fresh]

Immense and careless prodigality

Immense objects which dwarf us

Immersed in secret schemes

Immured in a trivial round of duty [immured = confine within]

Impassioned and earnest language

Impatient and authoritative tones

Impervious to the lessons of experience

Implying an immense melancholy

Imprisoned within an enchanted circle

In a deprecating tone of apology

In a flash of revelation

In a gale of teasing merriment

In a misery of annoyance and mortification

In a musing ecstasy of contemplation

In a sky stained with purple, the moon slowly rose

In a spirit of indulgent irony

In a strain of exaggerated gallantry

In a tone of after-dinner perfunctoriness [perfunctoriness = with little interest]

In a tone of musing surprise

In a tumult of self-approval and towering exultation

In a vague and fragmentary way

In a wise, superior, slightly scornful manner

In accents of menace and wrath

In its whole unwieldy compass

In moments of swift and momentous decision

In quest of something to amuse

In requital for various acts of rudeness

In the air was the tang of spring

In the dusky path of a dream

In the face of smarting disillusions

In the flush and heyday of youth and gaiety and loveliness

In the heyday of friendship

In the mild and mellow maturity of age

In the perpetual presence of everlasting verities

In this breathless chase of pleasure

In this chastened mood I left him

Incapable of initiative or boldness

Inconceivable perversion of reasoning

Indolently handsome eyes

Indulge in pleasing discursiveness

Ineffable sensation of irritability

Infantile insensibility to the solemnity of his bereavement

Infantine simplicity and lavish waste

Innumerable starlings
clove the air [clove = split]

Insensible to its subtle
influence

Inspired by the immortal
flame of youth

Intangible and
indescribable essence

Intense love of excitement
and adventure

Intimations of
unpenetrated mysteries

Into her eyes had come a
hostile challenge

Into the purple sea the
orange hues of heaven
sunk silently

Into the very vestibule of
death

Involuntarily she sighed

Involuntary awkwardness
and reserve

Involved in a labyrinth of
perplexities

It came to him with a stab
of enlightenment

It elicited a remarkably
clear and coherent
statement

It is a flight beyond the
reach of human
magnanimity

It is a thing infinitely
subtle

It is not every wind that
can blow you from your
anchorage

It lends no dazzling tints to
fancy

It moved me to a strange
exhilaration

It parted to a liquid horizon
and showed the gray rim of
the sea

It proved a bitter
disillusion

It seemed intolerably tragic

It seemed to exhale a silent
and calm authority

It was a breathless night of
suspense

It was a desolating vision

It was a night of little ease
to his toiling mind

It was a night of stupefying
surprises

It was all infinitely soft
and refreshing to the eye

It was an evening of great
silences and spaces, wholly
tranquil

It was sheer, exuberant,
instinctive, unreasoning,
careless joy

It was the ecstasy and
festival of summer

It was torture of the most
exquisite kind

J

Jealousies and animosities
which pricked their
sluggish blood to tingling

Joy rioted in his large dark
eyes

Judging without waiting to
ponder over bulky tomes

K

Kind of unscrupulous
contempt for gravity

Kiss-provoking lips

L

Laden with the poignant
scent of the garden
honeysuckle

Language of excessive
flattery and adulation

Lapped in soft music of
adulation

Lapse into pathos and
absurdity

Large, dark, luminous eyes
that behold everything
about them

Latent vein of whimsical humor

Lead to the strangest aberrations

Leaping from lambent flame into eager and passionate fire [lambent = effortlessly brilliant]

Leave to the imagination the endless vista of possibilities

Life flowed in its accustomed stream

Lights and shadows of reviving memory crossed her face

Lionized by fashionable society

Long intertangled lines of silver streamlets

Lost in a delirious wonder

Lost in irritable reflection

Love hovered in her gaze

Ludicrous attempts of clumsy playfulness and tawdry eloquence

Luke-warm assurance of continued love

Lulled by dreamy musings

Luminous with great thoughts

M

Magnanimous indifference to meticulous niceties

Making the ear greedy to remark offense

Marching down to posterity with divine honors

Marked out for some strange and preternatural doom

Mawkishly effeminate sentiment

Memories plucked from wood and field

Memory was busy at his heart

Merged in a sentiment of unutterable sadness and compassion

Microscopic minuteness of eye

Misgivings of grave kinds

Mockery crept into her tone

Molded by the austere hand of adversity

Moments of utter idleness and insipidity

Moods of malicious reaction and vindictive recoil

Morn, in yellow and white, came broadening out of the mountains

Mumble only jargon of dotage

My body is too frail for its moods

N

Nature seemed to revel in unwonted contrasts [unwonted = unusual]

New ambitions pressed upon his fancy

New dreams began to take wing in his imagination

Night after night the skies were wine-blue and bubbling with stars

Night passes lightly in the open world, with its stars and dews and perfumes

Nights of fathomless blackness

No mark of trick or artifice

Noble and sublime patience

Nursed by brooding thought

O

Obsessed with the modishness of the hour

Occasional flashes of tenderness and love

Oddly disappointing and fickle

One gracious fact emerges here

One long torture of soul

One of the golden twilights which transfigure the world

Oppressed and disheartened by an all-pervading desolation

Oppressed with a confused sense of cumbrous material [cumbrous = cumbersome]

Outweighing years of sorrow and bitterness

Over and over the paroxysms of grief and longing submerged her

Overhung and overspread with ivy

Overshadowed by a vague depression

P

Pale and vague desolation

Pallor of reflected glories

Palpitating with rage and wounded sensibility

Panting after distinction

Peace brooded over all

Pelted with an interminable torrent of words

Penetrate beneath the surface to the core

Peopled the night with thoughts

Perpetual gloom and seclusion of life

Pertinent to the thread of the discussion

Pervasive silence which wraps us in a mantle of content

Piles of golden clouds just peering above the horizon

Platitudinous and pompously sentimental

Plaudits of the unlettered mob

Pleasant and flower-strewn vistas of airy fancy

Pledged with enthusiastic fervor

Plumbing the depth of my own fears

Poignant doubts and misgivings

Power of intellectual metamorphosis

Power to assuage the thirst of the soul

Precipitated into mysterious depths of nothingness

Preening its wings for a skyward flight

Pressing cares absorbed him

Pride working busily within her

Proclaimed with joyous defiance

Prodigal of discriminating epithets

Prodigious boldness and energy of intellect

Products of dreaming indolence

Profound and chilling solitude of the spot

Proof of his imperturbability and indifference

Provocative of bitter hostility

Pulling the strings of many enterprises

Purge the soul of nonsense

Q

Quickened and enriched by new contacts with life and truth

Quivering with restrained grief

R

Radiant with the beautiful glamor of youth

Ransack the vocabulary

Red tape of officialdom

Redolent of the night lamp

Reflecting the solemn and unfathomable stars

Regarded with an exulting pride

Rehabilitated and restored to dignity

Remorselessly swept into oblivion

Resounding generalities and conventional rhetoric

Respect forbade downright contradiction

Restless and sore and haughty feelings were busy within

Retort leaped to his lips

Rigid adherence to conventionalities

Rudely disconcerting in her behavior

Rudely reminded of life's serious issues

S

Sacrificed to a futile sort of treadmill

Sadness prevailed among her moods

Scorched with the lightning of momentary indignation

Scorning such paltry devices

Scotched but not slain

Scrupulous morality of conduct

Seem to swim in a sort of blurred mist before the eyes

Seething with suppressed wrath

Seize on greedily

Sensuous enjoyment of the outward show of life

Serenity beamed from his look

Serenity of paralysis and death

Seriousness lurked in the depths of her eyes

Served to recruit his own jaded ideas

Set anew in some fresh and appealing form

Setting all the sane traditions at defiance

Shadowy vistas of sylvan beauty

She affected disdain

She assented in precisely the right terms

She bandies adjectives with the best

She challenged his dissent

She cherished no petty resentments

She curled her fastidious lip

She curled her lip with defiant scorn

She did her best to mask her agitation

She disarmed anger and softened asperity [asperity = harshness]

She disclaimed fatigue

She fell into a dreamy silence

She fell into abstracted reverie

She felt herself carried off her feet by the rush of incoherent impressions

She flushed an agitated pink

She forced a faint quivering smile

She frowned incomprehension

She had an air of restrained fury

She had an undercurrent of acidity

She hugged the thought of her own unknown and unapplauded integrity

She lingered a few leisurely seconds

She nodded mutely

She nourished a dream of ambition

She permitted herself a delicate little smile

She poured out on him the full opulence of a proud recognition

She questioned inimically [inimically = unfriendly; hostile]

She recaptured herself with difficulty

She regarded him stonily out of flint-blue eyes

She sat eyeing him with frosty calm

She seemed the embodiment of dauntless resolution

She seemed wrapped in a veil of lassitude

She shook hands grudgingly

She softened her frown to a quivering smile

She spoke with hurried eagerness

She spoke with sweet severity

She stilled and trampled on the inward protest

She stood her ground with the most perfect dignity

She strangled a fierce tide of feeling that welled up within her

She swept away all opposing opinion with the swift rush of her enthusiasm

She thrived on insincerity

She twitted him merrily

She was both weary and placated

She was conscious of a tumultuous rush of sensations

She was demure and dimly appealing

She was exquisitely simple

She was gripped with a sense of suffocation and panic

She was in an anguish of sharp and penetrating remorse

She was oppressed by a dead melancholy

She was stricken to the soul

She wore an air of wistful questioning

Sheer superfluity of happiness

Sickening contrasts and diabolic ironies of life

Silence fell

Singing lustily as if to exorcise the demon of gloom

Skirmishes and retreats of conscience

Slender experience of the facts of life

Slope towards extinction

Slow the movement was and tortuous

Slowly disengaging its significance from the thicket of words

So innocent in her exuberant happiness

Soar into a rosy zone of contemplation

Softened by the solicitude of untiring and anxious love

Solitary and sorely smitten souls

Some dim-remembered and dream-like images

Some exquisite refinement in the architecture of the brain

Some flash of witty irrelevance

Something curiously suggestive and engaging

Something eminently human beaconed from his eyes

Something full of urgent haste

Something indescribably reckless and desperate in such a picture

Something that seizes tyrannously upon the soul

Sore beset by the pressure of temptation

Specious show of impeccability

Spectacular display of wrath

Spur and whip the tired mind into action

Stale and facile platitudes

Stamped with unutterable and solemn woe

Startled into perilous activity

Startling leaps over vast gulfs of time

Stem the tide of opinion

Stern emptying of the soul

Stimulated to an ever deepening subtlety

Stirred into a true access of enthusiasm

Stony insensibility to the small pricks and frictions of daily life

Strange capacities and suggestions both of vehemence and pride

Strange laughing and glittering's of silver streamlets

Stripped to its bare skeleton

Strode forth imperiously [imperious = arrogantly overbearing]

Struck by a sudden curiosity

Struck dumb with strange surprise

Stung by his thoughts, and impatient of rest

Stung by the splendor of the prospect

Subdued passages of unobtrusive majesty

Sublime indifference to contemporary usage and taste

Submission to an implied rebuke

Subtle indications of great mental agitation

Subtle suggestions of remoteness

Such things as the eye of history sees

Such was the petty chronicle

Suddenly a thought shook him

Suddenly overawed by a strange, delicious shyness

Suddenly smitten with unreality

Suddenly snuffed out in the middle of ambitious schemes

Suffered to languish in obscurity

Sugared remonstrances and cajoleries

Suggestions of veiled and vibrant feeling

Summer clouds floating feathery overhead

Sunk in a phraseological quagmire

Sunk into a gloomy reverie

Sunny silence broods over the realm of little cottages

Supreme arbiter of conduct

Susceptibility to fleeting impressions

Sweet smoke of burning twigs hovered in the autumn day

Swift summer into the autumn flowed

T

Taking the larger sweeps in the march of mind

Tears of outraged vanity blurred her vision

Teased with impertinent questions

Tenderness breathed from her

Tense with the anguish of spiritual struggle

Terror filled the more remote chambers of his brain with riot

Tethered to earth

That which flutters the brain for a moment

The accelerated beat of his thoughts

The affluent splendor of the summer day

The afternoon was filled with sound and sunshine

The afternoon was waning

The air and sky belonged to midsummer

The air darkened swiftly

The air is touched with a lazy fragrance, as of hidden flowers

The air was caressed with song

The air was full of fugitive strains of old songs

The air was raw and pointed

The allurements of a coquette

The ambition and rivalship of men

The angry blood burned in his face

The anguish of a spiritual conflict tore his heart

The artificial smile of languor

The awful and implacable approach of doom

The babble of brooks grown audible

The babbledom that dogs the heels of fame

The bait proved incredibly successful

The balm of solitary musing

The beauty straightway vanished

The beckoning of alien appeals

The benign look of a father

The blandishments of pleasure and pomp of power

The blinding mist came down and hid the land

The blue bowl of the sky, all glorious with the blaze of a million worlds

The bound of the pulse of spring

The buzz of idolizing admiration

The caressing peace of bright soft sunshine

The chaotic sound of the sea

The chill of forlorn old age

The chill of night crept in from the street

The chivalric sentiment of honor

The chivalrous homage of respect

The clamorous agitation of rebellious passions

The clouded, restless, jaded mood

The constant iteration of the sea's wail

The contagion of extravagant luxury

The conversation became desultory [desultory = haphazardly; random]

The crowning touch of pathos

The current of his ideas flowed full and strong

The dance whizzed on with cumulative fury

The dawn is singing at the door

The day sang itself into evening

The day was at once redolent and vociferous [redolent = emitting fragrance; aromatic; suggestive; reminiscent] [vociferous = conspicuously and offensively loud]

The day was blind with fog

The day was gracious

The days passed in a stately procession

The days when you dared to dream

The debilitating fears of alluring fate

The deep and solemn purple of the summer night

The deep flush ebbed out of his face

The deep tranquility of the shaded solitude

The deepening twilight filled with shadowy visions

The deepest wants and aspirations of his soul

The delicatest reproof of imagined distrust

The demerit of an unworthy alliance

The desire of the moth for the star

The dimness of the sealed eye and soul

The dreamy solicitations of indescribable afterthoughts

The dying day lies beautiful in the tender glow of the evening

The early morning of the Indian summer day was tinged with blue mistiness

The earth looked despoiled

The east alone frowned with clouds

The easy grace of an unpremeditated agreeable talker

The easy-going indolence of a sedentary life

The echo of its wrathful roar surged and boomed among the hills

The empurpled hills standing up, solemn and sharp, out of the green-gold air

The enchanting days of youth

The eternal questioning of inscrutable fate

The evening comes with slow steps

The evening star silvery and solitary on the girdle of the early night

The exaggerations of morbid hallucinations

The excitement of rival issues

The extraordinary wistful look of innocence and simplicity

The eye of a scrutinizing observer

The eyes burnt with an amazing fire

The eyes filled with playfulness and vivacity

The father's vigil of questioning sorrow

The fine flower of culture

The first recoil from her disillusionment

The flawless triumph of art

The flight of the autumnal days

The flower of courtesy

The fluttering of untried wings

The foreground was incredibly shabby

The fragrance of a dear and honored name

The freshening breeze struck his brow with a cooling hand

The freshness of some pulse of air from an invisible sea

The fruit of vast and heroic labors

The general effect was of extraordinary lavish profusion

The give and take was delicious

The gloom of the afternoon deepened

The gloom of winter dwelt on everything

The gloomy insolence of self-conceit

The glow of the ambitious fire

The golden gloom of the past and the bright-hued hope of the future

The golden riot of the autumn leaves

The golden sunlight of a great summer day

The gray air rang and rippled with lark music

The grimaces and caperings of buffoonery

The grotesque nightmare of a haunting fear

The hand of time sweeps them into oblivion

The haunting melody of some familiar line of verse

The haunting phrase leaped to my brain

The headlong vigor of sheer improvisation

The heights of magnanimity and love

The high-bred pride of an oriental

The hills were clad in rose and amethyst

The hill-tops gleam in morning's spring

The hinted sweetness of the challenge aroused him

The hot humiliation of it overwhelmed her

The hungry curiosity of the mind

The idiosyncratic peculiarities of thought

The idle chatter of the crowd

The immediate tyranny of a present emotion

The inaccessible solitude of the sky

The incarnation of all loveliness

The incoherent loquacity of a nervous patient [loquacity = very talkative]

The indefinable air of good-breeding

The indefinable yearning for days that were dead

The indefinite atmosphere of an opulent nature

The intercepted glances of wondering eyes

The intrusive question faded

The invidious stigma of selfishness [invidious = rousing ill will]

The iron hand of oppression

The irresistible and ceaseless onflow of time

The irrevocable past and the uncertain future

The landscape ran, laughing, downhill to the sea

The leaden sky rests heavily on the earth

The leaves of time drop stealthily

The leaves syllabled her name in cautious whispers

The lights winked

The little incident seemed to throb with significance

The lofty grace of a prince

The loud and urgent pageantry of the day

The low hills on the horizon wore a haze of living blue

The machinations of a relentless mountebank [mountebank = flamboyant charlatan]

The machinations of an unscrupulous enemy

The magical lights of the horizon

The majestic solemnity of the moment yielded to the persuasive warmth of day

The marvelous beauty of her womanhood

The maximum of attainable and communicable truth

The melancholy day weeps in monotonous despair

The melodies of birds and bees

The memory of the night grew fantastic and remote

The meticulous observation of facts

The mind freezes at the thought

The mind was filled with a formless dread

The mocking echoes of long-departed youth

The moment marked an epoch

The moon is waning below the horizon

The more's the pity

The morning beckons

The morning droned along peacefully

The most servile acquiescence

The multiplicity of odors competing for your attention

The murmur of soft winds in the tree-tops

The murmur of the surf boomed in melancholy mockery

The murmuring of summer seas

The music and mystery of the sea

The music of her delicious voice

The music of her presence was singing a swift melody in his blood

The music of unforgotten years sounded again in his soul

The mute melancholy landscape

The mystery obsessed him

The naked fact of death

The nameless and inexpressible fascination of midnight music

The narrow glen was full of the brooding power of one universal spirit

The nascent spirit of chivalry

The night was drowned in stars

The old ruddy conviction deserted me

The onrush and vividness of life

The opulent sunset

The orange pomp of the setting sun

The oscillations of human genius

The outpourings of a tenderness reawakened by remorse

The pageantry of sea and sky

The palest abstractions of thought

The palpitating silence lengthened

The panorama of life was unrolled before him

The paraphernalia of power and prosperity

The parting crimson glory of the ripening summer sun

The past slowly drifted out of his thought

The pendulous eyelids of old age

The penetrating odors assailed his memory as something unforgettable

The pent-up intolerance of years of repression

The perfume of the mounting sea saturated the night with wild fragrance

The piquancy of the pageant of life [piquancy = tart spiciness]

The pith and sinew of mature manhood

The plenitude of her piquant ways [piquant = engagingly stimulating]

The presage of disaster was in the air

The pressure of accumulated misgivings

The preternatural pomposities of the pulpit

The pristine freshness of spring

The pull of soul on body

The pulse of the rebounding sea

The purging sunlight of clear poetry

The purple vaulted night

The question drummed in head and heart day and night

The question irresistibly emerged

The quick pulse of gain

The radiant serenity of the sky

The radiant stars brooded over the stainless fields, white with freshly fallen snow

The restlessness of offended vanity

The retreating splendor of autumn

The rising storm of words

The river ran darkly, mysteriously by

The river sang with its lips to the pebbles

The roar of the traffic rose to thunder

The romantic ardor of a generous mind

The room had caught a solemn and awful quietude

The rosy-hued sky went widening off into the distance

The rosy twilight of boyhood

The royal arrogance of youth

The sadness in him deepened inexplicably

The scars of rancor and remorse

The scent of roses stole in with every breath of air

The sea heaved silvery, far into the night

The sea slept under a haze of golden winter sun

The sea-sweep enfolds you, satisfying eye and mind

The sea-wind buffeted their faces

The secret and subduing charm of the woods

The see-saw of a wavering courage

The sentimental tourist will be tempted to tarry

The shadows of the night seemed to retreat

The shadows rested quietly under the breezeless sky

The shafts of ridicule

The sheer weight of unbearable loneliness

The shiver of the dusk passed fragrantly down the valley

The silence grew stolid

The silence was uncomfortable and ominous

The silent day perfumed with the hidden flowers

The silver silence of the night

The sinking sun made mellow gold of all the air

The sky grew brighter with the imminent day

The sky grew ensaffroned with the indescribable hue that heralds day

The sky put on the panoply of evening

The sky was a relentless, changeless blue

The sky was dull and brooding

The sky was heavily sprinkled with stars

The sky was turning to the pearly gray of dawn

The smiling incarnation of loveliness

The song of hurrying rivers

The sound of the sea waxed

The spacious leisure of the forest

The spell of a deathless dream was upon them

The star-strewn spaces of the night

The stars looked down in their silent splendor

The stars seemed attentive

The steadfast mind kept its hope

The steady thunder of the sea accented the silence

The still voice of the poet

The stillness of a forced composure

The stillness of the star-hung night

The strangest thought shimmered through her

The stream forgot to smile

The streams laughed to themselves

The strident discord seemed to mock his mood

The stunning crash of the ocean saluted her

The subtle emanation of other influences seemed to arrest and chill him

The sudden rush of the awakened mind

The summit of human attainment

The sun blazed torridly

The sun goes down in flame on the far horizon

The sun lay golden-soft over the huddled hills

The sunlight spread at a gallop along the hillside

The sunset was rushing to its height through every possible phase of violence and splendor

The suspicion of secret malevolence

The swelling tide of memory

The swing of the pendulum through an arch of centuries

The tempered daylight of an olive garden

The tender grace of a day that is fled

The tension of struggling tears which strove for an outlet

The thought leaped

The timely effusion of tearful sentiment

The tone betrayed a curious irritation

The torture of his love and terror crushed him

The trees rustled and whispered to the streams

The tumult in her heart subsided

The tumult in her mind found sudden speech

The tumult of pride and pleasure

The tune of moving feet in the lamplit city

The tyranny of nipping winds and early frosts

The unmasked batteries of her glorious gray eyes

The vacant fields looked blankly irresponsive

The vast and shadowy stream of time

The vast cathedral of the world

The vast unexplored land of dreams

The velvet of the cloudless sky grew darker, and the stars more luminous

The veneer of a spurious civilization

The very pulsation and throbbing of his intellect

The very silence of the place appeared a source of peril

The vision fled him

The vivifying touch of humor

The web of lies is rent in pieces

The wheel of her thought turned in the same desolate groove

The whispering rumble of the ocean

The white seething surf fell exhausted along the shore

The whole exquisite night was his

The whole sea of foliage is shaken and broken up with little momentary shivering's and shadows

The wide horizon forever flames with summer

The wild whirl of nameless regret and passionate sorrow

The wild winds flew round, sobbing in their dismay

The wind charged furiously through it, panting towards the downs

The wind piped drearily

The wind was in high frolic with the rain

The winnowed tastes of the ages

The woods were silent with adoration

The youth of the soul

The zenith turned shell pink

Their ephemeral but enchanting beauty had expired forever [ephemeral = markedly short-lived]

Their eyes met glancingly

Their troth had been plighted

There was a kind of exhilaration in this subtle baiting

There was a mild triumph in her tone

There was a mournful and dim haze around the moon

There was a strange massing and curving of the clouds

There was a thrill in the air

There was a time I might have trod the sunlit heights

There was no glint of hope anywhere

There was no menace in the night's silvern calmness

There was something so kindly in its easy candor

There was spendthrift grandeur

These qualities were raised to the white heat of enthusiasm

They became increasingly turbid and phantasmagorical [phantasmagorical = fantastic imagery]

They escaped the baffled eye

They sit heavy on the soul

They were vastly dissimilar

This exquisite conjunction and balance

This little independent thread of inquiry ran through the texture of his mind and died away

This shadowy and chilling sentiment unaccountably creeps over me

Thought shook through her in poignant pictures

Thoughts came thronging in panic haste

Thrilled by fresh and indescribable odors

Thrilled with a sense of strange adventure

Through a cycle of many ages

Through endless and labyrinthine sentences

Thrilled to the depths of her being

Time had passed unseen

Tinsel glitter of empty titles

Tired with a dull listless fatigue

To all intents and purposes

To speak with entire candor

To stay his tottering constancy

To the scourging he submitted with a good grace

Tossed disdainfully off from young and ardent lips

Touched every moment with shifting and enchanting beauty

Touched with a bewildering and elusive beauty

Transcendental contempt for money

Transformed with an overmastering passion

Trouble gathered on his brow

Turning the world topsy-turvy

Twilight creeps upon the darkening mind

U

Unapproachable grandeur and simplicity

Unaware of her bitter taunt

Under the vivifying touch of genius

Unearthly in its malignant glee

Unfathomed depths and impossibilities

Unforced and unstudied depth of feeling

Unspoiled by praise or blame

Unspoken messages from some vaster world

Unstable moral equilibrium of boyhood

Until sleep overtakes us at a stride

Untouched by the ruthless spirit of improvement

Upon the mountain-tops of meditation

Urbanely plastic and versatile

Uttering grandiose puerilities [puerilities = childishness, silly]

V

Vain allurements of folly and fashion

Variously ramified and delicately minute channels of expression

Varnished over with a cold repellent cynicism

Vast sweep of mellow distances

Veiled by some equivocation

Vibrant with the surge of human passions

Vicissitudes of wind and weather [vicissitudes = sudden or unexpected changes]

Vigor and richness of resource

Visible and palpable pains and penalties

Voices that charm the ear and echo with a subtle resonance in the soul

Volcanic upheavings of imprisoned passions

W

Wantonly and detestably unkind

Waylay Destiny and bid him stand and deliver

Wayward and strangely playful responses

Wearing the white flower of a blameless life

What sorry and pitiful quibbling

When a pleasant countryside tunes the spirit to a serene harmony of mood

When music is allied to words

When the frame and the mind alike seem unstrung and listless

When the profane voices are hushed

When the waves show their teeth in the flying breeze

Whilst the morn kissed the sleep from her eyes

Whistled life away in perfect contentment

Wholly alien to his spirit

With a vanquished and weary sigh

Womanly fickleness and caprice

Words and acts easily wrenched from their true significance

Worn to shreds by anxiety

Wrapped in a sudden intensity of reflection

Wrapped in an inaccessible mood

Wrapped in scudding rain

Wrapt in his odorous and many-colored robe

Wrapt in inward contemplation

Wrought of an emotion infectious and splendidly dangerous

Wrought out of intense and tragic experience

Y

Yielding to a wave of pity

Your mind enthroned in the seventh circle of content

SECTION VIII

STRIKING SIMILES

A

A blind rage like a fire swept over him

A book that rends and tears like a broken saw

A breath of melancholy made itself felt like a chill and sudden gust from some unknown sea

A cloud in the west like a pall creeps upward

A cloud like a flag from the sky

A cluster of stars hangs like fruit in the tree

A confused mass of impressions, like an old rubbish-heap

A cry as of a sea-bird in the wind

A dead leaf might as reasonably demand to return to the tree

A drowsy murmur floats into the air like thistledown

A face as imperturbable as fate

A face as pale as wax

A face tempered like steel

A fatigued, faded, lusterless air, as of a caged creature

A few pens parched by long disuse

A figure like a carving on a spire

A fluttering as of blind bewildered moths

A giant galleon overhead, looked like some misty monster of the deep

A glacial pang of pain like the stab of a dagger of ice frozen from a poisoned well

A glance that flitted like a bird

A great moon like a red lamp in the sycamore

A grim face like a carved mask

A hand icily cold and clammy as death

A heart from which noble sentiments sprang like sparks from an anvil

A jeweler that glittered like his shop

A lady that lean'd on his arm like a queen in a fable of old fairy days

A life, a Presence, like the air

A life as common and brown and bare as the box

of earth in the window there

A light wind outside the lattice swayed a branch of roses to and fro,

shaking out their perfume as from a swung censer

A lightning-phrase, as if shot from the quiver of infallible wisdom

A list of our unread books torments some of us like a list of murders

A little breeze ran through the corn like a swift serpent

A little weed-clogged ship, gray as a ghost

A long slit of daylight like a pointing finger

A memory like a well-ordered cupboard

A mighty wind, like a leviathan, plowed the brine

A mind very like a bookcase

A mystery, soft, soothing and gentle, like the whisper of a child murmuring its happiness in its sleep

A name which sounds even now like the call of a trumpet

A note of despairing appeal which fell like a cold hand upon one's living soul

A purpose as the steady flame

A question deep almost as the mystery of life

A quibbling mouth that snapped at verbal errors like a lizard catching flies

A radiant look came over her face, like a sudden burst of sunshine on a cloudy day

A reputation that swelled like a sponge

A ruby like a drop of blood

A shadow of melancholy touched her lithe fancies, as a cloud dims the waving of golden grain

A silver moon, like a new-stamped coin, rode triumphant in the sky

A slow thought that crept like a cold worm through all his brain

A smile flashed over her face, like sunshine over a flower

A soft and purple mist like a vaporous amethyst

A soft haze, like a fairy dream, is floating over wood and stream

A soul as white as heaven

A sound like the throb of a bell

A stooping girl as pale as a pearl

A sudden sense of fear ran through her nerves like the chill of an icy wind

A sweet voice caroling like a gold-caged nightingale

A thin shrill voice like the cry of an expiring mouse

A thing of as frail enchantment as the gleam of stars upon snow

A vague thought, as elusive as the smell of a primrose

A vanishing loveliness as tender as the flush of the rose leaf and as ethereal as the light of a solitary star

A voice as low as the sea

A voice soft and sweet as a tune that one knows

A white bird floats there, like a drifting leaf

Against a sky as clear as sapphire

Age, like winter weather

Agile as a leopard

Agitated like a storm-tossed ship

Air like wine

All around them like a forest swept the deep and empurpled masses of her tangled hair

All like an icicle it seemed, so tapering and cold

All my life broke up, like some great river's ice at touch of spring

All silent as the sheeted dead

All sounds were lost in the whistle of air humming by like the flight of a million arrows

All that's beautiful drifts away like the waters

All the world lay stretched before him like the open palm of his hand

All unconscious as a flower

Alone, like a storm-tossed wreck, on this night of the glad New Year

An anxiety hung like a dark impenetrable cloud

An ardent face out-looking like a star

An ecstasy which suddenly overwhelms your mind like an unexpected and exquisite thought

An envious wind crept by like an unwelcome thought

An ideal as sublime and comprehensive as the horizon

An immortal spirit dwelt in that frail body, like a bird in an outworn cage

An impudent trick as hackneyed as conjuring rabbits out of a hat

An indefinable resemblance to a goat

An isle of Paradise, fair as a gem

An old nodding negress whose sable head shined in the sun like a polished cocoanut

An omnibus across the bridge crawls like a yellow butterfly

An undefined sadness seemed to have fallen about her like a cloud

An unknown world, wild as primeval chaos

An unpleasing strain, like the vibration of a rope drawn out too fast

And a pinnace like a fluttered bird came flying from afar

And a tear like silver, glistened in the corner of her eye

And all our thoughts ran into tears like sunshine into rain

And at first the road comes moving toward me, like a bride waving palms

And Dusk, with breast as of a dove, brooded

And eyes as bright as the day

And fell as cold as a lump of clay

And her cheek was like a rose

And here were forests ancient as the hills

And many a fountain, rivulet, and pond, as clear as elemental diamond, or serene morning air

And melting like the stars in June

And night, as welcome as a friend

And silence like a poultice comes to heal the blows of sound

And spangled o'er with twinkling points, like stars

And the smile she softly uses fills the silence like a speech

As a child in play scatters the heaps of sand that he has piled on the seashore

As a cloud that gathers her robe like drifted snow

As a flower after a drought drinks in the steady plunging rain

As a leaf that beats on a mountain

As a lion grieves at the loss of her whelps

As a man plowing all day longs for supper and welcomes sunset

As a sea disturbed by opposing winds

As amusing as a litter of likely young pigs

As arbitrary as a cyclone and as killing as a pestilence

As austere as a Roman matron

As beautiful as the purple flush of dawn

As blind as a mole

As brief as sunset clouds in heaven

As bright as sunlight on a stream

As busy as a bee

As cattle driven by a gadfly

As chimney sweepers come to dust

As clear as a whistle

As clear as the parts of a tree in the morning sun

As close as oak and ivy stand

As delicate and as fair as a lily

As delightful to the mind as cool well-water to thirsty lip

As diamond cuts diamond

As direct and unvarying as the course of a homing bird

As distinct as night and morning

As dry as desert dust

As dumb as a fish

As easily as the sun shines

As easy as a turn of the hand

As elastic as a steel spring

As extinct as the dodo

As faint as the memory of a sound

As familiar to him as his alphabet

As fatal as the fang of the most venomous snake

As fleeting and elusive as our dreams

As foam from a ship's swiftness

As fresh and invigorating as a sea-breeze

As full of eager vigor as a mountain stream

As full of spirit as a gray squirrel

As gay and busy as a brook

As gently as the flower gives forth its perfume

As gently as withered leaves float from a tree

As graceful as a bough

As grave as a judge

As great as the first day of creation

As high as heaven

As I dropped like a bolt from the blue

As I dwelt like a sparrow among the spires

As if a door were suddenly left ajar into some world unseen before

As impossible as to count the stars in illimitable space

As in the footsteps of a god

As inaccessible to his feet as the clefts and gorges of the clouds

As inexorable as the flight of time

As innocent as a new laid egg

As iridescent as a soap bubble

As locusts gather to a stream before a fire

As mellow and deep as a psalm

As men strip for a race, so must an author strip for the race with time

As merry as bees in clover

As nimble as water

As one who has climbed above the earth's eternal snowline and sees only white peaks and pinnacles

As pale as any ghost

As patient as the trees

As quick as the movement of some wild animal

As quiet as a nun breathless with adoration

As radiant as the rose

As readily and naturally as ducklings take to water

As reticent as a well-bred stockbroker

As ruthlessly as the hoof of a horse tramples on a rose

As shallow streams run dimpling all the way

As simple as the intercourse of a child with its mother

As sleep falls upon the eyes of a child tired with a long summer day of eager pleasure and delight

As some vast river of unfailing source

As stars that shoot along the sky

As still as a stone

As stupid as a sheep

As sudden as a dislocated joint slipping back into place

As summer winds that creep from flower to flower

As supple as a step-ladder

As swaggering and sentimental as a penny novellete [novellete = short novel]

As swift as thought

As the accumulation of snowflakes makes the avalanche

As the bubble is extinguished in the ocean

As the dew upon the roses warms and melts the morning light

As the fair cedar, fallen before the breeze, lies self-embalmed amidst the moldering trees

As the light straw flies in dark'ning whirlwinds

As the lightning cleaves the night

As the loud blast that tears the skies

As the slow shadows of the pointed grass mark the eternal periods

As those move easiest who have learn'd to dance

As though a rose should shut, and be a bud again

As though Pharaoh should set the Israelites to make a pin instead of a pyramid

As unapproachable as a star

As weird as the elfin lights

As well try to photograph the other side of the moon

At extreme tension, like a drawn bow

Away he rushed like a cyclone

Awkward as a cart-horse

B

Babbling like a child

Balmy in manner as a bland southern morning

Be like the granite of thy rock-ribbed land

Beauteous she looks as a water-lily

Beautiful as the dawn, dominant as the sun

Beauty maddens the soul like wine

Beheld great Babel, wrathful, beautiful, burn like a blood-red cloud upon the plain

Beneath a sky as fair as summer flowers

Bent like a wand of willow

Black as a foam-swept rock

Black his hair as the wintry night

Blithe as a bird [blithe = carefree and lighthearted]

Bounded by the narrow fences of life

Bowed like a mountain

Breaking his oath and resolution like a twist of rotten silk

Breathed like a sea at rest

Bright as a diamond in the sun

Bright as a fallen fragment of the sky

Bright as the coming forth of the morning, in the cloud of an early shower

Bright as the sunbeams

Bright as the tear of an angel, glittered a lonely star

Brilliant and gay as a Greek

Brisk as a wasp in the sunshine

Brittle and bent like a bow

Bronze-green beetles tumbled over stones, and lay helpless on their backs with the air of an elderly clergyman knocked down by an omnibus

Brown as the sweet smelling loam

Brute terrors like the scurrying of rats in a deserted attic

Buried in his library like a mouse in a cheese

Burns like a living coal in the soul

But across it, like a mob's menace, fell the thunder

But thou art fled, like some frail exhalation

Butterflies like gems

C

Calm as the night

Calm like a flowing river

Calm like a mountain brooding o'er the sea

Calmly dropping care like a mantle from her shoulders

Cast thy voice abroad like thunder

Charm upon charm in her was packed, like rose-leaves in a costly vase

Chaste as the icicle

Cheeks as soft as July peaches

Chill breath of winter

Choked by the thorns and brambles of early adversity

Cities scattered over the world like ant-hills

Cities that rise and sink like bubbles

Clear and definite like the glance of a child or the voice of a girl

Clear as a forest pool

Clear as crystal

Clenched little hands like rumpled roses, dimpled and dear

Cloud-like that island hung afar

Clouds like the petals of a rose

Cloudy mirror of opinion

Cold and hard as steel

Cold as the white rose waking at daybreak

Cold, glittering monotony like frosting around a cake

Collapsed like a concertina

Colored like a fairy tale

Companionless as the last cloud of an expiring storm whose thunder is its knell

Consecration that like a golden thread
runs through the warp and woof of one's life

[warp = lengthwise threads]

[woof = crosswise threads]

Constant as gliding waters

Contending like ants for little molehill realms

Continuous as the stars that shine

Cowslips, like chance-found gold

Creeds like robes are laid aside

Creeping like a snail, unwillingly to school

Cruel as death

Curious as a lynx

Cuts into the matter as with a pen of fire

D

Dainty as flowers

Dance like a wave of the sea

Dark and deep as night

Dark as pitch

Dark trees bending together as though whispering secrets

Dazzling white as snow in sunshine

Deafening and implacable as some elemental force

Dear as remembered kisses after death

Dear as the light that visits these sad eyes

Dearer than night to the thief

Debasing fancies gather like foul birds

Deep as the fathomless sea

Deep dark well of sorrow

Delicate as nymphs

Delicate as the flush on a rose or the sculptured line on a Grecian urn

Denominational lines like stone walls

Dependency had dropped from her like a cast-off cloak

Despondency clung to him like a garment that is wet

Destructive as the lightning flash

Die like flies

Dip and surge lightly to and fro, like the red harbor-buoy

Disappearing into distance like a hazy sea

Dissatisfaction had settled on his mind like a shadow

Dissolve like some unsubstantial vision faded

Do make a music like to rustling satin

Dogging them like their own shadow

Dost thou not hear the murmuring nightingale like water bubbling from a silver jar?

Drop like a feather, softly
to the ground

Drowned like rats

Dull as champagne

E

Each like a corpse within
its grave

Each moment was an
iridescent bubble fresh-
blown from the lips of
fancy

Eager-hearted as a boy

Eager with the headlong
zest of a hunter for the
game

Ears that seemed as deaf as
dead man's ears

Easy as a poet's dream

Emotions flashed across
her face like the sweep of
sun-rent clouds over a
quiet landscape

Eternal as the skies

Evanescent as bubbles
[evanescent = vanishing
like vapor]

Every flake that fell from
heaven was like an angel's
kiss

Every lineament was clear
as in the sculptor's thought

[lineament = characteristic
feature]

Everyone on the watch,
like a falcon on its nest

Every phrase is like the
flash of a scimitar

Exploded like a penny
squib

Eyes as deeply dark as are
the desert skies

Eyes as luminous and
bright and brown as waters
of a woodland river

Eyes half veiled by
slumberous tears, like
bluest water seen through
mists of rain

Eyes like a very dark topaz

Eyes like deep wells of
compassionate gloom

Eyes like limpid pools in
shadow

Eyes like mountain water
that o'erflowing on a rock

F

Faces pale with bliss, like
evening stars

Fade away like a cloud in
the horizon

Faint and distant as the
light of a sun that has long
set

Faintly, like a falling dew

Fair and fleet as a fawn

Fair as a star when only
one is shining in the sky

Fallen like dead leaves on
the highway

Falling away like a speck
in space

Fanciful and extravagant
as a caliph's dream

Fawning like dumb
neglected lap-dogs

Felt her breath upon his
cheek like a perfumed air

Fields of young grain and
verdure pastures like
crushed velvet

Fierce as a bear in defeat

Fierce as the flames

Fills life up like a cup with
bubbling and sparkling
liquor

Fit closely together as the
close-set stones of a
building

Fixed like a beacon-tower
above the waves of a
tempest

Flame like a flag unfurled

Flap loose and slack like a
drooping sail

Flashed with the brilliancy of a well-cut jewel

Fled like sweet dreams

Fleet as an arrow

Flitted like a sylph on wings

Flowers as soft as thoughts of budding love

Fluent as a rill, that wanders silver-footed down a hill

Fluid as thought

Fluttered like gilded butterflies in giddy mazes

Fragile as a spider's web

Free as the air, from zone to zone I flew

Free as the winds that caress

Fresh and unworn as the sea that breaks languidly beside them

Fresh as a jewel found but yesterday

Fresh as the first beam glittering on a sail

Frightened like a child in the dark

Full-throated as the sea

Furious as eagles

G

Gazed like a star into the morning light

Glaring like noontide

Gleam like a diamond on a dancing girl

Glistening like threads of gold

Glitter like a swarm of fire-flies tangled in a silver braid

Glittering like an aigrette of stars [aigrette = ornamental tuft of upright plumes]

Gone astray as a sheep that is lost

Gone like a glow on the cloud at the close of day

Gone like tenants that quit without warning

Gorgeous as the hues of heaven

Grazing through a circulating library as contentedly as cattle in a fresh meadow

Great scarlet poppies lay in drifts and heaps, like bodies fallen there in vain assault

H

Hair as harsh as tropical grass and gray as ashes

Hangs like a blue thread loosen'd from the sky

Hard, sharp, and glittering as a sword

Harnessed men, like beasts of burden, drew it to the river-side

Haunts you like the memory of some former happiness

He began to laugh with that sibilant laugh which resembles the hiss of a serpent [sibilant = producing a hissing sound]

He bent upon the lightning page like some rapt poet o'er his rhyme

He bolted down the stairs like a hare

He clatters like a windmill

He danced like a man in a swarm of hornets

He fell as falls some forest lion, fighting well

He fell down on my threshold like a wounded stag

He had acted exactly like an automaton

He lay as straight as a mummy

He lay like a warrior taking his rest

He lived as modestly as a hermit

He looked fagged and sallow, like the day [fagged = worked to exhaustion]

He looked with the bland, expressionless stare of an overgrown baby

He played with grave questions as a cat plays with a mouse

He radiated vigor and abundance like a happy child

He sat down quaking like a jelly

He saw disaster like a ghostly figure following her

He snatched furiously at breath like a tiger snatching at meat

He spoke with a uniformity of emphasis that made his words stand out like the raised type for the blind

He swayed in the sudden grip of anger

He sweeps the field of battle like a monsoon

He that wavereth is like a wave of the sea, driven with the wind and tossed

He turned on me like a thunder-cloud

He turned white as chalk

He wandered restlessly through the house, like a prowling animal

He was as splendidly serious as a reformer

He was as steady as a clock

He was as wax in those clever hands

He was bold as the hawk

He was so weak now, like a shrunk cedar white with the hoar-frost

Hearts unfold like flowers before thee

Heavy was my heart as stone

Heeled like an avalanche to leeward

Her arms like slumber o'er my shoulders crept

Her banners like a thousand sunsets glow

Her beauty broke on him like some rare flower

Her beauty fervent as a fiery moon

Her breath is like a cloud

Her cheeks are like the blushing cloud

Her cheeks were wan and her eyes like coals

Her dusky cheek would burn like a poppy

Her expression changed with the rapidity of a kaleidoscope

Her eyes as bright as a blazing star

Her eyes as stars of twilight fair

Her eyes, glimmering star-like in her pale face

Her eyes were as a dove that sickeneth

Her face changed with each turn of their talk, like a wheat-field under a summer breeze

Her face collapsed as if it were a pricked balloon

Her face was as solemn as a mask

Her face was dull as lead

Her face was like a light

Her face was passionless, like those by sculptor graved for niches in a temple

Her hair dropped on her pallid cheeks, like sea-weed on a clam

Her hair hung down like summer twilight

Her hair shone like a nimbus

Her hair was like a coronet

Her hands are white as the virgin rose that she wore on her wedding day

Her hands like moonlight brush the keys

Her head dropped into her hands like a storm-broken flower

Her heart has grown icy as a fountain in the fall

Her holy love that like a vestal flame had burned

Her impulse came and went like fireflies in the dusk

Her lashes like fans upon her cheek

Her laugh is like a rainbow-tinted spray

Her lips are like two budded roses

Her lips like a lovely song that ripples as it flows

Her lips like twilight water

Her little lips are tremulous as brook-water is [tremulous = timid or fearful]

Her long black hair danced round her like a snake

Her mouth as sweet as a ripe fig

Her neck is like a stately tower

Her pale robe clinging to the grass seemed like a snake

Her pulses flutter'd like a dove

Her skin was as the bark of birches

Her sweetness halting like a tardy May

Her two white hands like swans on a frozen lake

Her voice cut like a knife

Her voice like mournful bells crying on the wind

Her voice was like the voice the stars had when they sang together

Her voice was rich and vibrant, like the middle notes of a 'cello

Her words sounding like wavelets on a summer shore

Herding his thoughts as a collie dog herds sheep

Here and there a solitary volume greeted him like a friend in a crowd of strange faces

Here in statue-like repose, an old wrinkled mountain rose

Hers was the loveliness of some tall white lily cut in marble, splendid but chill

His bashfulness melted like a spring frost

His brow bent like a cliff o'er his thoughts

His cheeks were furrowed and writhen like rain-washed crags [writhen = twisted]

His eyes blazed like deep forests

His eyes glowed like blue coals

His eyes were hollows of madness, his hair like moldy hay

His face burnt like a brand

His face was glad as dawn to me

His face was often lit up by a smile like pale wintry sunshine

His fingers were knotted like a cord

His formal kiss fell chill as a flake of snow on the cheek

His fortune melted away like snow in a thaw

His glorious moments were strung like pearls upon a string

His indifference fell from him like a garment

His invectives and vituperations bite and flay like steel whips [invective = abusive language] [vituperation = abusive language]

His mind murmurs like a harp among the trees

His mind was like a lonely wild

His mind was like a summer sky

His nerves thrilled like throbbing violins

His retort was like a knife-cut across the sinews

His revenge descends perfect, sudden, like a curse from heaven

His spirits sank like a stone

His talk is like an incessant play of fireworks

His voice is as the thin faint song when the wind wearily sighs in the grass

His voice rose like a stream of rich distilled perfumes

His voice was like the clap of thunder which interrupts the warbling birds among the leaves

His whole soul wavered and shook like a wind-swept leaf

His words gave a curious satisfaction, as when a coin, tested, rings true gold

Hopeful as the break of day

How like a saint she sleeps

How like a winter hath my absence been

How like the sky she bends over her child

Howling in the wilderness like beasts

Huge as a hippopotamus

Humming-birds like lake of purple fire

Hushed as the grave

Hushed like a breathless lyre

I

I had grown pure as the dawn and the dew

I have heard the Hiddon People like the hum of swarming bees

I have seen the ravens flying, like banners of old wars

I saw a face bloom like a flower

I saw a river of men marching like a tide

I saw his senses swim dizzy as clouds

I wandered lonely as a cloud

I was as sensitive as a barometer

I was no more than a straw on the torrent of his will

I will face thy wrath though it bite as a sword

Ideas which spread with the speed of light

Idle hopes, like empty shadows

Impassive as a statue

Impatient as the wind

Impregnable as Gibraltar

Impressive as a warrant of arrest for high treason

Incredible little white teeth, like snow shut in a rose

Infrequent carriages sped like mechanical toys guided by manikins

In honor spotless as unfallen snow

In that head of his a flame burnt that was like an altar-fire

In yonder cottage shines a light, far-gleaming like a gem

Instantly she revived like flowers in water

Intangible as a dream

It came and faded like a wreath of mist at eve

It cuts like knives, this air so chill

It drops away like water from a smooth statue

It pealed through her brain like a muffled bell

It poured upon her like a trembling flood

It racked his ears like an explosion of steam-whistles

It ran as clear as a trout-brook

It seems as motionless and still as the zenith in the skies

It set his memories humming like a hive of bees

It staggered the eye, like the sight of water running up hill

It stung like a frozen lash

It was as futile as to oppose an earthquake with argument

It was as if a door had been opened into a furnace, so the eyes blazed

It would collapse as if by enchantment

Its temples and its palaces did seem like fabrics of enchantment piled to Heaven

J

Jealousy, fierce as the fires

K

Kindle like an angel's wings the western skies in flame

Kindly mornings when autumn and winter seemed to go hand in hand like a happy aged couple

Kingdoms melt away like snow

L

Laboring like a giant

Languid streams that cross softly, slowly, with a sound like smothered weeping

Laughter like a beautiful bubble from the rosebud of baby-hood

Laughter like the sudden outburst of the glad bird in the tree-top

Lazy merchantmen that crawled like flies over the blue enamel of the sea

Leapt like a hunted stag

Let his frolic fancy play, like a happy child

Let in confusion like a whirling flood

Let thy mouth murmur like the doves

Life had been arrested, as the horologist, with interjected finger, arrests the beating of the clock [horologist = one who repairs watches]

Life stretched before him alluring and various as the open road

Life sweet as perfume and pure as prayer

Light as a snowflake

Lights gleamed there like stars in a still sky

Like a ball of ice it glittered in a frozen sea of sky

Like a blade sent home to its scabbard

Like a blast from a horn

Like a blast from the suddenly opened door of a furnace

Like a blossom blown before a breeze, a white moon drifts before a shimmering sky

Like a bright window in a distant view

Like a caged lion shaking the bars of his prison

Like a calm flock of silver-fleeced sheep

Like a cloud of fire

Like a cold wind his words went through their flesh

Like a crowd of frightened porpoises a shoal of sharks pursue

Like a damp-handed auctioneer

Like a deaf and dumb man wondering what it was all about

Like a dew-drop, ill-fitted to sustain unkindly shocks

Like a dipping swallow the stout ship dashed through the storm

Like a distant star glimmering steadily in the darkness

Like a dream she vanished

Like a festooned girdle encircling the waist of a bride

Like a flower her red lips parted

Like a game in which the important part is to keep from laughing

Like a glow-worm golden

Like a golden-shielded army

Like a great express train, roaring, flashing, dashing head-long

Like a great fragment of the dawn it lay

Like a great ring of pure and endless light

Like a great tune to which the planets roll

Like a high and radiant ocean

Like a high-born maiden

Like a jewel every cottage casement showed

Like a joyless eye that finds no object worth its constancy

Like a knight worn out by conflict

Like a knot of daisies lay the hamlets on the hill

Like a lily in bloom

Like a living meteor

Like a locomotive-engine with unsound lungs

Like a long arrow through the dark the train is darting

Like a mirage, vague, dimly seen at first

Like a miser who spoils his

coat with scanting a little cloth [scanting = short]

Like a mist the music drifted from the silvery strings

Like a moral lighthouse in the midst of a dark and troubled sea

Like a murmur of the wind came a gentle sound of stillness

Like a noisy argument in a drawing-room

Like a pageant of the Golden Year, in rich memorial pomp the hours go by

Like a pale flower by some sad maiden cherished

Like a poet hidden

Like a river of molten amethyst

Like a rocket discharging a shower of golden stars

Like a rose embower'd in its own green leaves

Like a sea of upturned faces

Like a shadow never to be overtaken

Like a shadow on a fair sunlit landscape

Like a sheeted ghost

Like a ship tossed to and fro on the waves of life's sea

Like a slim bronze statue of Despair

Like a snow-flake lost in the ocean

Like a soul that wavers in the Valley of the Shadow

Like a stalled horse that breaks loose and goes at a gallop through the plain

Like a star, his love's pure face looked down

Like a star that dwelt apart

Like a star, unhasting, unresting

Like a stone thrown at random

Like a summer cloud, youth indeed has crept away

Like a summer-dried fountain

Like a swift eagle in the morning glare breasting the whirlwind with impetuous flight

Like a thing at rest

Like a thing read in a book

or remembered out of the faraway past

Like a tide of triumph through their veins, the red, rejoicing blood began to race

Like a triumphing fire the news was borne

Like a troop of boys let loose from school, the adventurers went by

Like a vaporous amethyst

Like a vision of the morning air

Like a voice from the unknown regions

Like a wandering star I fell through the deeps of desire

Like a watch-worn and weary sentinel

Like a wave of the sea driven with the wind and tossed

Like a whirlwind they went past

Like a withered leaf the moon is blown across the bay

Like a world of sunshine

Like a yellow silken scarf the thick fog hangs

Like an alien ghost I stole away

Like an eagle clutching his prey, his arm swooped down

Like an eagle dallying with the wind

Like an engine of dread war, he set his shoulder to the mountain-side

Like an enraged tiger

Like an enthusiast leading about with him an indifferent tourist

Like an icy wave, a swift and tragic impression swept through him

Like an unbidden guest

Like an unbodied joy whose race is just begun

Like an unseen star of birth

Like an unwelcome thought

Like apparitions seen and gone

Like attempting to number the waves on the snore of a limitless sea

Like bells that waste the moments with their loudness

Like blasts of trumpets blown in wars

Like bright Apollo

Like bright lamps, the fabled apples glow

Like building castles in the air

Like bursting waves from the ocean

Like cliffs which have been rent asunder

Like clouds of gnats with perfect lineaments [lineaments = distinctive shape]

Like cobwebs woven round the limbs of an infant giant

Like crystals of snow

Like dead lovers who died true

Like Death, who rides upon a thought, and makes his way through temple, tower, and palace

Like dew upon a sleeping flower

Like dining with a ghost

Like drawing nectar in a sieve

Like earth's decaying leaves

Like echoes from a hidden lyre

Like echoes from an antenatal dream

Like fixed eyes, whence the dear light of sense and thought has fled

Like footsteps upon wool

Like fragrance from dead flowers

Like ghosts, from an enchanter fleeing

Like ghosts the sentries come and go

Like golden boats on a sunny sea

Like great black birds, the demons haunt the woods

Like green waves on the sea

Like having to taste a hundred exquisite dishes in a single meal

Like Heaven's free breath, which he who grasps can hold not

Like helpless birds in the warm nest

Like iridescent bubbles floating on a foul stream

Like kindred drops mingled into one

Like laying a burden on the back of a moth

Like lead his feet were

Like leaves in wintry weather

Like leviathans afloat

Like lighting a candle to the sun

Like making a mountain out of a mole-hill

Like mariners pulling the life-boat

Like mice that steal in and out as if they feared the light

Like mountain over mountain huddled

Like mountain streams we meet and part

Like music on the water

Like notes which die when born, but still haunt the echoes of the hill

Like oceans of liquid silver

Like one pale star against the dusk, a single diamond on her brow gleamed with imprisoned fire

Like one who halts with tired wings

Like one who talks of what he loves in dream

Like organ music came the deep reply

Like pageantry of mist on an autumnal stream

Like phantoms gathered by the sick imagination

Like planets in the sky

Like pouring oil on troubled waters

Like roses that in deserts bloom and die

Like rowing upstream against a strong downward current

Like scents from a twilight garden

Like separated souls

Like serpents struggling in a vulture's grasp

Like sheep from out the fold of the sky, stars leapt

Like ships that have gone down at sea

Like shy elves hiding from the traveler's eye

Like skeletons, the sycamores uplift their wasted hands

Like some grave night thought threading a dream

Like some new-gathered snowy hyacinth, so white and cold and delicate it was

Like some poor nigh-related guest, that may not rudely be dismist

Like some suppressed and hideous thought which flits athwart our musings, but can find no rest within a pure and gentle mind

Like some unshriven churchyard thing, the friar crawled

Like something fashioned in a dream

Like sounds of wind and flood

Like splendor-winged moths about a taper

Like stepping out on summer evenings from the glaring ball-room

upon the cool and still piazza

Like straws in a gust of wind

Like summer's beam and summer's stream

Like sunlight, in and out the leaves, the robins went

Like sweet thoughts in a dream

Like the awful shadow of some unseen power

Like the bellowing of bulls

Like the boar encircled by hunters and hounds

Like the bubbles on a river sparkling, bursting, borne away

Like the cold breath of the grave

Like the creaking of doors held stealthily ajar

Like the cry of an itinerant vendor in a quiet and picturesque town

Like the dance of some gay sunbeam

Like the dawn of the morn

Like the detestable and spidery araucaria [araucaria = evergreen trees of South America and Australia]

Like the dew on the mountain

Like the dim scent in violets

Like the drifting foam of a restless sea when the waves show their teeth in the flying breeze

Like the embodiment of a perfect rose, complete in form and fragrance

Like the faint cry of unassisted woe

Like the faint exquisite music of a dream

Like the fair flower dishevel'd in the wind

Like the fair sun, when in his fresh array he cheers the morn, and all the earth revealeth

Like the falling thud of the blade of a murderous ax

Like the fierce fiend of a distempered dream

Like the fitting of an old glove to a hand

Like the foam on the river

Like the great thunder sounding

Like the jangling of all the strings of some musical instrument

Like the jewels that gleam in baby eyes

Like the kiss of maiden love the breeze is sweet and bland

Like the long wandering love, the weary heart may faint for rest

Like the moon in water seen by night

Like the music in the patter of small feet

Like the prodigal whom wealth softens into imbecility

Like the quivering image of a landscape in a flowing stream

Like the rainbow, thou didst fade

Like the rustling of grain moved by the west-wind

Like the sap that turns to nectar, in the velvet of the peach

Like the sea whose waves are set in motion by the winds

Like the sea-worm, that perforates the shell of the mussel, which straightway closes the wound with a pearl

Like the setting of a tropical sun

Like the shadow of a great hill that reaches far out over the plain

Like the shadows of the stars in the upheaved sea

Like the shudder of a doomed soul

Like the silver gleam when the poplar trees rustle their pale leaves listlessly

Like the soft light of an autumnal day

Like the Spring-time, fresh and green

Like the stern-lights of a ship at sea, illuminating only the path which has been passed over

Like the sudden impulse of a madman

Like the swell of Summer's ocean

Like the tattered effigy in a cornfield

Like the vase in which roses have once been distill'd

Like the visits of angels, short and far between

Like the whole sky when to the east the morning doth return

Like thistles of the wilderness, fit neither for food nor fuel

Like those great rivers, whose course everyone beholds, but their springs have been seen by but few

Like thoughts whose very sweetness yielded proof

that they were born for immortality

Like to diamonds her white teeth shone between the parted lips

Like torrents from a mountain source, we rushed into each other's arms

Like troops of ghosts on the dry wind past

Like two doves with silvery wings, let our souls fly

Like two flaming stars were his eyes

Like vaporous shapes half seen

Like village curs that bark when their fellows do

Like wasted hours of youth

Like winds that bear sweet music, when they breathe through some dim latticed chamber

Like wine-stain to a flask the old distrust still clings

Like winged stars the fire-flies flash and glance

Like young lovers whom youth and love make dear

Lingering like an unloved guest

Lithe as a panther

Little white hands like pearls

Lofty as a queen

Loneliness struck him like a blow

Looked back with faithful eyes like a great mastiff to his master's face

Looking as sulky as the weather itself

Looking like a snarling beast baulked of its prey [baulked = checked, thwarted]

Loose clouds like earth's decaying leaves are shed

Lost like the lightning in the sullen clod

Love as clean as starlight

Love brilliant as the morning

Love had like the canker-worm consumed her early prime

Love is a changing lord as the light on a turning sword

Love like a child around the world doth run

Love like a miser in the dark his joys would hide

Love shakes like a windy reed your heart

Love smiled like an unclouded sun

Love that sings and has wings as a bird

Lovely as starry water

Lovely the land unknown and like a river flowing

M

March on my soul nor like the laggard stay

Me on whose heart as a worm she trod

Meaningless as the syllables of an unknown tongue

Men moved hither and thither like insects in their crevices

Mentality as hard as bronze

Mentally round-shouldered and decrepit

Merge imperceptibly into one another like the hues of the prism

Meteors that dart like screaming birds

Milk-white pavements, clear and richly pale, like alabaster

More variegated than the skin of a serpent

Motion like the spirit of that wind whose soft step deepens slumber

Motionless as a plumb line

Mountains like frozen wrinkles on a sea

Moving in the same dull round, like blind horses in a mill

Mute as an iceberg

My age is as a lusty Winter

My body broken as a turning wheel

My breath to Heaven like vapor goes

My head was like a great bronze bell with one thought for the clapper

My heart is as some famine-murdered land

My heart is like a full sponge and must weep a little

My heart like a bird doth hover

My heart will be as wind fainting in hot grass

My life floweth away like a river

My life was white as driven snow

My love for thee is like the sovereign moon that rules the sea

My love's like the steadfast sun

My lungs began to crow like chanticleer
[chanticleer = rooster]

My mind swayed idly like a water-lily in a lake

My muscles are as steel

My skin is as sallow as gold

My soul was as a lampless sea

My spirit seemed to beat the void, like the bird from out the ark

My thoughts came yapping and growling round me like a pack of curs

My thoughts ran leaping through the green ways of my mind like fawns at play

N

Night falls like fire

No longer shall slander's venomed spite crawl like a snake across his perfect name

Now every nerve in my body seemed like a strained harp-string ready to snap at a touch

Now like a wild nymph she veils her shadowy form

Now like a wild rose in the fields of heaven slipt forth the slender figure of the Dawn

Now memory and emotion surged in my soul like a tempest

Now thou seemest like a bankrupt beau, stripped of his gaudy hues

O

Obscured with wrath as is the sun with cloud

Odorous as all Arabia

Often enough life tosses like a fretful stream among rocky boulders

Oh, lift me as a wave, a leaf, a cloud

Old as the evening star

Old happy hours that have long folded their wings

Once again, like madness, the black shapes of doubt swing through his brain

One bleared star, faint glimmering like a bee

One bright drop is like the gem that decks a monarch's crown

One by one flitting like a mournful bird

One deep roar as of a cloven world

One winged cloud above like a spread dragon overhangs the west

Oppressed by the indefiniteness which hung in her mind, like a thick summer haze

Or shedding radiance like the smiles of God

Our enemies were broken like a dam of river reeds

Our hearts bowed down like violets after rain

Our sail like a dew-lit blossom shone

Overhead the intense blue of the noonday sky burst like a jewel in the sun

P

Pale and grave as a sculptured nun

Pale as a drifting blossom

Passed like a phantom into the shadows

Passive and tractable as a child

Peaceful as a village cricket-green on Sunday

Peevish and impatient, like some ill-trained man who is sick

Perished utterly, like a blown-out flame

Philosophy evolved itself, like a vast spider's loom

Pillowed upon its alabaster arms like to a child o'erwearied with sweet toil

Polished as the bosom of a star

Poured his heart out like the rending sea in passionate wave on wave

Pouting like the snowy buds o' roses in July

Presently she hovered like a fluttering leaf or flake of snow

Pride and self-disgust served her like first-aid surgeons on the battlefield

Proud as the proudest of church dignitaries

Pure as a wild-flower

Pure as the azure above them

Pure as the naked heavens

Pure as the snowy leaves that fold over the flower's heart

Purple, crimson, and scarlet, like the curtains of God's tabernacle

Put on gravity like a robe

Q

Quaking and quivering like a short-haired puppy after a ducking

Questions and answers sounding like a continuous popping of corks

Quiet as a nun's face

Quietly as a cloud he stole

Quietude which seemed to him beautiful as clear depths of water

Quivering like an eager race-horse to start

R

Rage, rage ye tears, that never more should creep like hounds about God's footstool

Ran like a young fawn

Rattle in the ear like a flourish of trumpets

Rays springing from the east like golden arrows

Red as the print of a kiss might be

Redolent with the homely scent of old-fashioned herbs and flowers

Reflected each in the other like stars in a lake

Refreshed like dusty grass after a shower

Refreshing as descending rains to sunburnt climes

Remote as the hidden star

Restless as a blue-bottle fly on a warm summer's day

Revealed his doings like those of bees in a glass hive

Rich as the dawn

Ride like the wind through the night

Rivers that like silver threads ran through the green and gold of pasture lands

Roared like mountain torrents

Rolling it under the tongue as a sweet morsel

Round my chair the

children run like little things of dancing gold

Ruddy as sunrise

Ruddy his face as the morning light

Ruffling out his cravat with a crackle of starch, like a turkey when it spreads its feathers

Running to and fro like frightened sheep

Rushing and hurrying about like a June-bug

S

Sanctuaries where the passions may, like wild falcons, cover their faces with their wings

Sayings that stir the blood like the sound of a trumpet

Scattered love as stars do light

Sea-gulls flying like flakes of the sea

Sentences level and straight like a hurled lance

Shadowy faces, known in dreams, pass as petals upon a stream

Shake like an aspen leaf

Shaken off like a nightmare

Shapeless as a sack of wool

Shattered like so much glass

She brightened like a child whose broken toy is glued together

She could summon tears as one summons servants

She danced like a flower in the wind

She disclaimed the weariness that dragged upon her spirits like leaden weights

She exuded a faint and intoxicating perfume of womanliness, like a crushed herb

She felt like an unrepentant criminal

She fled like a spirit from the room

She flounders like a huge conger-eel in an ocean of dingy morality

She gave him a surprised look, like a child catching an older person in a foolish statement

She gave off antipathies as a liquid gives off vapor

She has great eyes like the doe

She heard him like one in a dream

She let the soft waves of her deep hair fall like flowers from Paradise

She looked like a tall golden candle

She looked like the picture of a young rapt saint, lost in heavenly musing

She moved like mirth incarnate

She nestles like a dove

She played with a hundred possibilities fitfully and discursively as a musician runs his fingers over a key-board

She played with grave cabinets as a cat plays with a mouse

She saw this planet like a star hung in the glistening depths of even

She seemed as happy as a wave that dances on the sea

She shall be sportive as the fawn

She stood silent a moment, dropping before him like a broken branch

She that passed had lips like pinks

She walked like a galley-slave

She walks in beauty like the night

She was as brilliant, and as hard too, as electric light

She was silent, standing before him like a little statuesque figure

Shining like the dewy star of dawn

Shivering pine-trees, like phantoms

Showy as damask-rose and shy as musk

Shrill as the loon's call

Shrivel like paper thrust into a flame

Shy as the squirrel

Sights seen as a traveling swallow might see them on the wing

Silence deep as death

Silence now is brooding like a gentle spirit o'er the still and pulseless world

Silence that seemed heavy and dark; like a passing cloud

Sinks clamorous like mill-waters at wild play

Sits like the maniac on his fancied throne

Skies as clear as babies' eyes

Sleek and thick and yellow as gold

Slender and thin as a slender wire

Slowly as a tortoise

Slowly as the finger of a clock, her shadow came

Slowly moved off and disappeared like shapes breathed on a mirror and melting away

Slowly, unnoted, like the creeping rust that spreads insidious, had estrangement come

Small as a grain of mustard seed

Smooth as a pond

Smooth as the pillar flashing in the sun

Snug as a bug in a rug

Soaring as swift as smoke from a volcano springs

So elusive that the memory of it afterwards was wont to come and go like a flash of light

So my spirit beat itself like a caged bird against its prison bars in vain

Soft as a zephyr

Soft as sleep the snow fell

Soft as Spring

Soft as the down of the turtle dove

Soft as the landscape of a dream

Soft as the south-wind

Soft in their color as gray pearls

Soft vibrations of verbal melody, like the sound of a golden bell rung far down under the humming waters

Some gleams of feeling pure and warm as sunshine on a sky of storm

Some like veiled ghosts hurrying past as though driven to their land of shadows by shuddering fear

Some minds are like an open fire—how direct and instant our communication with them

Something divine seemed to cling around her like some subtle vapor

Something resistant and inert, like the obstinate rolling over of a heavy sleeper after he has been called to get up

Something sharp and brilliant, like the glitter of a sword or a forked flash of lightning

Sorrowful eyes like those of wearied kine spent from the plowing

[kine = cows]

Spread like wildfire

Squirrel-in-the-cage kind of movement

Stamping like a plowman to shuffle off the snow

Stared about like calves in a pen

Steadfast as the soul of truth

Steals lingering like a river smooth

Still as death

Stood like a wave-beaten rock

Straight as a ray of light

Straight as an arrow

Streamed like a meteor through the troubled air

Streamed o'er his memory
like a forest flame

Streaming tears, like pearl
drops from a flint

Striking with the force of
an engine of destruction

Strong as a bison

Style comes, if at all, like
the bloom upon fruit, or
the glow of health upon the
cheek

Subtle as jealousy

Sudden a thought came
like a full-blown rose,
flushing his brow

Sudden sprays of rain, like
volleys of sharp arrows,
rattled gustily against the
windows

Suddenly, like death, the
truth flashed on them

Sunbeams flashing on the
face of things like sudden
smilings of divine delight

Sunday mornings which
seem to put on, like a
Sabbath garment, an
atmosphere of divine
quietude

Supple and sweet as a rose
in bloom

Sway like blown moths
against the rosewhite flame

Sweet as a summer night
without a breath

Sweet as music she spoke

Sweet as the rain at noon

Sweet as the smile of a
fairy

Swift as a swallow heading
south

Swift as lightning

Swift as the panther in
triumph

Swifter than the twinkling
of an eye

T

Talking and thinking
became to him like the
open page of a monthly
magazine

Tall lance-like reeds wave
sadly o'er his head

That like a wounded snake
drags its slow length along

The anemone that weeps at
day-break, like a silly girl
before her lover

The army blazed and
glowed in the golden
sunlight like a mosaic of a
hundred thousand jewels

The army like a witch's
caldron seethed

The beating of her heart
was like a drum

The beauty of her quiet life
was like a rose in blowing

The billows burst like
cannon down the coast

The birds swam the flood
of air like tiny ships

The boat cuts its swift way
through little waves like
molten gold and opal

The boom of the surf grew
ever less sonorous, like the
thunder of a retreating
storm

The breast-plate of
righteousness

The breathless hours like
phantoms stole away

The breeze is as a pleasant
tune

The calm white brow as
calm as earliest morn

The camp fire reddens like
angry skies

The chambers of the house
were haunted by an
incessant echoing, like
some dripping cavern

The church swarmed like a
hive

The city is all in a turmoil;
it boils like a pot of lentils

The clouds that move like spirits o'er the welkin clear [welkin = sky]

The clustered apples burnt like flame

The colored bulbs swung noon-like from tree and shrub

The crimson close of day

The curl'd moon was like a little feather

The curling wreaths like turbans seem

The dark hours are swept away like crumbling ashes

The dark mass of her hair shook round her like a sea

The dawn is rising from the sea, like a white lady from her bed

The dawn had whitened in the mist like a dead face

The dawn with silver-sandaled feet crept like a frightened girl.

The day stunned me like light upon some wizard way

The day was sweeter than honey and the honey-comb

The day have trampled me like armed men

The dead past flew away over the fens like a flight of wild swans

The deep like one black maelstrom round her whirls

The deepening east like a scarlet poppy burnt

The desolate rocky hills rolled like a solid wave along the horizon

The dome of heaven is like one drop of dew

The dreams of poets come like music heard at evening from the depth of some enchanted forest

The eagerness faded from his eyes, leaving them cold as a winter sky after sunset

The earth was like a frying-pan, or some such hissing matter

The eternal sea, which like a childless mother, still must croon her ancient sorrows to the cold white moon

The evening sky was as green as jade

The excitement had spread through the whole house, like a piquant and agreeable odor

The excitement of the thought buoyed his high-strung temperament like a tonic

The feathery meadows like a lilac sea

The firm body like a slope of snow

The first whiff of reality dissipated them like smoke

The floor, newly waxed, gleamed in the candle-light like beaten moonbeams

The fragrant clouds of hair, they flowed round him like a snare

The gathering glory of life shone like the dawn

The gesture was all strength and will, like the stretching of a sea-bird's wings

The girl's voice rang like a bird-call through his rustling fancies

The glimmer of tall flowers standing like pensive moon-worshipers in an ecstasy of prayerless bloom

The guides sniffed, like chamois, the air
                    [chamois = extremely agile goat antelope]

The heavens are like a
scroll unfurled

The hills across the valley
were purple as thunder-
clouds

The hoofs of the horses
rang like the dumb cadence
of an old saga

The hours crawled by like
years

The hum of the camp
sounds like the sea

The hurrying crowds of
men gather like clouds

The ideas succeeded each
other like a dynasty of
kings

The impalpable presence
of the new century rose
like a vast empty house
through which

no human feet had walked

The inexorable facts closed
in on him like prison-
warders hand-cuffing a
convict

The lake glimmered as still
as a mirror

The land of gold seemed to
hold him like a spell

The land was like a dream

The level boughs, like bars
of iron across the setting
sun

The light of London flaring
like a dreary dawn

The lights blazed up like
day

The lilies were drooping,
white, and wan, like the
head and skin of a dying
man

The mellowing hand of
time

The melody rose tenderly
and lingeringly like a
haunting perfume of
pressed flowers

The Milky Way lay like
diamond-dust upon the
robe of some great king

The monk's face whitened
like sea-foam

The moon drowsed
between the trees like a
great yellow moth

The moon on the tower
slept soft as snow

The moonbeams rest like a
pale spotless shroud

The moonlight lay like
snow

The moonlight, like a fairy
mist, upon the mesa
spreads

The mortal coldness of the
soul, like death itself
comes down

The mountain shadows
mingling, lay like pools
above the earth

The mountains loomed up
dimly, like phantoms
through the mist

The music almost died
away, then it burst like a
pent-up flood

The name that cuts into my
soul like a knife

The nervous little train
winding its way like a
jointed reptile

The new ferns were spread
upon the earth like some
lacy coverlet

The night like a battle-
broken host is driven
before

The night yawned like a
foul wind

The ocean swelled like an
undulating mirror of the
bowl of heaven

The old books look
somewhat pathetically
from the shelves, like aged
dogs wondering why no
one takes them for a walk

The old infamy will pop

into daylight like a toad out of fissure in the rock

The penalty falls like a thunderbolt from heaven

The phrase was like a spear-thrust

The pine trees waved as waves a woman's hair

The place was like some enchanted town of palaces

The plains to northward change their color like the shimmering necks of doves

The poppy burned like a crimson ember

The prime of man has waxed like cedars

The public press would chatter and make odd ambiguous sounds like a shipload of monkeys in a storm

The purple heather rolls like dumb thunder

The rainbows flashed like fire

The river shouted as ever its cry of joy over the vitality of life, like a spirited boy before the face of inscrutable nature

The roofs with their gables like hoods

The roses lie upon the grass like little shreds of crimson silk

The satire of the word cut like a knife

The scullion with face shining like his pans

The sea reeled round like a wine-vat splashing

The sea-song of the trampling waves is as muffled bells

The sea spread out like a wrinkled marble floor

The sea, that gleamed still, like a myriad-petaled rose

The sea was as untroubled as the turquoise vault which it reflected

The setting of the sun is like a word of peace

The sharp hail rattles against the panes and melts on my cheeks like tears

The ships, like sheeted phantoms coming and going

The silence seemed to crush to earth like a great looking-glass and shiver into a million pieces

The silvery morning like a tranquil vision fills the world

The sky burned like a heated opal

The sky gleamed with the hardness and brilliancy of blue enamel

The sky was as a shield that caught the stain of blood and battle from the dying sun

The sky was clear and blue, and the air as soft as milk

The sky was like a peach

The sky where stars like lilies white and fair shine through the mists

The solid air around me there heaved like a roaring ocean

The solid mountains gleamed like the unsteady sea

The soul is like a well of water springing up into everlasting life

The sound is like a noon-day gale

The sound is like a silver-fountain that springeth in a golden basin

The sound of a thousand tears, like softly pattering wings

The sound of your running feet that like the sea-hoofs beat

The spear-tongued lightning slipped like a snake

The Spring breaks like a bird

The stacks of corn in brown array, like tattered wigwams on the plain

The stars come down and trembling glow like blossoms on the waves below

The stars lay on the lapis-lazuli sky
like white flower-petals on still deep water
    [lapis-lazuli = opaque to translucent blue,
    violet-blue, or greenish-blue gemstone]

The stars pale and silent as a seer

The strange cold sense of aloofness that had numbed her senses suddenly gave way like snow melting in the spring

The sudden thought of your face is like a wound when it comes unsought

The sun, like a great dragon, writhes in gold

The sun on the sea-wave lies white as the moon

The surf was like the advancing lines of an unknown enemy flinging itself upon the shore

The terrible past lay afar, like a dream left behind in the night

The tide was in the salt-weed, and like a knife it tore

The time, gliding like a dream

The torrent from the hills leaped down their rocky stairways like wild steeds

The tree whose plumed boughs are soft as wings of birds

The uproar and contention pierced him like arrows

The veiled future bowed before me like a vision of promise

The velvet grass that is like padding to earth's meager ribs

The villa dips its foot in the lake, smiling at its reflection like a bather lingering on the brink

The voice of Fate, crying like some old Bellman through the world

The voice that rang in the night like a bugle call

The warm kindling blood burned her cheeks like the breath of a hot wind

The waves were rolling in, long and lazy, like sea-worn travelers

The whole truth, naked, cold, and fatal as a patriot's blade

The wind all round their ears hissed like a flight of white-winged geese

The wind comes and it draws its length along like the genii from the earthen pot

The wine flows like blood

The woman seemed like a thing of stone

The words kept ringing in my ears like the tolling of a bell

The words of the wise fall like the tolling of sweet, grave bells upon the soul

The world had vanished like a phantasmagoria

The world is bitter as a tear

The world is in a simmer, like a sea

The world wavers within
its circle like a dream

The years stretched before
her like some vast blank
page out to receive the
record of her toil

The years vanished like a
May snowdrift

The yellow apples glowed
like fire

Their glances met like
crossed swords

Their joy like sunshine
deep and broad falls on my
heart

Their minds rested upon
the thought, as chasing
butterflies might rest
together on a flower

Their music frightful as the
serpent's hiss

Their touch affrights me as
a serpent's sting

Then fall unheeded like the
faded flower

Then felt I like some
watcher of the skies

Then it swelled out to rich
and glorious harmonies
like a full orchestra playing
under the sea

Then the lover sighing like
furnace

Theories sprouted in his
mind like mushrooms

There is an air about you
like the air that folds a star

There, like a bird, it sits
and sings

There seemed to brood in
the air a quiet benevolence
of a Father watching His
myriad children at play

There she soars like a
seraph

There she stood straight as
a lily on its stem

There slowly rose to sight,
a country like a dragon fast
asleep

There streamed into the air
the sweet smell of crushed
grass, as though many
fields had been pressed
between giant's fingers and
so had been left

These eyes like stars have
led me

These final words snapped
like a whip-lash

These thoughts pierced me
like thorns

They are as cruel as
creeping tigers

They are as white foam on
the swept sands

They are as white swans in
the dusk, thy white hands

They are painted sharp as
death

They broke into pieces and
fell on the ground, like a
silvery, shimmering
shower of hail

They dropped like panthers

They fly like spray

They had hands like claws

They had slipped away like
visions

They have as many
principles as a fish has
bones

They have faces like
flowers

They hurried down like
plovers that have heard the
call [plovers = wading
birds]

They look like rose-buds
filled with snow

They seem like swarming
flies, the crowd of little
men

They seemed like floating
flowers

They shine as sweet as
simple doves

They stand like solitary mountain forms on some hard, perfectly transparent day

They vanished like the shapes that float upon a summer's dream

Thick as wind-blown leaves innumerable

Thickly the flakes drive past, each like a childish ghost

Thine eyes like two twin stars shining

This life is like a bubble blown up in the air

This love that dwells like moonlight in your face

This thought is as death

This tower rose in the sunset like a prayer

Those ancestral themes past which so many generations have slept like sea-going winds over pastures

Those death-like eyes, unconscious of the sun

Those eyelids folded like a white rose-leaf

Those eyes like bridal beacons shine

Thou art to me but as a wave of the wild sea

Thou as heaven art fair and young

Thou hadst a voice whose sound was like the sea

Thou must wither like a rose

Thou shalt be as free as mountain winds

Thou wouldst weep tears bitter as blood

Though bright as silver the meridian beams shine

Though thou be black as night

Thoughts vague as the fitful breeze

Three-cornered notes fly about like butterflies

Through the forest, like a fairy dream through some dark mind, the ferns in branching beauty stream

Through the moonlit trees, like ghosts of sounds haunting the moonlight, stole the faint tinkle of a guitar

Through the riot of his senses, like a silver blaze, ran the legend

Thy beauty like a beast it bites

Thy brown benignant eyes have sudden gleams of gladness and surprise, like woodland brooks that cross a sunlit spot

Thy carven columns must have grown by magic, like a dream in stone

Thy favors are but like the wind that kisses everything it meets

Thy heart is light as a leaf of a tree

Thy name burns like a gray and flickering candle flame

Thy name will be as honey on men's lips

Till death like sleep might steal on me

Till he melted like a cloud in the silent summer heaven

Time drops in decay, like a candle burnt out

Time like a pulse shakes fierce

To drag life on, which like a heavy chain lengthens behind with many a link of pain

To forsake as the trees drop their leaves in autumn

Toys with smooth trifles like a child at play

Transitory as clouds without substance

Transparent like a shining sun

Tree and shrub altered their values and became transmuted to silver sentinels

Trees that spread their forked boughs like a stag's antlers

Trembling like an aspen-leaf

Truths which forever shine as fixed stars

Turning easily and securely as on a perfect axle

U

Unbends like a loosened bow

Unbreakable as iron

Unconscious as an oak-tree of its growth

Under the willow-tree glimmered her face like a foam-flake drifting over the sea

Unheralded, like some tornado loosed out of the brooding hills, it came to pass

Unknown, like a seed in fallow ground, was the germ of a plan

Unmoving as a tombstone

Untamable as flies

Unutterable things pressing on my soul like a pent-up storm craving for outlet

Upcast like foam of the effacing tide

Uplifting the soul as on dovelike wings

Uplifting their stony peaks around us like the walls and turrets of a gigantic fortress

Urgent as the seas

Uttering wild cries like a creature in pain

V

Vague as a dream

Vague thoughts that stream shapelessly through her mind like long sad vapors through the twilight sky

Vanish into thin air, like ghosts at the cockcrow

Vanished like snow when comes a thaw

Vanished like vapor before the sun

Vibrations set quivering like harp strings struck by the hand of a master

Vociferous praise following like a noisy wave

W

Walking somewhat unsteadily like a blind man feeling his way

Waves glittered and danced on all sides like millions of diamonds

We left her and retraced our steps like faithless hounds

Weak and frail like the vapor of a vale

Wearing their wounds like stars

Weary wind, who wanderest like the world's rejected guest

When a draft might puff them out like a guttering candle
    [guttering = To melt through the side of the hollow in a candle
    formed by a burning wick; to burn low and unsteadily; flicker]

When arm in arm they
both came swiftly running,
like a pair of turtle-doves
that could not live asunder
day or night

When cards, invitations,
and three-corn'd notes fly
about like white butterflies

When she died, her breath
whistled like the wind in a
keyhole

When the fever pierced me
like a knife

Where a lamp of deathless
beauty shines like a beacon

Where heroes die as leaves
fall

Where the intricate wheels
of trade are grinding on,
like a mill

Where the source of the
waters is fine as a thread

Whilst the lagging hours of
the day went by like
windless clouds o'er a
tender sky

Whistled sharply in the air
like a handful of vipers

White as a ghost from
darkness

White as chalk

White as dove or lily, or
spirit of the light

White as the driven snow

White as the moon's white
flame

White as the sea-bird's
wing

White clouds like daisies

White hands she moves
like swimming swans

White hands through her
hair, like white doves
going into the shadow of a
wood

White like flame

White sails of sloops like
specters

Whose bodies are as strong
as alabaster

Whose hair was as gold
raiment on a king

Whose laugh moves like a
bat through silent haunted
woods

Whose little eyes glow like
the sparks of fire

Whose music like a robe of
living light reclothed each
new-born age

Windy speech which hits
all around the mark like a
drunken carpenter

Winged like an arrow to its
mark

With a sting like a
scorpion

With all the complacency
of a homeless cat

With an angry broken roar,
like billows on an unseen
shore, their fury burst

With hate darkling as the
swift winter hail

With music sweet as love

With sounds like breakers

With strength like steel

With the whisper of leaves
in one's ear

With words like honey
melting from the comb

Wits as sharp as gimlets
[gimlet = small hand tool
for boring holes]

Women with tongues like
polar needles

Words as fresh as spring
verdure [verdure = lush
greenness of flourishing
vegetation]

Words as soft as rain

Words like the gossamer
film of the summer

Words sweet as honey
from his lips distill'd

Words were flashing like brilliant birds through the boughs overhead

Wordsworth, thy music like a river rolls

Worthless like the conjurer's gold

Wrangle over details like a grasping pawnbroker

Wrinkled and scored like a dried apple

Writhing with an intensity that burnt like a steady flame

Y

Yielding like melted snow

Yonder flimsy crescent, bent like an archer's bow above the snowy summit

You are as gloomy to-night as an undertaker out of employment

You are as hard as stone

You gave me such chill embraces as the snow-covered heights receive from clouds

Your blood is red like wine

Your charms lay like metals in a mine

Your eyes are like fantastic moons that shiver in some stagnant lake

Your eyes as blue as violets

Your eyes they were green and gray like an April day

Your frail fancies are swallowed up, like chance flowers flung upon the river's current

Your hair was golden as tints of sunrise

Your heart is as dry as a reed

Your locks are like the raven

Your love shall fall about me like sweet rain

Your step's like the rain to summer vexed farmer

Your thoughts are buzzing like a swarm of bees

Your tongue is like a scarlet snake

Your voice had a quaver in it just like the linnet [linnet = small finch]

Youth like a summer morn

SECTION IX

CONVERSATIONAL PHRASES

A

A most extraordinary idea!

A thousand hopes for your success

Accept my best wishes

All that is conjecture

Allow me to congratulate you

An unfortunate comparison, don't you think?

And even if it were so?

And how am I to thank you?

And in the end, what are you going to make of it?

And yet the explanation does not wholly satisfy me

Apparently I was wrong

Are we wandering from the point?

Are you a trifle—bored?

Are you fully reconciled?

Are you not complicating the question?

Are you prepared to go to that length?

Are you still obdurate? [obdurate = Hardened in wrongdoing; stubbornly impenitent]

As it happens, your conjecture is right

Assuredly I do

At first blush it may seem fantastic

B

Banish such thoughts

But are you not taking a slightly one-sided point of view?

But consider for a moment

But I look at the practical side

But I wander from my point

But now I'll confide something to you

But perhaps I'm hardly fair when I say that

But seriously speaking, what is the use of it?

But surely that is inconsistent

But that's a tremendous hazard

But the thing is simply impossible

But there's one thing you haven't said

But, wait, you haven't heard the end

But what do you yourself think about it?

But who could foresee what was going to happen?

But you are open to persuasion?

But you do not know for certain

But you must tell me more

By a curious chance, I know it very well

By no means desirable, I think

C

Can I persuade you?

Can you imagine anything so horrible?

Certain circumstances make it undesirable

Certainly not, if it displeases you

Certainly, with the greatest pleasure

Come, where's your sense of humor?

Consult me when you want me—at any time

D

Decidedly so

Dine with me to-morrow night?—if you are free?

Do I presume too much?

Do I seem very ungenerous?

Do not misunderstand me

Do not the circumstances justify it?

Don't be so dismal, please

Don't delude yourself

Don't let me encroach on your good nature

Don't think I am unappreciative of your kindness

Do you attach any particular meaning to that?

Do you know, I envy you that

Do you know what his chief interests are now?

Do you mind my making a suggestion?

Do you press me to tell?

Do you really regard him as a serious antagonist?

Do you think there is anything ominous in it?

Does it please you so tremendously?

Does it seem incredible?

E

Either way is perplexing

Eminently proper, I think

Everyone looks at it differently

Excuse my bluntness

F

Fanciful, I should say

For the simplest of reasons

Forgive me if I seem disobliging

Fortunate, to say the least

Frankly, I don't see why it should

Frugal to a degree

Fulsome praise, I call it

G

Give me your sympathy and counsel

Glorious to contemplate

Good! that is at least something

Gratifying, I am sure

H

Happily there are exceptions to every rule

Has it really come to that?

Have I incurred your displeasure?

Have you any rooted objection to it?

Have you anything definite in your mind?

Have you reflected what the consequences might be to yourself?

He does me too much honor

He feels it acutely

He has a queer conception of the proprieties

He is a poor dissembler [dissemble = conceal behind a false appearance]

He is anything but obtuse

He is so ludicrously wrong

He is the most guileless of men

He was so extremely susceptible

He writes uncommonly clever letters

Heaven forbid that I should wound your sensibility

His sense of humor is unquenchable

How amiable you are to say so

How can I tell you how much I have enjoyed it all?

How can I thank you?

How can you be so unjust?

How delightful to meet you

How does the idea appeal to you?

How droll you are!

How extraordinary!

How intensely interesting!

How perfectly delightful!

How utterly abominable

How very agreeable this is!

How very interesting

How very surprising

How well you do it!

However, I should like to hear your views

Human nature interests me very much indeed

I

I admire your foresight

I admit it most gratefully

I agree—at least, I suppose I do

I agree that something ought to be done

I always welcome criticism so long as it is sincere

I am absolutely bewildered

I am afraid I am not familiar enough with the subject

I am afraid I cannot suggest an alternative

I am afraid I've allowed you to tire yourself

I am afraid I must confess my ignorance

I am afraid you will call me a sentimentalist

I am always glad to do anything to please you

I am anxious to discharge the very onerous debt I owe you

I am appealing to your sense of humor

I am at your service

I am bound to secrecy

I am compelled to, unluckily

I am curious to learn what his motive was

I am deeply flattered and grateful

I am delighted to hear you say so

I am dumb with admiration

I am entirely at your disposal

I am extremely glad you approve of it

I am far from believing the maxim

I am fortunate in being able to do you a service

I am glad to be able to think that

I am glad to have had this talk with you

I am glad to say that I have entirely lost that faculty

I am glad you can see it in that way

I am glad you feel so deeply about it

I am giving you well-deserved praise

I am going to make a confession

I am grateful for your good opinion

I am honestly indignant

I am, I confess, a little discouraged

I am in a chastened mood

I am inclined to agree with you

I am incredulous

I am indebted to you for the suggestion

I am listening—I was about to propose

I am lost in admiration

I am luckily disengaged to-day

I am more grieved than I can tell you

I am naturally overjoyed

I am not a person of prejudices

I am not an alarmist

I am not as unreasonable as you suppose

I am not at all in the secret of his ambitions

I am not capable of unraveling it

I am not going into sordid details

I am not going to let you evade the question

I am not going to pay you any idle compliments

I am not impervious to the obligations involved

I am not in sympathy with it

I am not in the least surprised

I am not inquisitive

I am not prepared to say

I am not sure that I can manage it

I am not vindictive

I am overjoyed to hear you say so

I am perfectly aware of what I am saying

I am persuaded by your candor

I am quite convinced of that

I am quite discomfited

I am quite interested to see what you will do

I am quite ready to be convinced

I am rather of the opinion that I was mistaken

I am ready to make great allowances

I am really afraid I don't know

I am really gregarious

I am sensible of the flattery

I am seriously annoyed with myself about it

I am so glad you think that

I am so sorry—so very sorry

I am sorry to disillusionize you

I am sorry to interrupt this interesting discussion

I am sorry to say it is impossible

I am speaking plainly

I am still a little of an idealist

I am suppressing many of the details

I am sure it sounds very strange to you

I am sure you could pay me no higher compliment

I am sure you will hear me out

I am surprised, I confess

I am sustained by the prospect of a good dinner

I am vastly obliged to you

I am vastly your debtor for the information

I am very far from being a fanatic

I am very glad of this opportunity

I am very grateful—very much flattered

I am wholly in agreement with you

I am willing to accept all the consequences

I am wonderfully well

I am wondering if I may dare ask you a very personal question?

I am your creditor unawares

I anticipate your argument

I appreciate your motives

I assure you it is most painful to me

I assure you my knowledge of it is limited

I bear no malice about that

I beg your indulgence

I beg your pardon, but you take it too seriously

I brazenly confess it

I can easily understand your astonishment

I can explain the apparent contradiction

I can find no satisfaction in it

I can hardly agree with you there

I can never be sufficiently grateful

I can only tell you the bare facts

I can scarcely accept the offer

I can scarcely boast that honor

I can scarcely imagine anything more disagreeable

I can sympathize with you

I cannot altogether acquit myself of interested motives

I cannot explain it even to myself

I cannot find much real satisfaction in it

I cannot forbear to press my advantage

I cannot imagine what you mean

I cannot precisely determine

I can't pretend to make a jest of what I'm going to say

I cannot say definitely at the moment

I cannot say that in fact it is always so

I cannot see how you draw that conclusion

I cannot thank you enough for all your consideration

I compliment you on your good sense

I confess, I find it difficult

I could ask for nothing better

I could never forgive myself for that

I dare say your intuition is quite right

I decline to commit myself beforehand

I detest exaggeration

I didn't mean that—exactly

I do not comprehend your meaning

I don't deny that it is interesting

I don't doubt it for a moment

I do not doubt the sincerity of your arguments

I do not exactly understand you

I do not feel sure that I entirely share your views

I don't feel that it is my business

I do not find it an unpleasant subject

I don't insist on your believing me

I don't justify my presumption

I don't know quite why you should say that

I don't know that I can do that

I don't know when I have heard anything so lamentable

I don't know why you should be displeased

I don't make myself clear, I see

I don't pretend to explain

I don't see anything particularly wonderful in it

I don't underrate his kindness

I don't want to disguise that from you

I don't want to exaggerate

I don't want to seem critical

I doubt the truth of that saying

I endorse it, every word

I entirely approve of your plan

I fancy it's just that

I fear I cannot help you

I fear that's too technical for me

I feel a certain apprehension

I feel an unwonted sense of gaiety [unwonted = unusual]

I feel it my duty to be frank with you

I feel myself scarcely competent to judge

I feel very grateful to you for your kind offer

I find it absorbing

I find it rather monotonous

I find this agreeable mental exhilaration

I frankly confess that

I generally trust my first impressions

I give my word gladly

I give you my most sacred word of honor

I had better begin at the beginning

I had no intention of being offensive

I hadn't thought of it in that light

I hardly think that could be so

I have a hundred reasons for thinking so

I have a peculiar affection for it

I have an immense faith in him

I have been constrained by circumstances

I have been decidedly impressed

I have been longing to see more of you

I have been puzzling over a dilemma

I have every reason to think so

I have given you the best proof of it

I have gone back to my first impressions

I have known striking instances of the kind

I have never heard it put so well

I have no delusions on that score

I have not succeeded in convincing myself of that

I have not the influence you think

I have not the least doubt of it

I haven't the remotest idea

I have often a difficulty in deciding

I have often marveled at your courage

I have quite changed my opinion about that

I have something of great importance to say to you

I have sometimes vaguely felt it

I have the strongest possible prejudice against it

I heartily congratulate you

I hope it will not seem unreasonable to you

I hope we may meet again

I hope you will forgive an intruder

I hope you will not think me irreverent

I hope you will pardon my seeming carelessness

I indulge the modest hope

I know it is very presumptuous

I know my request will appear singular

I like it immensely

I like your frankness

I make no reflection whatever

I mean it literally

I might question all that

I mistrust these wild impulses

I most certainly agree with you

I most humbly ask pardon

I must add my congratulations on your taste

I must apologize for intruding upon you

I must ask you one more question, if I may

I must confess I have never thought of that

I must refrain from any comment

I must respectfully decline to tell you

I must take this opportunity to tell you

I need not remind you that you have a grave responsibility

I never heard anything so absurd

I offer my humblest apologies

I owe the idea wholly to you

I partly agree with you

I personally owe you a great debt of thankfulness

I place myself entirely at your service

I place the most implicit reliance on your good sense

I prefer to reserve my judgment

I purposely evaded the question

I quite appreciate the very clever way you put it

I quite see what the advantages are

I really am curious to know how you guessed that

I realize how painful it must be to you

I recollect it clearly

I rely on your good sense

I remember the occasion perfectly

I resent that kind of thing

I respect you for that

I respect your critical faculty

I say it in all modesty

I see disapproval in your face

I see it from a different angle

I see you are an enthusiast

I see your point of view

I seem to have heard that sentiment before

I shall at once proceed to forget it

I shall await your pleasure

I shall be glad if you will join me

I shall be interested to watch it develop

I shall be most proud and pleased

I shall certainly take you at your word

I shall feel highly honored

I shall make a point of thinking so

I shall never forget your kindness

I shall respect your confidence

I should appreciate your confidence greatly

I should be very ungrateful were I not satisfied with it

I should feel unhappy if I did otherwise

I should like your opinion of it

I should not dream of asking you to do so

I should think it very unlikely

I simply cannot endure it

I spoke only in jest

I stand corrected

I suppose I ought to feel flattered

I surmised as much

I sympathize deeply with you

I take that for granted

I think extremely well of it

I think he has very noble ideals

I think I can answer that for you

I think I know what you are going to say

I think it has its charm

I think it is superb!

I think it quite admirable

I think its tone is remarkably temperate

I think that is rather a brilliant idea

I think what you say is reasonable

I think you are quibbling

I think you are rather severe in your opinions

I think you have great appreciation of values

I think you have summed it up perfectly

I think your candor is charming

I thoroughly agree with you

I thought it most amusing

I thought you were seriously indisposed

I trust you will not consider it an impertinence

I understand exactly how you feel about it

I understand your delicacy of feeling

I venture to propose another plan

I very rarely allow myself that pleasure

I want to have a frank understanding with you

I was at a loss to understand the reason for it

I was hoping that I could persuade you

I was on the point of asking you

I was speaking generally

I watched you with admiration

I will answer you frankly

I will listen to no protestations

I will take it only under compulsion

I will tell you what puzzles me

I will think of it, since you wish it

I will, with great pleasure

I wish I could explain my point more fully

I wish I knew what you meant by that

I wish to be perfectly fair

I wish to put things as plainly as possible

I wonder how much truth there is in it?

I wonder if you have the smallest recollection of me?

I would agree if I understood

I wouldn't put it just that way

If ever I can repay it, command me

If I mistake not you were there once?

If I speak strongly, it is because I feel strongly

If I were disposed to offer counsel

If I were sure you would not misunderstand my meaning

If you don't mind my saying so

If you insist upon it

If you will pardon me the frankness

In a manner that sometimes terrifies me

In one respect you are quite right

In that case let me rob you of a few minutes

In what case, for example?

Incredible as it sounds, I had for a moment forgotten

Indeed, but it is quite possible

Indeed! How?

Indeed, you are wholly wrong

Indifferently so, I am afraid

Irony was ten thousand leagues from my intention

Is it sane—is it reasonable?

Isn't it amazing?

Isn't it extraordinarily funny?

Isn't it preposterous?

Isn't that a trifle unreasonable?

Isn't that rather a hasty conclusion?

Is that a fair question?

It always seemed to me impossible

It amuses you, doesn't it?

It blunts the sensibilities

It could never conceivably be anything but popular

It depends on how you look at it

It depends upon circumstances

It doesn't sound plausible to me

It has a lovely situation as I remember it

It has amused me hugely

It has been a relief to talk to you

It has been an immense privilege to see you

It has never occurred to me

It is a curious fact

It is a great pleasure to meet you

It is a huge undertaking

It is a most unfortunate affair

It is a perfectly plain proposition

It is a rather melancholy thought

It is a truth universally acknowledged

It is all very inexcusable

It is all very well for you to be philosophical

It is altogether probable

It is an admirable way of putting it

It is an error of taste

It is an extreme case, but the principle is sound

It is an ingenious theory

It is an uncommonly fine description

It is extremely interesting, I can assure you

It is for you to decide

It is historically true

It is I who should ask forgiveness

It is incredible!

It is indeed generous of you to suggest it

It is inexplicable

It is interesting, as a theory

It is literally impossible

It is merely a mood

It is most unfortunate

It is my deliberately formed opinion

It is my opinion you are too conscientious

It is nevertheless true

It is not a matter of the slightest consequence

It is not always fair to judge by appearances

It is not so unreasonable as you think

It is often very misleading

It is one of the grave problems of the day

It is only a fancy of mine

It is perfectly defensible

It is perfectly trite

It is permissible to gratify such an impulse

It is possible, but I rather doubt it

It is quite an easy matter

It is quite conceivable

It is quite too absurd

It is rather startling

It is really impressive

It is really most callous of you to laugh

It is sheer madness

It is sickening and so insufferably arrogant

It is simply a coincidence

It is the most incomprehensible thing in the world

It is to you that I am indebted for all this

It is true, I am grieved to say

It is true none the less

It is very amusing

It is very far from being a fiction

It is very good of you to do this for my pleasure

It is very ingenious

It is very splendid of you

It is wanton capriciousness

It is your privilege to think so

It's a difficult and delicate matter to discuss

It's a matter of immediate urgency

It's absolute folly

It's absurd—it's impossible

It's all nonsense

It's as logical as it can be under the circumstances

It's been a strange experience for you

It's deliciously honest

It's going to be rather troublesome

It's inconceivable that it should ever be necessary

It's mere pride of opinion

It's my chief form of recreation

It's not a matter of vast importance

It's past my comprehension

It's quite wonderful how logical and simple you make it

It's really very perplexing

It's so charming of you to say that

It's so kind of you to come

It's such a bore having to talk about it

It's the natural sequence

It's too melancholy

It's very wonderful

It makes it all quite interesting

It may sound strange to you

It must be a trifle dull at times

It must be fascinating

It must be very gratifying to you

It must have been rather embarrassing

It seems an age since we've last seen you

It seems entirely wonderful to me

It seems incredible

It seems like a distracting dream

It seems preposterous

It seems the height of absurdity

It seems to me that you have a perfect right to do so

It seems unspeakably funny to me

It seems very ridiculous

It shall be as you wish

It should not be objectionable

It sounds plausible

It sounds profoundly interesting

It sounds rather appalling

It sounds very alluring

It strikes me as rather pathetic

It was an unpardonable liberty

It was inevitable that you should say that

It was most stupid of me to have forgotten it

It was not unkindly meant

It was peculiarly unfortunate

It was really an extraordinary experience

It was so incredible

It was the most amazing thing I ever heard

It was very good of you to come out and join us

It will create a considerable sensation

It will divert your thoughts from a mournful subject

It will give me pleasure to do it

It will not alter my determination

It would be ill-advised

It would interest me very much

It would seem to be a wise decision

It would take too long to formulate my thought

J

Join us, please, when you have time

Just trust to the inspiration of the moment

Justify it if you can

L

Let me persuade you

Let me say how deeply indebted I feel for your kindness

Let me speak frankly

Let us grant that for the sake of the argument

Let us take a concrete instance

M

Many thanks—how kind and good you are!

May I ask to whom you allude?

May I be privileged to hear it?

May I speak freely?

May I venture to ask what inference you would draw from that?

Might I suggest an alternative?

Most dangerous!

My attitude would be one of disapproval

My confidence in you is absolute

My idea of it is quite the reverse

My information is rather scanty

My meaning is quite the contrary

My point of view is different, but I shall not insist upon it

My views are altered in many respects

N

No, I am speaking seriously

No, I don't understand it

Not at all

Not to my knowledge

Nothing could be more delightful

Now is it very plain to you?

Now you are flippant

O

Obviously the matter is settled

Of course, but that again isn't the point

Of course I am delighted

Of course I don't want to press you against your will

Of course you will do what you think best

Oh, certainly, if you wish it

Oh, do not form an erroneous impression

Oh, I appreciate that in you!

Oh, that's mere quibbling

Oh, that's splendid of you!

Oh, that was a manner of speaking

Oh, yes, I quite admit that

Oh, yes, you may take that for granted

Oh, you are very bitter

Oh, you may be as scornful as you like

On the contrary, I agree with you thoroughly

On the face of it, it sounds reasonable

One assumption you make I should like to contest

One has no choice to endure it

One must be indulgent under the circumstances

One thing I beg of you

P

Pardon me, but I don't think so

Pardon me, I meant something different

Perhaps I am indiscreet

Perhaps not in the strictest sense

Perhaps you do not feel at liberty to do so

Perhaps you think me ungrateful

Personally I confess to an objection

Please continue to be frank

Please do not think I am asking out of mere curiosity

Please forgive my thoughtlessness

Please make yourself at home

Pray don't apologize

Pray forgive me for intruding on you so unceremoniously

Pray go on!

Precisely, that is just what I meant

Put in that way it certainly sounds very well

Q

Question me, if you wish

Quibbling, I call it

Quite so

Quite the wisest thing you can do

R

Rather loquacious, I think [loquacious = very talkative]

Reading between the lines

Really? I should have thought otherwise

Really—you must go?

Reassure me, if you can

Reflect upon the possible consequences

Relatively speaking

Reluctantly I admit it

Reverting to another matter

S

Shall we have a compact?

She has an extraordinary gift of conversation

She is easily prejudiced

She seems uncommonly appreciative

She will be immensely surprised

Show me that the two cases are analogous

So far so good

So I inferred

So much the better for me

So you observe the transformation?

Something amuses you

Sometimes the absurdity of it occurs to me

Speaking with all due respect

Still, you might make an exception

Strangely it's true

Such conduct seems to me unjustifiable

Surely there can be no question about that

Surely we can speak frankly

Surely you sound too harsh a note

Surely you would not countenance that

T

Tell me in what way you want me to help you

Thank you for telling me that

Thank you for your good intentions

That, at least, you will agree to

That depends on one's point of view

That doesn't sound very logical

That is a counsel of perfection

That is a fair question, perhaps

That is a question I have often proposed to myself

That is a stroke of good fortune

That is a superb piece of work

That is a very practical explanation

That is admirably clear

That is certainly ideal

That is eminently proper

That is hardly consistent

That is inconceivable

That is just like you, if you will forgive me for saying so

That is most fortunate

That is most kind of you

That is most unexpected and distressing

That is not fair—to me

That is not to be lightly spoken of

That is precisely what I mean

That is quite true, theoretically

That is rather a difficult question to answer

That is rather a strange request to make

That is rather awkward

That is really good of you

That is the prevailing idea

That is tragic

That is true and I think you are right

That is very amiable in you

That is very curious

That is very felicitous

That is very gracious

That is what I call intelligent criticism

That is what I meant to tell you

That is a humiliating thought

That is a most interesting idea

That is such a hideous idea

That is the most incredible part of it

That might involve you in life-long self-reproach

That must be exceedingly tiresome

That ought to make you a little lenient

That reassures me

That shows the infirmity of his judgment

That theory isn't tenable

That was exceedingly generous

That was intended ironically

That was very thoughtful of you

That was very well reasoned

That will blast your chances, I am afraid

That will suit me excellently

That would be somewhat serious

That would be very discreditable

The agreement seems to be ideal

The idea is monstrous

The inference is obvious

The notion is rather new to me

The pleasure is certainly not all on your side

The reason is not so far to seek

The same problem has perplexed me

The sentiment is worthy of you

The simplest thing in the world

The situation is uncommonly delicate

The story seems to me incredible

The subject is extremely interesting

The tone of it was certainly hostile

The very obvious moral is this

The whole thing is an idle fancy

Then I have your permission?

Then you're really not disinclined?

Then you merely want to ask my advice?

There are endless difficulties

There are reasons which make such a course impossible

There is a good deal of sense in that

There is a grain of truth in that, I admit

There is food for reflection in that

There is my hand on it

There is no resisting you

There is nothing I should like so much

There is one inevitable condition

There is something almost terrifying about it

There must be extenuating circumstances

They amuse me immensely

This is a most unexpected pleasure

This is charmingly new to me

This is indeed good fortune

This is really appalling

This is really not a laughing matter

Those are my own private feelings

Those things are not forgotten at once

To me it's simply outrageous

To speak frankly, I do not like it

True, I forgot!

U

Undeniably true

Unfortunately I must decline the proposal

Unlikely to be so

Unquestionably superior

Unwholesome influence, I would say

V

Very good, I'll do so

Very well, I will consent

Vivacity is her greatest charm

Virtually accomplished, I believe

Vouch for its truth

W

We are all more or less susceptible

We are drifting away from our point

We are impervious to certain rules

We are merely wasting energy in this duel

We can safely take it for granted

We couldn't have a better topic

We had better agree to differ

We have had some conclusions in common

We must judge it leniently

We must not expose ourselves to misinterpretation

We owe you a debt of gratitude

We shall be glad to see you, if you care to come

We will devoutly hope not

Well, as a matter of fact, I have forgotten

Well done! I congratulate you

Well, I'm not going to argue that

Well, I call it scandalous

Well, I confess they don't appeal to me

Well, more's the pity

Well, perhaps it is none of my affair

Well, that is certainly ideal!

Well, this is good fortune

Well, yes—in a way

Well, you are a dreamer!

What a beautiful idea

What a charming place you have here

What a curious coincidence!

What a pretty compliment!

What a tempting prospect!

What an extraordinary idea!

What are your misgivings?

What can you possibly mean?

What conceivable reason is there for it?

What do you imagine my course should be?

What do you propose?

What is the next step in your argument?

What is there so strange about that?

What, may I ask, is your immediate object?

What unseemly levity on his part

What very kind things you say to me

What would you expect me to do?

What you have just said is even truer than you realize

What you propose is utterly impossible

Who is your sagacious adviser? [sagacious = sound judgment, wise]

Why ask such embarrassing questions?

Why did you desert us so entirely?

Why do you take it so seriously?

Will you allow me to ask you a question?

Will you be more explicit?

Will you have the kindness to explain?

Will you pardon my curiosity?

Will you permit me a brief explanation?

Would you apply that to everyone?

Would you mind telling me your opinion?

Y

Yes and no

Yes, but that is just what I fail to comprehend

Yes, I dare say

Yes, if you will be so good

Yes, it was extraordinarily fine

Yes, that is my earnest wish

Yes, that's undeniable

Yes? You were saying?

You agree with me, I know

You are a profound philosopher

You are a severe critic

You are delightfully frank

You are greatly to be envied

You are heartily welcome

You are incomprehensible

You are incorrigible

You are kind and comforting

You are most kind

You are not consistent

You are not serious, I hope

You are not seriously displeased with me?

You are quite delightful

You are rather puzzling to-day

You are right to remind me of that

You are unduly distressing yourself

You are very complimentary

You are very gracious

You're so tremendously kind about it

You're succeeding admirably

You're taking it all much too seriously

You're talking nonsense!

You're very good, I'm sure

You ask me—but I shouldn't wonder if you knew better than I do

You astonish me greatly

You behaved with great forbearance

You can hardly be serious

You cannot regret it more than I do

You could not pay me a higher compliment

You did it excellently

You did not clearly understand what I meant

You don't seem very enthusiastic

You excite my curiosity

You flatter my judgment

You have a genius for saying the right thing

You have asked me a riddle

You have asked the impossible

You have been wrongly informed

You have done me a great service

You have had a pleasant time, I hope

You have my deepest sympathy

You have my unbounded confidence

You have received a false impression

You have such an interesting way of putting things

You interest me deeply

You judge yourself too severely

You know I'm in an agony of curiosity

You know I'm not given to sentimentality

You know the familiar axiom

You leave no alternative

You look incredulous

You may be sure of my confidence

You may rely on me absolutely

You might make an exception

You must have misunderstood me

You must not fail to command me

You overwhelm me with your kindness

You really insist upon it?

You rebuke me very fairly

You say that as though you were surprised

You see how widely we differ

You see, it's all very vague

You see things rose-colored

You seem to be in a happy mood

You seem to take a very mild interest in what I propose

You shock me more than I can say

You speak in enigmas

You speak with authority

You surely understand my position

You take a great deal for granted

You take a pessimistic view of things

You take me quite by surprise

You will admit I have some provocation

You will become morbid if you are not careful

You will have ample opportunity

You will, of course, remember the incident

You will please not be flippant

You will understand my anxiety

Your argument is facile and superficial

Your consideration is entirely misplaced

Your judgments are very sound

Your logic is as clever as possible

Your opinion will be invaluable to me

Your request is granted before it is made

Your statement is somewhat startling

SECTION X

PUBLIC SPEAKING PHRASES

A

A fact of vast moment

A few words will suffice to answer

A further objection is

A great many people have said

A little indulgence may be due to those

A majority of us believe

A man in my situation has

A more plausible objection is found

A proof of this is

A servile mind can never know

A short time since

A specific answer can be given

A thought occurred to me

Able men have reasoned out

Above all things, let us not forget

Absolutely true it is

Abundant reason is there

Accordingly by reason of this circumstance

Add this instance to

After a careful study of all the evidence

After full deliberation

After reminding the hearer

After this it remains only to say

Again, can we doubt

Again, I ask the gentleman

Again, in this view

Again, it is quite clear that

Again, it is urged

Again, let us compare

Again, very numerous are the cases

Again, we have abundant instances

Against all this concurring testimony

All confess this to be true

All I ask is

All of us know

All that I will say now

All the facts which support this

All the signs of the time indicate

All these things you know

All this being considered

All this is historical fact

All this is very well

All this suggests

All this we take for granted

Allow me for a moment to turn to

Allow me to tell a story

Although I say it to myself

Amazing as it may seem

Am I mistaken in this

Among many examples

Among the distinguished guests who honor

Among the problems that confront us

An answer to this is now ready

An argument has often been put forward

An example or two will illustrate

An indescribably touching incident

An opinion has now become established

And again, it is said

And again, it is to be presumed

And coming nearer to our own day

And did a man try to persuade me

And do you really think

And everybody here knows

And for myself, as I said

And further, all that I have said

And hence the well-known doctrine

And here again, when I speak

And here allow me to call your attention

And here I am led to observe

And here I come to the closing evidence

And here I have an opportunity

And here I reproach

And here I wish you to observe

And here let me define my position

And here let me give my explanation

And here let us recall to mind

And how is it possible to imagine

And I am bound to say

And I beg of you

And I call on you

And I might say this

And I refuse assent

And I rejoice to know

And I say, it were better for you

And I should in like manner repudiate

And I speak with reverence

And I submit to you

And I trust that you will consider

And I will make a practical suggestion

And I will tell you why

And I would, moreover submit

And if a man could anywhere be found

And if any of you should question

And if I know anything of my countrymen

And if I may presume to speak

And if I take another instance

And if this be true

And if you come to a decision

And if you think it your duty

And in conclusion

And in like manner

And in order to see this

And in thus speaking, I am not denying

And is not this lamentable

And is there not a presumption

And it happens

And it is certainly true

And it is doubtful if

And it is not difficult to see

And it is not plain

And it is one of the evidences

And it is precisely in this

And it is strikingly suggested to us

And it is undeniable, I say

And it is well that this should be so

And last of all

And lest anyone should marvel

And let it be observed

And lo! and behold

And more than this

And next I would ask

And now allow me to call attention

And now behold a mystery

And now consider

And now having discussed

And now I beg that I may be permitted

And now I go back to the statement

And now I have completed my review

And now I have said enough to explain

And now I must touch upon one point

And now if I may take for granted

And now it would be very pleasant for me

And now observe how

And now, sir, what I had first to say

And now supposing this point to be settled

And now that I have mentioned

And now the chief points of it

And now the question is asked me

And now, to close, let me give you

And now, to what purpose do I mention

And, of course, you are aware

And of this I am perfectly certain

And quite as difficult is it to create

And right here lies the cause

And, sir, a word

And so, again, as regard

And so I am reminded of a story

And so I leave these words with you

And so I may point out

And so I might recount to you

And so, in the other cases, I have named

And so in the present case

And so on

And so through all phases

And so, upon every hand

And sometimes it will be difficult

And that gave another distorted view

And the reason is very obvious

And the same holds good

And then again

And then hastily to conclude

And then I may be reminded

And then there is another thought

And then when it is said

And there are reasons why

And there is also this view

And therefore am I truly glad

And therefore it is not unfrequently quoted

And therefore it is not without regret

And this brings me to the last thing

And this is really the sense

And this leads me to say a word

And thus consistently

And thus it is conceivable

And thus it seems to me

And thus we are led on then to further question

And to all this must be added

And to return to the topic

And to this conclusion you must come

And unquestionably

And we are brought to the same conclusion

And what do you suppose will be

And when I have shown to you

And when I recall that event

And when we pass beyond the bounds of

And where, let me ask

And why should I insist

And will you still insist

And with these thoughts come others

And yet I can not but reflect

And yet I feel justified in believing

And yet I think we all feel

And yet let me say to you

And yet one more quotation

And yet this notion is, I conceive

And yet though this be true

And yet we ought, if we are wise

And you may also remember this

Another circumstance that adds to the difficulty

Another consideration which I shall adduce [adduce = cite as an example]

Another instance of signal success

Another of these presumptions

Another point is made as clear as crystal

Another reason of a kindred nature

Another reflection which occurs to me

Another sign of our times

Another signal advantage

Another striking instance

Answers doubtless may be given

Are there not many of us

Are we content to believe

Are we forever to deprive ourselves

Are we not startled into astonishment

Are we satisfied to assume

As a general rule I hold

As a last illustration

As a matter of fact

As a proof of this

As an illustration of this truth

As briefly as I may

As far as my limits allow

As far as this is true

As far as this objection relates

As far as we know

As for the rest

As I have now replied to

As I look around on this assembly

As I rise to respond to the sentiment

As I understand this matter

As memory scans the past

As society is now constituted

As some one has well said

As the foregoing instances have shown

As to the particular instance before us

As well might we compare

As we shall see in a few moments

Assuredly it is this

At the outset of this inquiry

At the risk of digression

At the same time, I candidly state

At the utmost we can say

At this juncture

At this solemn moment

Away then with the notion

B

Be assured, then

Be confident, therefore

Be it so

Be not deceived

Be sure that in spite of

Be these things as they may

Be your interests what they may be

Bear with me for a few moments

Bearing on this point

Before attempting to answer this question

Before going further

Before I close I will particularly remark

Before I come to the special matter

Before I proceed to compare

Being fully of the opinion

Being persuaded then

Believing, as I do

Beyond all question we

Bidden by your invitation to a discussion

Broadly speaking

But, above all things, let us

But after all, I think no one can say

But again, when we carefully consider

But am I wrong in saying

But apart from the fact

But besides these special facts

But can this question

But depend upon it

But despite all this

But do not let us depend

But do you imagine

But doubts here arise

But even admitting these possibilities

But everyone who deserves

But first of all, remark, I beg you

But, further, I shall now demonstrate

But, gentlemen, I must be done

But grave problems confront us

But here I am discussing

But here let me say

But how can we pass over

But how shall I describe my emotions

But however that may be

But I am bound to say

But I am certain from my own experience

But I am very sorry to say

But I am willing enough to admit

But I can at least say

But I cannot conceive

But I can promise

But I cherish the hope

But I confess that I should be glad

But I digress

But I do not propose all these things

But I do say this

But I have been insisting simply

But I have heard it argued

But I have no fear of the future

But I leave this train of thought

But I may be permitted to speak

But I may say in conclusion

But I need hardly assert

But I pass that over

But I propose to speak to you

But I repeat

But I resist the temptation

But I return to the question

But I shall go still further

But I simply ask

But I submit the whole subject

But I trust that you will all admit

But I venture to assure you

But I will allude

But I will not further impress any idea

But I would earnestly impress upon you

But if I may even flatter myself

But if I seek for illustrations

But if you want more evidence

But if you wish to know

But in making this assertion

But in my opinion there is no need

But in the course of time

But is it quite possible to hold

But is this any reason why

But it does not follow from this

But it happens very fortunately

But it has been suggested to me

But it is a fact

But it is impossible for one

But it is necessary to explain

But it is no use protesting

But it is not fair to assert

But it is not my intention

But it is not necessary to suppose

But it is not possible to believe

But it is not really so

But it is otherwise with

But it is sometimes said

But it may be doubted whether

But it may happen that I forgot

But it will be a misfortune

But it will naturally be asked

But it will perhaps be argued

But it would be vain to attempt

But let me ask you to glance

But let me before closing refer

But let none of you think

But let us also keep ever in mind

But let us look a little further

But lo! all of a sudden

But mark this

But more than all things else

But my allotted time is running away

But my answer to this objection

But, my friends, pause for a moment

But never was a grosser wrong

But not for one moment

But notwithstanding all this

But now look at the effect

But now take notice of

But on the other hand

But on what ground are we

But passing these by

But perhaps I ought to speak distinctly

But perhaps you are not yet weary

But putting these questions aside

But quite contrary to this, you will find

But recollect, I pray you, how

But, sir, it is manifest

But some other things are to be noted

But some will ask me

But sooner or later

But still, I repeat

But suppose the fact

But surely, you can not say

But that I may not divert you from

But that is not all

But that must be always the impression

But the fact is

But the final value

But the greatest proof of all

But the most formidable problem

But the necessity of the case

But the question may arise

But, then, let us ask ourselves

But there is another duty imposed

But there is much more than this

But this I do not hesitate to say

But this I fearlessly affirm

But this I know

But this is a circuitous argument

But this is no place for controversy

But this is not all

But this is what I mean

But this much I affirm as true

But this warns me

But this we may put aside

But to go still further

But to say the truth

But we are met with the assertion

But we are to recollect

But we ask, perhaps

But we may depend upon it

But we think it is not wise

But we want something more for explanation

But what a blunder would be yours

But what is the fact

But what we must needs guard against

But when it is declared

But when we look a little deeper

But while it may be admitted

But who has not seen

But why do I numerate these details

But with these exceptions

But yet nothing can be more splendid

But you should know

By no means

By the way, I have not mentioned

By this time it will be suspected

C

Can it be supposed

Can the long records of humanity teach us

Can there be a better illustration

Can we pretend

Can you lightly contemplate

Can you yield yourselves

Cautious and practical thinkers ask

Certain it is

Certainly I am not blind to the faults

Certainly, one can conceive

Clearly enough

Coming back to the main subject

Coming down to modern times

Coming to present circumstances

Common sense indicates

Consequently, I am not discussing this matter

Consider, I beg you, what

Contemplating these marvelous changes

D

Delude not yourselves with the belief

Depend upon it

Did it ever occur to you

Difficult then as the question may be

Do I need to describe

Do me the honor of believing

Do not imagine

Do not let us conceal from ourselves

Do not suppose for a moment

Do not talk to me of

Do not think me guilty of

Do we not know

Do what you will

Do you ask how that can be

Do you believe this can be truthfully said

Do you not know I am speaking of

Do you remember a concrete instance

Do you think, then

Does any man say

Does it ever occur to you

Does it not seem something like idiocy to

Does it not shock you to think

Does not the event show

Does not the nature of every man revolt

Doubtless the end is sought

E

Every now and then you will find

Every one has asked himself

Every one therefore ought to look to

Every reader of history can recall

F

Far from it

Few indeed there are

Few subjects are more fruitful

Few things impress the imagination more

Finally, it is my most fervent prayer

First in my thoughts are

First of all I ask

For, be assured of this

For behold

For I must tell you

For if any one thinks that there is

For, in truth, if you please to recollect

For instance, I can fancy

For is it not true

For it is not right to

For let it be observed first

For mark you

For my own part, I believe

For myself, certainly I think

For observe what the real fact is

For one I deny

For, perhaps, after all

For, perhaps, some one may say

For so it generally happens

For the sake of my argument

For this is what I say

For this reason, indeed, it is

For we all know

Fortunately for us

Fortunately I am not obliged

From one point of view we are

From the circumstances already explained

From the standpoint of

From this statement you will perceive

G

Generally speaking

God be praised

Grant this true

Granting all this

H

Had I time for all that might be said

Had my limits allowed it

Happily for us

Hardly less marvelous

Hardly will anyone venture to say

Have I exaggerated

Have you ever noticed

Having taken a view of

Having thus described what appears to me

He is the best prophet who

He seems at times to confuse

He was an eminent instance of

He who is insensible to

Hence arises a grave mischief

Hence, as I have said

Hence it follows

Here again the testimony corroborates

Here arises the eternal question

Here comes the practical matter

Here for a moment I seem

Here, however, it may be objected

Here I am considering

Here I end my illustrations

Here I must pause for a moment

Here I only insist upon

Here I ought to stop

Here is another strange thing

Here is good hope for us

Here is no question

Here let me meet one other question

Here, then, I am brought to the consideration

Here then I take up the subject

Here then is the key

Here, then, it is natural at last

Here then, we are brought to the question

Here, then, we are involved

Here undoubtedly it is

Here we cannot but pause to contemplate

Here we come into direct antagonism with

Here we come to the very crux of

Here we have it on high authority

History is replete with predictions

Hitherto I have spoken only of

Holding this view, I am concerned

How can we help believing

How do you account for

How does it happen

How human language staggers when

How infinitely difficult it is

How infinitely superior must it appear

How is this to be explained

How many a time

How momentous, then

How much better, I say, if

How much more rational it would be

How shall I attempt to enumerate

How shall I describe to you

However, I am viewing the matter

However, I will not in any way admit

However, it is to me a very refreshing thing

I

I abide by my statement

I add a few suggestions

I adduce these facts [adduce = cite as an example]

I admire the main drift of

I admit, of course, at once

I admit the extreme complexity

I again ask

I allude to

I always delight to think

I always will assert the right to

I am a great admirer

I am a little at a loss to know

I am about to supplement

I am agitated by conflicting emotions

I am alarmed, indeed, when I see

I am also bound to say

I am also satisfied

I am apprehensive

I am asked to-night to propose

I am assured and fully believe

I am at a loss for adequate terms

I am bold to say

I am but saying

I am by no means certain

I am certain that you will give me credit

I am certainly in earnest sympathy

I am confronted by the hope

I am conscious of the fact

I am convinced by what I have seen

I am deeply imbued with the conviction

I am deeply insensible of the compliment

I am determined

I am even bold enough to hazard

I am exceeding my necessary limits

I am exceedingly glad of this opportunity

I am extremely obliged to you

I am familiar with

I am far from asserting

I am filled with admiration

I am firmly convinced

I am free to admit

I am fully convinced

I am giving voice to what you all feel

I am glad of this public opportunity

I am glad to answer to the toast

I am glad to express the belief

I am glad to notice

I am going to spare you and myself

I am grateful to you for this honor

I am greatly alarmed

I am greatly indebted to you

I am happy to be with you

I am here by the favor of your invitation

I am here the advocate of

I am here to introduce

I am in favor of

I am in sympathy with

I am inclined sometimes to believe

I am inclined to suspect

I am indebted for the honor

I am, indeed, most solicitous

I am informed

I am led on by these reflections

I am led to believe

I am mainly concerned

I am most deeply sensible of the welcome

I am most grateful for the opportunity

I am myself greatly indebted

I am nevertheless too sensible

I am not a stranger to

I am not at liberty to discuss

I am not at present concerned

I am not about to defend

I am not advocating

I am not altogether clear

I am not aware of a single instance

I am not blind to the faults of

I am not bold enough to

I am not catching at sharp arguments

I am not concerned to argue

I am not defending myself

I am not dreaming of denying

I am not going into vexed questions

I am not going to reproach

I am not here to defend

I am not insensible

I am not of those who pretend

I am not prepared to dispute the word

I am not presumptuous to assert

I am not proposing to set forth

I am not ripe to pass sentence

I am not so unreasonable as to tell you

I am not surprised

I am not taking into account

I am not unaware

I am not undertaking to deliver

I am now going to attempt

I am obliged to add

I am obliged to go still further

I am often reminded

I am old enough to remember

I am one of those who believe

I am only too sensible of the fact

I am perfectly willing to admit

I am persuaded

I am prepared to back that opinion by

I am privileged to speak to

I am quite conscious that

I am rather disposed to think

I am ready to do battle

I am reassured by the presence here

I am reluctantly but forcibly reminded

I am resolved not to permit

I am sensible, sir

I am simply endeavoring to show

I am so surrounded on every hand

I am sometimes inclined to think

I am somewhat relieved to know

I am sorry to say

I am suggesting the reason why

I am sure, at any rate

I am sure every impartial man will agree

I am sure I feel no hostility

I am sure that I echo the sentiment

I am sure this generous audience will pardon me

I am sure you all hope

I am sure you feel the truth

I am sure you will acquit me

I am sure you will be kind enough

I am sure you will do me the justice

I am sure you will not be surprised

I am surely not here to assert

I am tempted further to offer to you

I am thankful for the privilege

I am thoroughly convinced

I am to speak to you this evening

I am to urge the interest of

I am told occasionally

I am told on authority

I am too well aware of the difficulties

I am totally at a loss to conceive

I am trespassing too long on your time

I am unable to understand

I am unconscious of intentional error

I am under a very great obligation

I am under the deepest feeling of gratitude

I am under the impression

I am unwillingly bound to add

I am uttering no paradox when I say

I am very far from thinking.

I am very glad to have the honor

I am very happy to be here

I am very much in the condition of

I am very sure that if you ponder

I am very sure you will believe

I am well aware

I am willing to know

I anticipate with pleasing expectation

I appeal in the first place

I appeal to any man to say

I appeal to the better judgment

I appreciate the significance

I argue this cause

I ask again

I ask no greater blessing

I ask permission to speak to you

I ask the attention

I ask the audience

I ask the audience to return with me

I ask this of you

I ask you calmly and dispassionately

I ask you gentlemen, do you think

I ask you if it is possible

I ask you, if you please, to rise and give the toast

I ask you in all candor

I ask you now to follow me

I ask you to consider

I ask you to join me in drinking a toast

I ask you to pledge with me

I ask your attention

I ask your indulgence

I assert, sir, that it is

I assure myself

I assure you, of my own personal knowledge

I attribute it to

I avail myself of the opportunity

I beg again to thank you for the honor

I beg all to remember

I beg and implore of you

I beg emphatically to say

I beg leave to make some observations

I beg of you to remember

I beg to tender my most fervent wishes

I beg you not to mistake my meaning

I beg you to accept my grateful expression

I begin by observing

I begin with expressing a sentiment

I believe from my own personal experience

I believe I can speak for all

I believe I shall make it clear to you

I believe I voice the sentiment

I believe it to be the simple truth

I believe most profoundly

I believe that I am within the mark

I believe that in this instance

I bid you a most cordial and hearty welcome

I bow with you in reverent commemoration

I call on you to answer

I call to mind how

I can by no calculation justify

I call hardly conceive

I can make allowance for

I can most truthfully assure you

I call never sufficiently express my gratitude

I cannot allow myself to believe

I cannot avoid confessing

I cannot be content with

I cannot believe, I will not believe

I cannot better illustrate this argument

I cannot better sum up

I cannot boast of

I cannot bound my vision

I cannot but reflect

I cannot but see what mischief

I cannot charge myself with

I cannot close without giving expression

I cannot conceive a greater honor

I cannot feel any doubt myself

I cannot forbear from offering

I cannot give you a better illustration

I cannot help expressing a wish

I cannot help speaking urgently

I cannot here go into details

I cannot hesitate to say

I cannot hope adequately to respond

I cannot justly be responsible because

I cannot let this opportunity pass

I cannot persuade myself

I cannot prevail on myself

I cannot refrain from saying for myself

I cannot resist the train of thought

I cannot say how glad I am

I cannot say with confidence

I cannot stop to give in detail

I cannot sufficiently thank you

I cannot take back my word

I cannot take it for granted

I cannot thank you enough

I cannot well avoid saying

I can only congratulate you

I can only hope for indulgence

I can readily understand

I can scarcely concede anything more important

I can scarcely find fitting words

I can strongly recommend

I can understand, moreover

I can with propriety speak here

I certainly have not so good an opinion

I challenge any man

I cheerfully own

I cheerfully submit myself

I claim a share also for

I class them altogether under the head

I close with the words

I close with this sentiment

I come at length to

I come next to the question of

I come to the other assumption

I conceive this to be

I confess I feel not the least alarmed

I confess I have had my doubts

I confess I have little sympathy

I confess it affects me very deeply to

I confess it is very difficult to

I confess that I do not entirely approve

I confess that it is a comfort to me

I confess that my notions are widely different

I confess to a little embarrassment

I confess to you that I have no fear

I confine myself to saying

I congratulate you upon the auspicious character

I consider I have said enough in proof

I consider it amply explains

I contend

I content myself with pursuing

I could do no less than

I could easily mention

I could enlarge upon it

I could never understand

I could wish that this belief

I dare say you know

I dare venture the remark

I declare to you

I deem it both necessary and just

I deem it proper here to remind

I deem myself honored

I deny, once and for all

I deny the inference

I desire to be brief

I desire to bear my testimony

I desire to call attention

I desire to know

I desire to lay emphatic stress

I dissent from the opinion

I distrust all general theories of

I do again and again urge upon you

I do, indeed, recollect

I do not absolutely assert

I do not advocate

I do not argue

I do not ask you to

I do not at this moment remember

I do not believe it possible

I do not belong to those who

I do not choose to consume

I do not complain of

I do not consider it necessary

I do not contend

I do not countenance for a moment

I do not deem it incumbent upon me

I do not depreciate for a moment

I do not desire to call in question

I do not desire to put too much emphasis

I do not despair of surmounting

I do not disguise the fact

I do not enter into the question

I do not fail to admire

I do not fear a contradiction

I do not feel at liberty

I do not forget the practical necessity

I do not hesitate to say

I do not imagine

I do not in the least degree

I do not indeed deny

I do not indulge in the delusion

I do not know how anyone can believe

I do not know whether you are aware of it

I do not know why

I do not know with what correctness

I do not mean anything so absurd

I do not mean now to go further than

I do not mean to impute

I do not merely urge

I do not mistrust

I do not myself pretend to be

I do not need to remind you

I do not, of course, deny

I do not pretend to argue

I do not propose to take up your time

I do not question for a moment

I do not recount all

I do not say anything about the future

I do not say this with any affectation

I do not see how it is possible

I do not see much difference between

I do not seek to palliate

I do not speak exclusively

I do not stop to discuss

I do not, therefore, wonder

I do not think it necessary to warn you

I do not think it possible

I do not think it unfair reasoning

I do not think myself obliged to dwell

I do not think that I need further discuss

I do not think this at all an exaggeration

I do not think we can go far wrong

I do not think you will often hear

I do not understand how it can apply

I do not vouch for

I do not want to discourage you

I do not wish to be considered egotistic

I do not wish to be misrepresented

I do not wonder

I doubt very much whether

I dwell with pleasure on the considerations

I earnestly maintain

I embrace with peculiar satisfaction

I end as I began

I entertain great apprehension for

I entertain no such chimerical hopes [chimerical = highly improbable]

I entertain the hope and opinion

I entirely dissent from the view

I especially hail with approval

I even add this

I even venture to deny

I fancy I hear you say

I fear I may seem trifling

I fear lest I may

I fearlessly appeal

I fearlessly challenge

I feel a great necessity to

I feel bound to add my expression

I feel constrained to declare

I feel entirely satisfied

I feel I have a right to say

I feel it a proud privilege

I feel keenly myself impelled by every duty

I feel only a great emotion of gratitude

I feel respect and admiration

I feel some explanation is due

I feel sure

I feel tempted to introduce here

I feel that I have a special right to

I feel that it is not true

I feel the greatest satisfaction

I feel the task is far beyond my power

I fervently trust

I find it difficult to utter in words

I find it more easy

I find my reference to this

I find myself called upon to say something

I find myself in the position of

I find no better example than

I find no fault with

I find numberless cases

I flatter myself

I, for my part, would rather

I, for one, greatly doubt

I forbear to inquire

I foresaw the consequence

I fully recognize

I gave notice just now

I give you, in conclusion, this sentence

I go further

I grant all this

I grant with my warmest admiration

I gratefully accept

I greatly deplore

I had a kind of hope

I had almost said

I had in common with others

I had occasion to criticize

I happen to differ

I hardly dare to dwell longer

I hardly know anything more strange

I hasten to concede

I have a dark suspicion

I have a great admiration for

I have a pleasing and personal duty

I have a profound pity for those

I have a right to consider

I have a strong belief

I have a very high respect for

I have abstained from

I have acquired some useful experience

I have all along implied

I have all but finished

I have already alluded to

I have already shown the ground of my hope

I have already stated, and now repeat

I have always been under the impression

I have always listened with the greatest satisfaction

I have always maintained

I have another objection

I have another observation to add

I have anticipated the objection

I have assumed throughout

I have attempted thus hastily

I have barely touched some of the points

I have been allowed the privilege

I have been asked several times

I have been extremely anxious

I have been given to understand

I have been glad to observe

I have been heretofore treating

I have been insisting then on this

I have been interested in hearing

I have been pointing out how

I have been profoundly moved

I have been requested to say a word

I have been told by an eminent authority

I have been too long accustomed to hear

I have been touched by the large generosity

I have been trying to show

I have before me the statistics

I have but one more word to add

I have demonstrated to you

I have depicted

I have endeavored to emphasize

I have enlarged on this subject

I have felt it almost a duty to

I have found great cause for wonder

I have frequently been surprised at

I have gazed with admiration

I have generally observed

I have gone so far as to suggest

I have good reason for

I have had steadily in mind

I have had the honor

I have had to take a long sweep

I have heard it objected

I have heard with relief and pleasure

I have hitherto been adducing instances [adduce = cite as an example]

I have hitherto been engaged in showing

I have in a measure anticipated

I have in my possession

I have incidentally dwelt on

I have introduced it to suggest

I have labored to maintain

I have laid much stress upon

I have lately observed many strong indications

I have listened with the utmost interest

I have little hope that I can add anything

I have lived to see

I have long ago insisted

I have long been of the conviction

I have never heard it suggested

I have never whispered a syllable

I have no acquaintance with

I have no doubt whatever

I have no excuse for intruding

I have no fear of myself

I have no fears for the success

I have no hesitation in asserting

I have no intention to moralize

I have no particular inclination

I have no prejudice on the subject

I have no pretention to be regarded

I have no reason to think

I have no scruple in saying

I have no such gloomy forebodings

I have no sympathy with the men

I have no thought of venturing to say

I have no wish at all to preach

I have not accustomed myself

I have not allowed myself

I have not been able to deny

I have not particularly referred to

I have not said anything yet

I have not the means of forming a judgment

I have not the right to reproach

I have not time to present

I have nothing more to say

I have noticed of late years

I have now explained to you

I have now made bold to touch upon

I have now rather more than kept my word

I have now said all that occurs to me

I have often been impressed with

I have often been struck with the resemblance

I have often lingered in fancy

I have one step farther to go

I have only partially examined

I have partly anticipated

I have pleasant memories of

I have pointed out

I have pride and pleasure in quoting

I have racked this brain of mine

I have read with great regret

I have said and I repeat

I have said over and over again

I have said what I solemnly believe

I have scant patience

I have seen for myself

I have seen it stated in a recent journal

I have seen some signs of encouragement

I have shown

I have some sort of fear

I have sometimes asked myself

I have sometimes fancied

I have sometimes wondered whether

I have still two comments to make

I have taken pains to know

I have the confident hope

I have the greatest possible confidence

I have the honor to propose

I have then to investigate

I have thought it incumbent on me

I have thought it right on this day

I have thought it well to suggest

I have throughout highly appreciated

I have thus been led by my feelings

I have thus stated the reason

I have to confess with a feeling of melancholy

I have to force my imagination

I have touched very cursorily

I have tried to convey to you

I have undertaken to speak

I have very much less feeling of

I have watched with some attention

I have witnessed the extraordinary

I have yet a more cogent reason

I have yet to learn

I hazard nothing in saying

I hear it sometimes said

I hear you say to yourselves

I heartily feel the singular claims

I hesitate to take an instance

I hold it to be clearly expedient

I hold myself obliged to

I hold the maxim no less applicable

I hold this to be a truth

I hold to the principle

I hope by this time we are all convinced

I hope for our own sakes

I hope I have expressed myself explicitly

I hope I may be allowed to intimate

I hope I shall not be told

I hope it is no disparagement

I hope most sincerely and truly

I hope none who hear me

I hope not to occupy more than a few minutes

I hope that I shall not be so unfortunate

I hope the day may be far distant

I hope the time may come again

I hope to be excused if

I hope to be forgiven if

I hope we may forget

I hope you will not accuse me

I imagine that no one will be disposed

I insist upon it

I intend to propose

I know from experience how

I know full well

I know I am treading on thin ice

I know it has been questioned

I know it is said

I know it will be said

I know many reasons why

I know not how else to express

I know not in what direction to look

I know not of my own knowledge

I know not where else to find

I know perfectly well

I know that it is impossible for me to

I know that this is the feeling

I know that what I may say is true

I know there are some who think

I know there is a theory among us

I know too well

I know very well the difference between

I know well it is not for me

I know well the sentiments

I know you are all impatient to hear

I know you will do all in your power

I know you will interpret what I say

I labor under a degree of prejudice

I lately heard it affirmed

I lay it down as a principle

I leave history to judge

I leave it to you

I leave the arduous task

I leave to others to speak

I long to speak a word or two

I look hopefully to

I look in vain

I look with encouragement

I look with inexpressible dread

I look with mingled hope and terror

I make my appeal to

I make no extravagant claim

I make this abrupt acknowledgment

I marvel that

I may add, speaking for my own part

I may be allowed to make one remark

I may be permitted to add

I may confess to you

I may safely appeal

I may say to you calmly

I may seem to have been diffuse

I may take as an instance

I may venture upon a review

I mean by this

I mean, moreover

I mean something more than that

I mention it to you to justify

I mention these facts because

I mention this, not by way of complaint

I might bring you another such case

I might deny that

I might enter into such detail

I might go further

I might go on indefinitely

I might go on to illustrate

I might of course point first

I might reasonably question the justice

I might try to explain

I might venture to claim

I might well have desired

I might well think

I must ask an abrupt question

I must be careful about what I say

I must be contented with

I must be excused if I say

I must bow in reverence

I must call your attention for a moment

I must conclude abruptly

I must confess that I became rather alarmed

I must consider this as

I must crave your indulgence

I must express to you again

I must fairly tell you

I must find some fault with

I must for want of time omit

I must here admit

I must lament

I must leave any detailed development

I must mention with praise

I must not allow myself to indulge

I must not for an instant be supposed

I must not overlook

I must now beg to ask

I must pause a moment to

I must proceed

I must qualify the statement

I must remind my hearers of

I must reply to some observations

I must return to the subject

I must say that I am one of those

I must speak plainly

I must suppose, however

I must take occasion to say

I must thank you once more

I must try to describe to you

I myself have boundless faith

I need not assure this brilliant company

I need not dwell

I need not enter into

I need not follow out the application

I need not, I am certain, assure you

I need not say how much I thank you

I need not show how inconsistent

I need not specially recommend to you

I need not wander far in search

I need only to observe

I need say nothing in praise

I need scarcely observe

I need to guard myself right here

I neither affirm nor deny

I next come to the implicit assumption

I note with particular pleasure

I notice it as affording an instance

I noticed incidentally the fact

I now address you on a question

I now come, sir, to the second head

I now have the pleasure of presenting to you

I now pass to the question of

I now proceed to inquire

I now reiterate

I object strongly to the use

I observe, then, in the first place

I only ask a favorable construction of

I only marvel

I only wish you to recognize

I open the all-important question

I ought to give an illustration

I own I cannot help feeling

I particularly allude to

I pass on from that

I pass then to our second division

I pause for a moment to say

I pause to confess once more

I pay tribute to

I personally know that it is so

I pray God I may never

I predict that you will

I prefer a practical view

I presume I shall have to admit

I presume that I shall not be disbelieved

I proceed to another important phase

I profess

I propose briefly to glance at

I propose, therefore to consider

I protest I never had any doubt

I purposely have avoided

I question whether

I quite endorse what has been said

I rather look forward to a time

I readily grant

I really can not think it necessary to

I really do not know

I really thought that you would excuse me

I recall another historical fact

I recognize the high compliment conveyed

I recollect hearing a sagacious remark [sagacious = sound judgment]

I refer especially

I refuse to believe

I regard as an erroneous view

I regard it as a tribute

I regard it as a very great honor

I regret that I am not able to remember

I regret that it is not possible for me

I regret the time limits me

I regret this the less

I rejoice in an occasion like this

I rejoice that events have occurred

I rejoice to think I remark here

I remember a reference made

I remember an intimation

I remember full well

I remember the enjoyment with which

I remember to have heard

I repeat, I am not speaking

I repeat my statement in another form

I respectfully counsel

I respectfully submit

I rest my opinion on

I rise in behalf

I rise to express my disapprobation [approbation = warm approval; praise]

I rise to thank you

I rise with some trepidation

I return, in conclusion, to

I return you my most grateful thanks

I said a little way back

I said it would be well

I said that I thought

I salute with profound reverence

I sanction with all my heart

I saw an ingenious argument the other day

I say frankly

I say in moderation

I say it is extremely important

I say it most confidently

I say no more of these things

I say not one syllable against

I say, then, my first point is

I say this is no disparagement of

I say this the more gladly

I say without fear of contradiction

I see around me

I see as clearly as any man possibly can

I see little hope of

I see no exception

I see no possibility of

I see no reason for doubting

I seem to hear you say

I seize upon this opportunity

I seriously desire

I set out with saying

I shall add a few words

I shall address myself to a single point

I shall ask you to look very closely

I shall be told

I shall best attain my object

I shall bestow a little attention upon

I shall certainly admit

I shall consider myself privileged

I shall desist from

I shall endeavor to be guided

I shall give it in the words of

I shall here briefly recite the

I shall here use the word to denote

I shall hope to interest you

I shall invite you to follow me

I shall just give the summary of

I shall never believe

I shall never cease to be grateful

I shall not acknowledge

I shall not attempt a detailed narrative

I shall not end without appealing

I shall not enlarge upon

I shall not force into the discussion

I shall not go so far as to say

I shall not hesitate to say something

I shall not tax your patience

I shall not undertake to prophesy

I shall not weary your patience

I shall now give you some instances

I shall now proceed to show

I shall often have to advert to

I shall pass by all this

I shall presently show

I shall proceed without further preface

I shall recur to certain questions

I shall say all this without entering into

I shall show that I am not

I shall speak first about

I shall speak with becoming frankness

I shall take a broader view of the subject

I shall take it for granted here

I shall therefore endeavor

I shall touch upon one or two questions

I shall waste no time in refuting

I shall with your sanction

I should be false to my own manhood

I should be surprised if

I should be the last man to deny

I should fail in my duty if

I should find it hard to discover

I should have forfeited my own self-respect

I should like at least to mention

I should like to emphasize

I should like to go a step farther

I should like to refer to two events

I should like to see that view answered

I should like to-day to examine briefly

I should much prefer

I should not be satisfied with myself

I should think it too absurd

I shrink from the contemplation

I shudder at the doctrine

I simply lay my finger on a fact

I simply pause here to ask

I sincerely regret the absence

I sincerely wish it were in my power

I solemnly declare

I sometimes hear a wish expressed

I sorrowfully call to mind

I speak forth my sentiment

I speak from no little personal observation

I speak of this to show

I speak the fact when I tell you

I speak the secret feeling of this company

I speak what I know when I say

I speak wholly without authority

I speak with feeling upon this point

I speak with some degree of encouragement

I speak with the utmost sincerity

I speak within the hearing of

I stand in awed amazement before

I stand in the midst of men

I still view with respect

I submit it to every candid mind

I submit that in such a case

I submit that it is high time

I submit this proposition

I summon you to do your share

I suppose it is right to answer

I suppose it to be entirely true

I suppose most men will recollect

I suppose that everyone who listens to me

I suppose there is no one here

I suppose we are all of one opinion

I suspect that is why we so often

I sympathize most heartily

I take a broader and bolder position

I take it for granted

I take leave to say

I take one picture as an illustration

I take pleasure in saying

I take the liberty of observing

I take this instance at random

I take two views of

I tell him in reply

I tell you, gentlemen

I tender my thanks to you

I thank you for having allowed me

I thank you for the appreciative tone

I thank you for the honor

I thank you for your most generous greeting

I thank you for your thoughtful courtesy

I thank you from the bottom of my heart

I thank you very gratefully

I thank you very sincerely for the honor

I think I am correct in saying

I think I am not the first to utter

I think I can claim a purpose

I think I can sincerely declare

I think I have a right to look upon

I think I have rightly spoken

I think I might safely say

I think I need not say more

I think it is not too much to say

I think it is quite right

I think it may be necessary to consider

I think it might be said with safety

I think it my duty to

I think it observable

I think it probable

I think it will astonish you

I think it will be granted

I think no Wise man can be indifferent

I think, on the contrary

I think something may be said in favor of

I think that all will agree

I think that I can explain

I think that I can venture to say

I think that, in these last years

I think that none of us will deny

I think there is no better evidence

I think there is no call on me to listen

I think we are justified

I think we can hardly hope

I think we may all easily see

I think we may ask in reply

I think we may safely conclude

I think we may say, therefore

I think we may well be proud of

I think we may well congratulate each other

I think we must draw a distinction

I think we need neither doubt nor fear

I think we ought to recur a moment to

I think we shall all recognize

I think we should do well to call to mind

I think we take too narrow a view

I think when we look back upon

I think you may well rejoice in

I think you will all agree

I think you will pardon my saying

I think you will see

I thus explicitly reply

I tremble at the task

I tremble to think

I trust I may be indulged

I trust it is not presumptuous

I trust that as the years roll on

I trust that I shall have the indulgence

I trust that this will not be regarded as

I turn, gentlemen, to the case

I use the word advisedly

I use the word in the sense

I use very plain language

I utter this word with the deepest affection

I value very much the honor

I venture to ask permission

I venture to say

I verily believe

I very confidently submit

I view that prospect with the greatest misgiving

I want to bespeak your attention

I want to know the character

I want to make some simple applications

I want to say just a few words

I want to say one word more

I want to say to you seriously

I want to think with you

I warn and exhort you

I was astonished to learn

I was constantly watchful to

I was exceedingly interested

I was honored with the acquaintance

I was lost in admiration

I was not slow to accept and believe

I was not without some anxiety

I was overwhelmed

I was sincerely astonished

I was very much interested

I was very much thrilled

I well recollect the time

I well remember an occasion

I will accept the general proposition

I will add the memorable words

I will ask the indulgence

I will ask you to accompany me

I will ask you to bear witness

I will dwell a little longer

I will endeavor in a brief way

I will endeavor to illustrate

I will endeavor to show you

I will enlarge no further

I will even express a hope at the outset

I will even go further and say

I will first call your attention to

I will give one more illustration

I will illustrate this point by

I will merely mention

I will neither affirm nor deny

I will not allude

I will not argue this

I will not attempt to note

I will not be content until

I will not condescend to

I will not enumerate at present

I will not pause to maintain

I will not positively say

I will not pretend to inquire into

I will not quarrel with

I will not relinquish the confidence

I will not repeat the arguments here

I will not try to gauge

I will now consider with you

I will now leave this question

I will now take an instance

I will only speak to one point

I will only sum up my evidence

I will only take an occasion to express

I will only venture to remind you

I will point out to your attention

I will say at once

I will speak but a word or two more

I will speak plainly

I will state with perfect distinctness

I will suppose the objection to be

I will take one more instance

I will take the precaution to add

I will tell you what I think of

I will try to make the thing intelligible

I will venture a single remark

I will venture to add

I will venture to express the hope

I will yield the whole question

I willingly admit

I wish also to declare positively

I wish at the outset

I wish emphatically to reaffirm

I wish I had the time and the power

I wish it first observed

I wish rather to call your attention

I wish, sir, that justice might be done

I wish to ask if you honestly and candidly believe

I wish to be allowed to enforce in detail

I wish to begin my statement

I wish to confine what I have to say

I wish to do full justice to

I wish to draw your attention

I wish to express my profound gratification

I wish to give these arguments their full weight

I wish to know whether

I wish to offer a few words relative to

I wish to remind you in how large a degree

I wish to say a word or two

I wish to state all this as a matter of fact

I wish you success and happiness

I wish you to observe

I would also gratefully acknowledge

I would as soon believe

I would desire to speak simply and directly

I would enter a protest

I would further point out to you

I would have you understand

I would infinitely rather

I would like to say one word just here

I would not be understood as belittling

I would not dwell upon that matter if

I would not push the suggestion so far

I would now gladly lay before you

I would rather a thousand times

I would recommend to your consideration

I would suggest first of all

I would that my voice could reach the ear

I would urge and entreat you

I would urge upon you

I would venture to point out

I yielded to the earnest solicitations

If any man be so persuaded

If anyone could conceive

If anyone is so dim of vision

If any other answer be made

If at first view this should seem

If, however, you determine to

If I am asked for the proof

If I am wrong

If I can carry you with me

If I can succeed in describing

If I could find words

If I have done no more than view the facts

If I have in any way deserved

If I may be allowed a little criticism

If I may be allowed modestly to suggest

If I may be allowed to refer

If I may reverently say so

If I may say so without presumption

If I may so speak

If I may take for granted

If I may venture to say anything

If I mistake not the sentiment

If I recollect aright

If I understand the matter at all

If I venture a few remarks

If I were asked

If I were to act upon my conviction

If I were to recapitulate

If I wished to prove my contention

If, in consequence we find it necessary

If in the glow of conscious pride

If in the years of the future

If it be difficult to appreciate

If it be so

If it be true

If it is contended

If it means anything, it means this

If more were needed to illustrate.

If my opinions are true

If on the contrary, we all foresee

If, on the other hand, I say

If one seeks to measure

If only we go deep enough

If still you have further doubt

If the bare facts were studied

If the experience of the world is worth anything

If, then, I am asked

If, then, I should here rest my cause

If there be any among us

If there be one lesson more than another

If this be so

If this seems doubtful to anyone

If, unhappily, the day should ever come

If we accept at all the argument

If we are not blind to

If we are rightly informed

If we are to reason on the fact

If we cast our glance back

If we embark upon a career

If we had the whole case before us

If we isolate ourselves

If we may trust to experience

If we pursue a different course

If we pursue our inquiries through

If we sincerely desire

If we survey

If we would not be beguiled

If what has been said is true

If you remain silent

If you seek the real meaning of

If you think for a moment

If you want to look

If you were asked to point out

If you will allow me to prophesy

If you will forgive me the expression

If you wish for a more interesting example

If you wish to get at the bottom of facts

If you would see the most conclusive proof

If your view is right

In a significant paragraph

In a wider sense

In a word, gentlemen

In a word, I conceive

In actual life, I suspect

In addition to these arguments

In addressing myself to the question

In addressing you I feel

In agreement with this obvious conclusion

In all ages of the world

In all or any of these views

In all times and places

In an unguarded moment

In answering the inquiry

In any view of the case

In closing my speech, I ask each of you

In conclusion, let me say

In conclusion, may I repeat

In consequence it becomes a necessity

In contemplating the causes

In days to come

In examining this part of the subject

In fine, it is no extravagance to say

In former ages and generations

In further illustration

In further proof of my assertion

In illustration of what I have said

In like manner are to be explained

In like manner I would advise

In listening to the kind words

In looking about me

In many instances

In meeting this difficulty, I will not urge

In most cases I hold

In my estimation

In my humble opinion

In my view

In offering to you these counsels

In one other respect

In one point I wish no one to mistake me

In one sense this is undoubtedly true

In order to appreciate the force of

In order to complete the proof

In order to do justice to the question

In order to prove plainly and intelligibly

In order to realize adequately

In other words

In our estimate of the past

In point of fact

In precisely the same way

In pursuance of these views

In pursuing the great objects

In regard to

In rising to return my sincere thanks

In saying all of this, I do not forget

In saying this, I am not disposed to deny

In short, I say

In solving this difficulty

In something of a parallel way

In spite of the fact

In such cases, strictly speaking

In support of this assertion

In that matchless epitome

In that mood of high hope

In the anomalies of fortune

In the course of these remarks

In the existing circumstances

In the first place, therefore, I consider

In the first place we see

In the first place, we should be all agreed

In the fullest sense

In the fullness of time

In the last suggestion

In the meantime I will commend to you

In the next place, be assured

In the presence of this vast assembly

In the present situation

In the progress of events

In the remarks I have made

In the same manner I rely

In the second place it is quite clear

In the suggestion I have made

In the very brief space at our disposal

In these extraordinary circumstances

In these sentiments I agree

In this brief survey

In this connection, I may be permitted to refer

In this connection I remind myself

In this necessarily brief and imperfect review

In this rapid and slight enumeration

In this respect

In this sense only

In this there is no contradiction

In very many instances

In very truth

In view of these reflections

In what has now been said

In what I have now further to say

In widening our view

Indeed, can anyone tell me

Indeed, I am not convinced

Indeed, I can not do better

Indeed, I have heard it whispered

Indeed, I may fairly say

Indeed, it will generally be found

Indeed we know

Instances abound

Is it logically consistent

Is it not legitimate to recognize

Is it not marvelous

Is it not obvious

Is it not quite possible

Is it not, then, preposterous

Is it not universally recognized

Is it not wise to argue

Is it possible, can it be believed

Is it, then, any wonder

Is not that the common sentiment

Is there any evidence here

Is there any language of reproach

Is there any possibility of mistaking

Is there any reason in the world

It affords me gratification

It also pleases me very much

It amounts to this

It appears from what has been said

It appears to me, on the contrary

It can rightly be said

It certainly follows, then

It comes to this

It could not be otherwise

It does not necessarily follow

It exhibits a state of mind

It follows as a matter of course

It follows inevitably

It gives us an exalted conception

It grieves me to relate

It hardly fits the character

It has at all times been a just reproach

It has been a very great pleasure for me

It has been generally assumed

It has been justly objected

It has been my privilege

It has been suggested fancifully

It has been well said

It has ever been my ambition

It has struck me very forcibly

It is a circumstance of happy augury [augury = sign of something coming; omen]

It is a common error

It is a curious trait

It is a fact well known

It is a falsehood to say

It is a familiar charge against

It is a good augury of success [augury = sign of something coming; omen]

It is a great pleasure to me

It is a living truth

It is a matter of absorbing interest

It is a matter of amusement

It is a matter of fact

It is a matter of just pride

It is a melancholy story

It is a memory I cherish

It is a mischievous notion

It is a mistake to suppose

It is a most extraordinary thing

It is a most pertinent question

It is a noble thing

It is a peculiar pleasure to me

It is a perversion of terms

It is a pleasing peculiarity

It is a popular idea

It is a rare privilege

It is a recognized principle

It is a remarkable and striking fact

It is a strange fact

It is a sure sign

It is a theme too familiar

It is a thing commonly said

It is a touching reflection

It is a true saying

It is a very significant fact

It is a vision which still inspires us

It is a wholesome symptom

It is, all things considered, a fact

It is all very fine to think

It is all very well to say

It is almost proverbial

It is also possible

It is also probably true

It is always pleasant to respond

It is amazing how little

It is an easy matter

It is an egregious mistake [egregious = conspicuously and outrageously reprehensible]

It is an established rule

It is an incredible thing

It is an interesting fact

It is an unforgivable offense

It is an unquestionable truth

It is appropriate that we should celebrate

It is asserted

It is assumed as an axiom

It is at once inconsistent

It is but fair to say

It is but too true

It is by no means my design

It is certainly especially pleasant

It is certainly remarkable

It is common in these days to lament

It is commonly assumed

It is comparatively easy

It is curious sophistry

It is curious to observe

It is desirable for us

It is difficult for me to respond fitly

It is difficult to avoid saying

It is difficult to describe

It is difficult to overstate

It is difficult to put a limit

It is difficult to surmise

It is doubtful whether

It is easy enough to add

It is easy to instance cases

It is easy to understand

It is eminently proper

It is every man's duty to think

It is evident that the answer to this

It is evidently supposed by many people

It is exceedingly gratifying to hear

It is exceedingly unfortunate

It is fair that you should hear

It is fair to suppose

It is far from me to desire

It is fatal to suppose

It is fitting

It is for me to relate

It is for others to illustrate

It is for this reason

It is for us to ask

It is greatly assumed

It is gratifying to have the honor

It is hardly for me

It is hardly necessary to pass judgment

It is idle to think of

It is immaterial whether

It is impossible to avoid saying

It is in every way appropriate

It is in the highest degree worthy

It is in this characteristic

It is in vain

It is in your power to give

It is indeed a strange doctrine

It is indeed not a little remarkable

It is indeed true

It is indeed very clear

It is indispensable to have

It is interesting and suggestive

It is interesting to know

It is just so far true

It is likewise necessary

It is made evident

It is manifest

It is manifestly absurd to say

It is merely common sense to say

It is more than probable

It is my agreeable duty

It is my belief

It is my earnest wish

It is my grateful duty to address you

It is my hope

It is my present purpose

It is natural to ask the question

It is necessary to refer

It is necessary to take some notice

It is needful to a complete understanding

It is needless before this audience to repeat

It is no doubt true

It is no exaggeration to say

It is no part of my business

It is no significant thing

It is no small indication

It is no wonder

It is not a practical question

It is not altogether satisfactory

It is not an unknown occurrence

It is not by any means

It is not difficult to comprehend

It is not difficult to discern

It is not easy for me to find words

It is not enough to say

It is not entirely clear to me

It is not evident

It is not for me on this occasion

It is not given to many men

It is not likely that any of you

It is not logical to say

It is not my intention to enter into

It is not my purpose to discuss

It is not necessarily true

It is not necessary for me even to sketch

It is not necessary for our purpose

It is not often in these modern days

It is not ours to pronounce

It is not out of place to remind you

It is not possible to recount

It is not quite clear

It is not to me so very surprising

It is not too much to say

It is not unknown to you

It is not within the scope of this address

It is now high time for me

It is now perfectly plain

It is observable enough

It is obvious

It is of course difficult

It is of great importance to show

It is of no moment

It is of very little importance

It is often remarked

It is on these grounds

It is one of the burning questions of the day

It is one of the most natural visions

It is one of the most significant things

It is one of the queerest freaks of fate

It is only a few short years since

It is only just to say

It is our duty to examine

It is ours to bear witness

It is owing to this truth

It is peculiarly befitting at this time

It is perfectly apparent

It is pitiable to reflect

It is pleasant to meet this brilliant company

It is rather a pleasant coincidence

It is rather an arduous task

It is rather startling

It is related

It is ridiculous to say

It is said, and I think said truly

It is said to be impossible

It is satisfactory to notice

It is scarcely necessary to insist

It is scarcely questioned

It is self-evident

It is sometimes hard to determine

It is still an open question

It is still more surprising

It is substantially true

It is surely necessary for me

It is the clear duty of

It is the doctrine of

It is the fashion to extol

It is the universal testimony

It is therefore evident

It is therefore necessary

It is this which lies at the foundation

It is to be expected

It is to be remembered

It is to me a very sincere satisfaction

It is told traditionally

It is too plain to be argued

It is true

It is unnecessary for me to remind you

It is upon this line of reasoning

It is very common to confuse

It is very doubtful whether

It is very interesting and pleasant

It is well known

It is with great pleasure

It is with pity unspeakable

It is within the memory of men now living

It is worth while to notice

It may appear absurd

It may at first sight seem strange

It may be added

It may be conjectured

It may be imagined

It may be plausibly objected

It may be rightly said

It may be useful to trace

It may be worth your while to keep in view

It may indeed be unavoidable

It may not be altogether certain

It may not be uninteresting to any of you

It may or may not be true

It may, perhaps, seem wonderful

It may seem a little strange

It may still more probably be said

It must be a cause of delight

It must be borne in mind

It must be the verdict of history

It must create astonishment

It must doubtless be admitted

It must ever be recollected

It must never be forgotten

It must not be supposed

It must seem to every thoughtful man

It needs scarcely be said

It now becomes my pride and privilege

It only remains now to speak

It ought to animate us

It proves a great deal

It remains only to speak briefly

It remains that I inform you of

It remains that I should say a few words

It reminds me of an anecdote

It reminds one of the compliment

It requires no effort of imagination

It scarcely seems to be in keeping

It seems almost desperate to think of

It seems almost incredible

It seems now to be generally admitted

It seems strange to be told

It seems then that on the whole

It seems to me a striking circumstance

It seems to me idle to ask

It seems to me singularly appropriate

It seems to me the primary foundation

It seems to me unphilosophical

It should always be borne in mind

It should be remembered

It so happens

It sometimes seems to me

It still remains to be observed

It strikes me with wonder

It suggests at the outset

It summons our imagination

It surely is not too much to expect

It therefore astonishes me

It used to be a reproach

It was a brilliant answer

It was a fine and delicate rebuke

It was a fit and beautiful circumstance

It was a propitious circumstance [propitious = auspicious, favorable]

It was certainly a gracious act

It was in the full understanding

It was my good fortune

It was not to be expected

It was said by one who ought to know

It was, therefore, inevitable

It was under these circumstances

It will appeal to

It will appear from what has been said

It will be asked me how

It will be easy to say too much

It will be easy to trace the influence

It will be evident to you

It will be idle to imply

It will be interesting to trace

It will be just as reasonable to say

It will be rather to our advantage

It will be recollected

It will be seen at a glance

It will be well and wise

It will carry out my meaning more fully

It will, I suppose, be denied

It will not be expected from me

It will not be safe

It will not do for a man to say

It will not, I trust, be concluded

It will not surely be objected

It will not take many words to sum up

It will thus be seen

It would be a misfortune

It would be a proud distinction

It would be a very remarkable fact

It would be absurd to pretend

It would be an inexcusable omission

It would be idle for me

It would be imprudent in me

It would be invidious for me [invidious = rousing ill will, animosity]

It would be natural on such an occasion

It would be no less impracticable

It would be out of place here

It would be preposterous to say

It would be presumptuous in me

It would be the height of absurdity

It would be unfair to praise

It would be unjust to deny

It would be well for us to reflect

It would indeed be unworthy

It would seem perhaps most fitting

J

Just the reverse is true

L

Language is inadequate to voice my appreciation

Lastly, I do not understand

Lastly, it can not be denied

Less than this could not be said

Lest I should be accused of quibbling

Let all of us labor in this work

Let anyone imagine to himself

Let anyone who doubts

Let everyone consider

Let it be clearly understood, I repeat it

Let it be remembered

Let it not be objected

Let it not be supposed that I impute [impute = relate to a particular cause or source]

Let me add another thing

Let me add my final word

Let me add one other hint

Let me also say a word in regard

Let me answer these questions

Let me ask you to imagine

Let me ask your leave to propose

Let me be allowed to devote a few words

Let me call attention to another fact

Let me commend to you

Let me direct your attention now to

Let me entreat you to examine

Let me give one more instance

Let me give one parting word

Let me give you an illustration

Let me here make one remark

Let me here say

Let me hope that I have said enough

Let me illustrate again

Let me make myself distinctly understood

Let me make use of an illustration

Let me not be thought offensive

Let me now conclude with

Let me once more urge upon you

Let me protest against the manner

Let me quite temperately defend

Let me rather make the supposition

Let me say a practical word

Let me simply declare

Let me tell you an interesting reminiscence

Let me thank you once more

Let me urge you earnestly

Let no man congratulate himself

Let our conception be enlarged

Let our object be

Let that question be answered by

Let the facts be granted

Let these instances suffice

Let this be the record made

Let this inspire us with abhorrence of

Let us approach the subject from another side

Let us attempt a survey

Let us be perfectly just

Let us be quite practical

Let us bear perpetually in mind

Let us begin at the beginning

Let us begin by examining

Let us briefly review

Let us brush aside once for all

Let us cherish

Let us confirm our opinion

Let us consider for a moment

Let us devote ourselves

Let us discard all prejudice

Let us do all we can

Let us draw an illustration

Let us endeavor to understand

Let us enumerate

Let us figure to ourselves

Let us for the moment put aside

Let us get a clear understanding

Let us heed the voice

Let us hope and believe

Let us hope that future generations

Let us imitate

Let us inquire also

Let us labor and pray

Let us likewise remember

Let us look briefly at a few particulars

Let us look nearer home

Let us not be fearful

Let us not be misled

Let us not be misunderstood

Let us not flatter ourselves

Let us not for a moment forget

Let us not limit our view

Let us now apply the views presented

Let us now consider the characteristics

Let us now see the results

Let us now turn our consideration

Let us observe this analogy

Let us pass on to another fact

Let us pause a moment

Let us push the inquiry yet further

Let us rather listen to

Let us reflect how vain

Let us remember this

Let us remind ourselves

Let us resolve

Let us scrutinize the facts

Let us suppose, for argument's sake

Let us suppose the case to be

Let us take, for instance

Let us, then, be assured

Let us, then, be worthy of

Let us, therefore, say once for all

Let us try to form a mental picture

Let us turn to the contemplation of

Let your imagination realize

Like all citizens of high ideals

Likely enough

Little wonder therefore

Long have I been convinced

Look at it in another way

Look at some of these questions

Look at the situation

M

Mainly, I believe

Making allowances for differences of opinion

Many of us have had the good fortune

Many of you, perhaps, recollect

May I ask you to believe

May I not speak here

May I try to show that every effort

May I venture to suggest

May it not also be advanced

May the day come quickly

Meantime it is encouraging to think

Meanwhile let us freely recognize

Men are in the habit of saying

Men are telling us nowadays

Men everywhere testify

More and more it is felt

More than once have I had to express

More than this need not be said

Moreover, I have insisted

Moreover, I would counsel you

Moreover, when we pass judgment

Much has been said and written about

My appreciation has been quickened

My belief, therefore, is

My duty is to endeavor to show

My experience tells me

My first duty is to express to you

My friends, do you really believe

My friends, I propose

My heart tells me

My idea, therefore, is

My last criticism upon

My mind is not moved by

My mind most perfectly acquiesces

My next objection is

My own private opinion is

My present business is

My regret is intensified by the thought

N

Nay, I boldly say

Nay, it will be a relief to my mind

Nay, there is a general feeling

Need I say that I mean

Neither should you deceive

Never before have I so strongly felt

Never can I cease to feel

Never did there devolve

Never for a moment believe

Never have I felt so forcibly

Never was a weaker defense attempted

Never was there a greater mistake

Never was there an instance

Nevertheless we can admit

Next, from what has been said it is plain

Next, I consider

Next, it will be denied

No argument can overwhelm a fact

No defense is to be found

No distinct test can be named

No doubt, in the first instance

No doubt there are many questions

No doubt to most of us

No finer sentence has come down to us

No greater service could be rendered

No longer do we believe

No man regrets more than I do

No one can feel this more strongly

No one can, I think, pretend

No one can see the end

No one here, I am sure

No one, I suppose, would say

No one, I think, can fail to observe

No one, I think, will dispute the statement

No one need to exaggerate

No one will accuse me

No true man ever believes

None can have failed to observe

Nor am I disparaging or discouraging

Nor can I forget either

Nor can it justly be said

Nor can we afford to waste time

Nor can we forget how long

Nor can we now ask

Nor do I believe

Nor do I doubt

Nor do I pretend

Nor do I think there can be found

Nor does it matter much

Nor has there been wanting

Nor indeed am I supposing

Nor is it a fair objection

Nor is it probable

Nor is this all

Nor let me forget to add here

Nor must I be understood as saying

Nor must it be forgotten

Nor need we fear to speak

Nor should any attempt be made

Nor will history fail to record

Nor will I enlarge on the matter

Not at all

Not only so

Not that I quarrel with

Nothing but the deepest sense

Nothing can be further from the truth

Nothing could be clearer

Nothing could be more striking

Nothing is more common in the world

Nothing that you can do

Notwithstanding all that has been said

Notwithstanding all this, I hold

Now, bear with me when I say

Now comes the question

Now, comparing these instances together

Now, from these instances it is plain

Now, having spoken of

Now, I admit

Now, I am far from denying

Now, I am far from undervaluing

Now, I am justified in calling this

Now, I am obliged to say

Now, I do not wish you to believe

Now, I have a closing sentence or two

Now, I pass on to consider

Now, I shall not occupy your time

Now, I understand the argument

Now, I will undertake to say

Now, I wish to call your attention

Now, if you will clearly understand

Now, is there any ground or basis for

Now, it is an undoubted fact

Now, it is evident

Now, it is not at all strange

Now, it is unquestioned

Now, let me speak with the greatest care

Now, let me stop a moment

Now, let us consider

Now, observe, my drift

Now, sir, I am truly horrified

Now, the answer we should give

Now, the question here at issue

Now, the world will say

Now, there is a close alliance between

Now, this is precisely the danger

Now, this is to some extent

Now, understand me definitely

Now, we do not maintain

Now, we will inquire

Now, what I want you to realize

Now, with regard to

Now, you will allow me to state

Now, you will understand from this

O

Observe again

Occasionally you ought to read

Of course I am aware

Of course I am putting an impossible case

Of course I can not be taken to mean

Of course I do not maintain

Of course I do not stop here

Of course I would not allow

Of course much may be said

Of course these remarks hold good

Of course we may, if we please

Of course you will sympathize

Of one thing, however, I am certain

Of this briefly

Of this statement I will only say

Of this truth I shall convince you by

On a review of the whole subject

On occasions of this kind

On such a day as this

On the contrary, I am assuming

On the occasion to which I refer

On the other hand, it is clear

On the whole, then, I observe

On this auspicious occasion

On this point I do not mean to dwell

On this subject you need not suspect

Once again, there are those

Once more I emphasize

Once more let me try to put into words

One additional remark

One almost wishes

One cannot decline to note

One concluding remark has to be made

One fact is clear and indisputable

One further word

One important topic remains

One is fairly tempted to wish

One lesson history may be said to repeat

One might be challenged to produce

One of the ancients said

One of the most commonly known

One of the most extraordinary incidents

One of the things I recollect with most pride

One of these signs is the fact

One or two points are made clear

One other circumstance

One other remark suggests itself

One remark I will make

One thing more will complete this question

One thing which always impressed me

One very striking tendency

One word in courtesy I must say

One word more in a serious vein

One would naturally suppose

Only so much do I know

Opinions are divided as to whether

Or to come nearer home

Or to take but one other example

Ordinarily speaking, such deductions

Others may hold other opinions

Ought we not to think

Our thoughts wander back

Over and above all this

P

Pardon me if

Perhaps another reason why

Perhaps, however, in speaking to you

Perhaps, however, some among you will be

Perhaps I may be best able to illustrate

Perhaps I ought to say

Perhaps it may be doubted

Perhaps, sir, I am mistaken in

Permit me frankly to say

Permit me to add another circumstance

Permit me to bring home to you

Personally, I am far too firm a believer

Pray, sir, let me say

R

Read but your history aright

Recollect, sir

Reflections such as these

Rely upon it

Remember, I do not seek to

Remembering some past occurrences

Returning, then, to the consideration

S

Seriously, then, do I beg you

Shall I tell you

Shall we complain

Should there be objection, I answer

Since, then, it is provided

Since, then, this is the case

Sir, with all my heart, I respond

So accustomed are we

So at least it seems to me

So far as I know

So far as my observation and experience goes

So far in general

So I say to you

So it comes to pass

So long as we continue to love truth and duty

So men are asking

So much at first sight

So much on this subject

So that I may venture to say

So that if you were persuaded

So then ought we also

So, to add one other example

So, too, I may go on to speak

So when I hear people say

Some have insisted

Some of you can recall the time

Some of you may think this visionary

Some of you will remember

Some one will perhaps object

Some prejudice is attached

Some writer has said

Sometimes I venture to think

Sometimes it may happen

Speaking in this place

Startling as this may appear to you

Stating only the truth, I affirm

Still another encouraging fact

Still further

Still I can not part from my subject

Still I have generally found

Still I imagine you would consider it

Still I know what answer I can make to

Still it may with justice be said

Still one thing more

Still we ought to be grateful

Strange as it may seem

Strictly in confidence, I do not think

Strictly speaking, there is no such thing

Such a doctrine is essentially superficial

Such are the rather tolerant ideas

Such considerations as these

Such, I believe, would be the consequences

Such illustrations are not frequent

Such, in brief, is the story

Such is steadfastly my opinion

Such is the deep prejudice now existing

Such is the intellectual view we take

Such is the lesson which I am taught

Such is the progress

Such is the truth

Such, sir, I conceive to be

Such, then, is the true idea

Such, too, is the characteristic of

Suffer me to point out

Suffice it to say here

Summing up what I have said

Suppose we turn our eyes to

Surely I do not misinterpret

Surely it is a paradox

Surely it is not too much for me to say

T

Take another instance

Take one of the most recent cases

Take the simple fact

Take this example

Taking a broader view

Taking the facts by themselves

That is a further point

That is a natural boast

That is a pure assumption

That is all that it seems necessary to me

That is all very good

That is far from my thoughts

That is final and conclusive

That is the lesson of history

That is the question of questions

That you may conceive the force of

The answer is easy to find

The answer is ready

The belief is born of the wish

The broad principle which I would lay down

The circumstances under which we meet

The climax of my purpose in this address

The common consent of civilized mankind

The conclusion is irresistible

The confusing assertion is sometimes made

The day is at hand

The decided objection is raised

The doctrine I am combating

The doctrine is admirable

The effect too often is

The evolution of events has brought

The fact has made a deep impression on me

The fact has often been insisted

The fact to be particularly noted

The facts are clear and unequivocal

The facts may be strung together

The first business of every man

The first counsel I would offer

The first great fact to remember is

The first point to be ascertained

The first practical thought is

The first remarkable instance was

The first thing I wish to note

The first thing that we have to consider

The future historian will, no doubt

The generous feeling that has promoted you

The great mass of the people

The hour is at hand

The illustration is analogous

The important thing is

The instance I shall choose

The irresistible tendency of

The kindness with which I have been received

The last and distinguishing feature is

The latest inclination I have seen

The lesson which we should take most to heart

The main cause of all this

The more you examine this matter

The most concise tribute paid

The most reasonable anticipation

The most remarkable step forward

The most striking characteristic

The most sublime instance that I know

The next point is

The next question to be considered is

The next thing I consider indispensable

The occasion that calls us together

The one central difference between

The only course that remains open

The only plea to be offered

The other day I observed

The paramount consideration is

The perils that beset us here

The pleasing duty is assigned me

The point I have urged upon you is

The point I wish a little further to speak of

The point to which I shall call your attention

The popular notion is

The practical inference from all this

The presence of this brilliant assemblage

The pressing question is

The prevalent opinion, no doubt

The proof of this statement is to be found

The question is deeply involved

The question, then, recurs

The remedy I believe to be

The result, I fancy, has been

The result of the whole

The rule will always hold good

The sacred voice of inspiration

The same is true in respect of

The scene all comes back

The sentiment to which I am to respond

The sentiment which you have expressed

The simple rule and test

The simple truth is

The soundness of this doctrine depends

The strongest proof I have

The subject of the evening's address

The subject which has been assigned to me

The task has been placed in my hands

The testimony of history is

The theory seems at first sight

The thought with which I shall close

The time has manifestly now arrived

The time is not far distant

The time is now come for me

The times are full of signs and warnings

The toast I am about to propose to you

The vain wish has sometimes been indulged

The view I have been enforcing

The view is more misleading

The warmth and kindness of your reception

The welcome that has been extended to me

The whole story of civilization

Then again, in corroboration

Then again, when men say

Then take the other side of the argument

Then the question arises

Then there is another story

Then, too, it must be remembered

There are certain old truths

There are few spectacles

There are hopeful signs of

There are, I believe, many who think

There are, indeed, exceptions

There are, indeed, persons who profess

There are many educated and intelligent people

There are people in every community

There are several reasons why

There are some slight modifications

There are some who are fond of looking at

There are some who have an idea

There are those of us who can remember

There are those who wish

There are two conflicting theories

There can be but one answer

There can be no doubt

There has been a great deal of discussion lately

There has been no period of time

There have been differences of opinion

There is a characteristic saying

There is a class of person

There is a common saying

There is a conviction

There is a degree of evidence

There is a genuine grief

There is a great deal of rash talking

There is a growing disposition

There is a large class of thinkers

There is a lesson of profound interest

There is a more important question

There is a most serious lesson

There is a multitude of facts

There is a question of vital importance

There is a very common tendency

There is a vital difference of opinion

There is an analogy in this respect

There is an ancient story to the effect

There is an eternal controversy

There is another class of men

There is another factor

There is another object equally important

There is another point of view

There is another remarkable analogy

There is another sense in which

There is, at any rate, to be said

There is but one consideration

There is certainly no reason

There is hardly any limit

There is, however, another opinion

There is, however, one caution

There is little truth in

There is no field of human activity

There is no good reason

There is no justification for

There is no mistaking the purpose

There is no more insidious peril

There is no more striking exemplification

There is no occasion to exaggerate

There is no page of history

There is no sense in saying

There is no worse perversion

There is not a shadow of evidence

There is nothing more repulsive

There is nothing overstated in this description

There is nothing to show

There is one story which it is said

There is only one sense in which

There is some difference of opinion

There is something strangely interesting

There is yet another distinction

There is yet one other remark

There ought certainly to be

There was but one alternative

There was one remarkable incident

There will always be a number of men

There will be no difficulty

There yet remains

Therefore, there is no possibility of a doubt

Therein lies your responsibility

These alone would not be sufficient

These are enough to refute the opinion

These are general counsels

These are generalizations

These are my reasons for

These are points for consideration

These considerations have great weight with me

These exceptions do not hold in the case of

These ideas naturally present themselves

These instances are far from common

These instances are indications

These last words lead me to say

These objections only go to show

These questions I shall examine

These various partial views

They mistake the intelligence

They would persuade you to

Think for a moment

Think of the cool disregard

This absurdity arises

This appeal to the common sense

This argument is especially

cogent [cogent = powerfully persuasive]

This, at least, is sure

This being the case

This being true

This being undeniable, it is plain

This being understood, I ask

This brings me to a single remark

This brings us to a subject

This episode goes to prove

This fact was soon made manifest

This from the nature of the case

This I conceive to be the business

This I consider to be my own case

This I have told you

This is a general statement

This is a very one-sided conception

This is a very serious situation

This is an astonishing announcement

This is conceded by

This is contrary to all argument

This is doubtless the truth

This is especially the case

This is essentially an age of

This is in the main just

This is like saying

This is not all

This is not the main point of objection

This is not the occasion or the place

This is obvious

This is on the whole reasonable

This is only another illustration of

This is owing in great measure to

This is precisely what we ought to do

This is said in no spirit of

This is suggested to us

This is the design and intention

This is the great fact

This is the main point on which the inquiry turns

This is the meaning of

This is the obvious answer

This is the point I want to impress upon you

This is the point of view

This is the position of our minds

This is the radical question

This is the sentiment of mankind

This is the starting-point

This is the sum

This is to be found in the fact

This is what I am led to say

This is what may be objected

This is why I take the liberty

This language is plain

This leads me to the question

This leads us to inquire

This may be said without prejudice

This might be illustrated at length

This much is certain

This sentiment was well-nigh universal

This, surely, is the conclusion

This, then, is the answer

This, then, is the drift of my illustration

This, then, is what I mean by saying

This will be evident at once

This you can not deny

Those who have watched the tendencies

Thus a great deal may be done

Thus analogy suggests

Thus far, I willingly admit

Thus I am led on to another remark

Thus if you look into

Thus instances occur now and then

Thus it comes to pass

Thus my imagination tells me

Thus much, however, I may say

Thus much I may be allowed to say

Thus much may be sufficient to recall

Thus we see

Time would not permit me

To a man of the highest public spirit

To avoid all possibility of being misunderstood

To be more explicit

To be sure, we sometimes hear

To bring the matter nearer home

To convince them of this

To feel the true force of this argument

To illustrate

To make my story quite complete

To me, however, it would appear

To my way of conceiving such matters

To prevent misapprehension

To some it may sound like a paradox

To sum up all that has been said

To sum up in one word

To take a very different instance

To the conclusion thus drawn

To the enormous majority of persons

To these general considerations

To this I answer

To this it will be replied

To what other cause can you ascribe

To-day, as never before

Treading close upon the heels

Tried by this standard

True it is

True, there are difficulties

Truly it is a subject for astonishment

Two things are made very clear

U

Under all the circumstances

Under these favoring conditions

Under this head

Undoubtedly we may find

Unfortunately it is a truth

Unless I could be sure

Up to this moment I have stated

V

Very strange is this indeed

W

We all agree as to

We all feel the force of the maxim

We all in equal sincerity profess

We almost shudder when we see

We are accustomed to lay stress upon

We are all familiar with

We are approaching an era

We are apt to forget

We are assembled here to-day

We are beginning to realize

We are bound to give heed

We are constantly being told

We are fulfilling what I believe to be

We are in the habit of saying

We are met to-night

We are not able to prove

We are not disinterested

We are quite unable to speculate

We are told emphatically

We are tolerably certain

We believe with a sincere belief

We can but pause to contemplate

We can imagine the amazement of

We cannot but be struck with

We cannot escape the truth

We cannot have this too deeply fixed

We cannot too highly honor the temper of

We cannot wonder

We can only applaud the sentiment

We can only bow with awe

We can presume

We can remember with pride

We can see to some extent

We continually hear nowadays

We deeply appreciate the circumstances of

We do not quarrel with those

We do not question the reality

We do well to recall

We easily persuade ourselves

We feel keenly about such things

We grope blindly along

We have a firm assurance

We have a right to claim

We have an overpowering sense

We have been accustomed to

We have been told by more than one

We have come together to-night

We have great reason to be thankful

We have heard lately

We have here plain proof

We have need to examine

We have no means of knowing

We have no other alternative

We have not yet solved the problem

We have sought on this occasion

We have the evidence of this

We have the good fortune to-night

We have to admit

We have witnessed on many occasions

We hear it is said sometimes

We hear no complaint

We heartily wish and mean

We hold fast to the principle

We laugh to scorn the idea

We may all of us agree

We may be permitted to remember

We may contemplate with satisfaction

We may have a deep consciousness

We may indeed consider

We may not know precisely how

We must also look

We must constantly direct our purpose

We must not be deceived

We must not mistake

We must realize conscientiously

We must remember

We need no proof to assure us

We need not look far for reasons

We need not trouble ourselves

We of this generation

We often hear persons say

We ought in strict propriety

We pride ourselves upon the fact

We rightly pay all honor

We see in a variety of ways

We shall all doubtless concede

We shall be blind not to perceive

We shall do well to remember

We shall have no difficulty in determining

We should be convinced

We should contemplate and compare

We should dread nothing so much

We should lend our influence

We should not question for a moment

We should not, therefore, question

We stand astonished at

We stumble and falter and fall

We take it for granted

We will not stop to inquire

Weighty as these conditions are

Well, gentlemen, it must be confessed

Well may we explain

Well, now, let us propose

Well, that being the case, I say

Were I to enter into a detailed description

Were I to speculate

What are the precise characteristics

What are we to think of

What are you going to do

What can avail

What can be more intelligible

What can be more monstrous than

What can I say better

What commonly happens is this

What could be more captivating

What could be more true

What do we gain by

What do we understand to have been

What I mean is this

What I now say is

What I object to is

What I propose to do is

What I shall actually attempt to show here

What I suggest is

What is more important

What is more remarkable

What is the pretext

What is this but to say

What more shall I say

What remains but to wish you

What strikes the mind so forcibly

What, then, are we to believe

What, then, can be the reason

What, then, I may be asked

What, then, is the use

What, then, was the nature of

What was the consequence of

What we are concerned to know is

What we have most to complain of

What would you say

Whatever a man thinks

Whatever difference of opinion may exist

Whatever opinion I may express

Whatever the truth may be

When I am told

When I hear it said

When I remember the history

When I review these circumstances

When I speak of this question

When I thus profess myself

When one remembers

When we consider the vastness

When we contemplate

When we get so far as this

When we look closely at

When will men understand

When you are assured

When you did me the honor to invite me

Whence it is, I say

Whence was the proof to come

While acknowledging the great value

While I feel most keenly the honor

While I have hinted to you

Whilst I am on this matter

Who can deny the effect

Who can say in a word

Who does not like to see

Who has not felt the contrast

Who that reads does not see

Who will accuse me

Why, again, should I take notice

Why need you seek to disprove

Will any gentleman say

Will anyone answer

Will it be whispered

Will it not be well for us

Will you allow me to present to you

Will you bear with me

Will you mistake this

Will you permit me to thank you

With all my heart I share

With possibly a single exception

With respect to what has been said

With this ideal clearly before us

With whatever opinions we come here

Without going into any details

Without my saying a word more

Y

Yet I am convinced

Yet I am willing to admit

Yet I am willing to conclude

Yet I feel quite free to say

Yet I, for one, do not hesitate to admit

Yet I have never been thoroughly satisfied

Yet I suppose it is worth while

Yet I would have to think

Yet if you were to ask the question

Yet it is instructive and interesting

Yet it is no less true

Yet it is perfectly plain

Yet let me consider what consequences must

Yet may I not remind you

You all know the history of

You and I are always contrasting

You are at a parting of the ways

You are now invited to do honor

You can never forget

You cannot assert

You do not need to be told

You have all read the story

You have been gracious enough to assign to me

You have been mindful

You have been pleased to confer upon me

You have but to observe

You have done me great honor

You have no right

You have not forgotten

You have often pondered over

You have sometimes been astonished

You know that it is impossible to

You know the legend which has grown up

You know very well

You may also be assured

You may be acquainted with

You may be sure

You may depend upon it

You may remember

You may well be proud

You may well study the example

You might apply to yourselves

You must not forget

You must understand I do not mean to claim

You ought not to disregard what I say

You remember how

You will allow me to say with becoming brevity

You will be pleased to hear

You will bear me out when I say

You will clearly understand

You will expect me to say something about

You will forgive me

You will join with me, I trust

You will observe

You will pardon me, I am sure

You will scarcely be surprised

You would never dream of urging

You yourselves are the evidence

Your friendly and generous words

Your good sense must tell you

Your presence seems to say

SECTION XI

MISCELLANEOUS PHRASES

A

A bewildering labyrinth of facts

A blank absence of interest or sympathy

A bloodless diplomatist

A breach of confidence

A brilliant and paradoxical talker

A burning sense of shame and horror

A century of disillusionment

A certain catholicity of taste [catholicity = universality]

A cheap and coarse cynicism

A civilizing agency of conspicuous value

A cleanness and probity of life [probity = integrity; uprightness]

A commendable restraint

A condescending and patronizing spirit

A confused and troublesome time

A conscientious anxiety to do the right thing

A conspicuous and crowning service

A constant source of surprise and delight

A contemptible species of mockery

A convenient makeshift

A copious torrent of pleasantry

A course of arrogant obstinacy

A crumb of consolation

A crystallized embodiment of the age

A cynical and selfish hedonist

A dangerous varnish of refinement

A dead theological dogma

A decorous and well-intentioned person

A deep and most impressive solemnity

A deep and strange suggestiveness

A deep authentic impression of disinterestedness

A dereliction of duty

A disaster of the first magnitude

A distorted and pessimistic view of life

A dogmatic and self-righteous spirit

A duel of brains

A dull collocation of words

A fastidious sense of fitness

A fatal moral hollowness

A feeling of lofty remoteness

A feminine excess of inconsequence

A final and irrevocable settlement

A firmness tempered by the most scrupulous courtesy

A fitting interval for penitence

A flippant rejoinder

A flood of external impressions

A flourish of rhetoric

A fund of curious information

A furtive groping after knowledge

A gambler's desperate chance

A ghastly mixture of defiance and conceit

A glaring example of rapacity [rapacity = plundering]

A graceful nonentity

A great and many-sided personality

A great capacity for generous indignation

A great source of confusion

A gross piece of stupidity

A habit of riding a theory too hard

A habit of rigorous definition

A happy and compensating experience

A haughty self-assertion of equality

A hideous absurdity

A hideous orgy of massacre and outrage

A high pitch of eloquence

A homelike and festive aspect

A hopeless enigma

A hotbed of disturbance

A hushed rustle of applause testified to a widespread approbation [approbation = warm approval; praise]

A keenly receptive and intensely sensitive temperament

A kind of fantastic patchwork

A kind of surly reluctance

A laudable stimulus

A law of retributive justice

A less revolutionary innovation

A life of studious contemplation

A limpidity and lucidity of style [limpidity = transparent clarity; easily intelligible]

A lingering tinge of admiration

A lively sense of what is dishonorable

A long accumulating store of discontent and unrest

A long tangle of unavoidable detail

A look threatening and

peremptory [peremptory = ending all debate or action]

A many-sided and far-reaching enthusiasm

A marvelous sharpener of the faculties

A melancholy preponderance of mischief

A memory-haunting phrase

A mercenary marriage

A mere conjectural estimate

A microscopic care in the search of words

A misconception which is singularly prevalent

A mixture of malignancy and madness

A modicum of truth

A monstrous travesty

A mood of hard skepticism

A more than ordinary share of baseness and depravity

A most laudable zeal

A most repulsive and incomprehensible idiom

A most unseasonable piece of impertinence

A multitude of groundless alarms

A murderous tenacity about trifles

A mysterious and an intractable pestilence

A mysterious and inscrutable power

A narrow and superficial survey

A nature somewhat frivolous and irresolute

A needlessly offensive manner

A nimble interchange of uninteresting gossip

A noble and puissant nation [puissant = with power, might]

A novel and perplexing course

A numerous company

A painful and disconcerting deformity

A partial disenchantment

A passage of extraordinary daring

A patchwork of compromises

A permanent and habitual state of mind

A pernicious and growing tendency

A perversion of judgment

A phantom of the brain

A piece of grotesque stupidity

A pleasant flow of appropriate language

A pompous failure

A potential menace to life

A powerful and persuasive orator

A prevalent characteristic of her nature

A prey to the tongue of the public

A pristine vigor of style

A profusion of compliments

A proposition inherently vicious

A puerile illusion [puerile = immature; childish]

A quenchless thirst for expression

A rage akin to frenzy

A rare precision of insight

A rather desperate procedure

A reckless fashion

A recrudescence of superstition [recrudescence = recurrence of a pathological symptoms after a period of improvement]

A relish for the sublime

A reversion to the boldest paganism

A rigid avoidance of extravagance and excess

A ripple of applause

A restraining and conservative force

A robust and consistent application

A sacred and indissoluble union

A sane philosophy of life

A secluded dreamer of dreams

A secret and wistful charm

A sense of deepening discouragement

A sense of indescribable reverence

A series of brief and irritating hopes

A settled conviction of success

A sharp difference of opinion

A sharp pang of regretful surprise

A shrewd eye to the main chance

A signal deed of justice

A skeptical suspension of judgment

A slight and superficial tribute

A slowly subsiding frenzy

A snare and a delusion

A somewhat complicated and abstruse calculation [abstruse = difficult to understand]

A sordid and detestable motive

A sort of incredulous stupefaction

A source of unfailing delight and wonder

A species of moral usurpation

A spirit inimical to learning

A spirit of complacent pessimism

A startling and unfortunate digression

A state of scarcely veiled insurrection

A state of urgent necessity

A stern decree of fate

A stern foe of snobbishness

A storm of public indignation

A strange mixture of carelessness, generosity, and caprice

A strangely perverse and poverty stricken imagination

A strong assumption of superiority

A subjugated and sullen population

A sudden revulsion

A supposed ground of affinity

A synonym for retrogression

A taunting accusation of falsehood

A tedious and needless drudgery

A temper which brooked no resistance

A temporary expedient

A tender tone of remonstrance

A theme of endless meditation

A thing of moods and moments

A thoroughly sincere and unaffected effort

A thousand mangled delusions

A tissue of dull excuses

A tone of exaggerated solicitude

A touch of exquisite pathos

A trace of obvious sarcasm

A transcript of the common conscience

A trifle prim and puritanic

A truth begirt with fire

A unique and overwhelming charm

A vague aversion

A variety of conflicting and profound emotions

A variety of enfeebling amendments

A vast multitude of facts

A vastly extended vision of opportunity

A vehement and direct attack

A very elusive and delicate thought

A very formidable problem

A vigilant reserve

A violent and base calumniator [calumniator = makes malicious or knowingly false statements]

A voice of matchless compass and eloquence

A warmth of seemingly generous indignations

A wealth of resource that seemed inexhaustible

A welcome release from besetting difficulties

A whole catalog of disastrous blunders

A whole whirlpool of various emotions

Abounding bodily vigor

Above and beyond and before all else

Absurd and inconsequential career

Abundant and congenial employment

Accidental rather than intentional

Accustomed to ascribe to chance

Acquired sentiments of propriety

Activities of the discursive intellect

Actuated by an unduly anxious desire

Acute sensibility coupled with quickness of intellect

Adhere too tenaciously to forms and modes

Admirable mastery of technique

Admit the soft impeachment

Admitted with a childlike cheerfulness

Advance by leaps and bounds

Advancing to dignity and honor

Adventitious aids to memory [adventitious = Not inherent; added extrinsically]

Affectation and superfluous ornament

Aggravated to an unspeakable degree

Agitated and perplexed by a dozen cross-currents of conflicting tendency

Agreeable and humanizing intercourse

Aided by strong mental endowments

Airy swiftness of treatment

Alien to the purpose

All sorts of petty tyrannies

All the resources of a burnished rhetoric

Allied by taste and circumstances

Allied with a marked imperiousness [imperious = arrogantly overbearing]

Almost incredible obtuseness

Altogether monstrous and unnatural

Always observant and discriminating

Amaze and confound the imagination

Amiable and indulgent hostess

Amid many and pressing avocations

Amid the homeliest details of daily life

Amid the rush and roar of life

Ample scope for the exercise of his astonishing gifts

An abandoned and exaggerated grief

An accidental encounter

An act of folly amounting to wickedness

An afternoon of painfully constrained behavior

An agreeable image of serene dignity

An air of artificial constraint

An air of round-eyed profundity

An alarmed sense of strange responsibilities

An almost excessive exactness

An almost sepulchral regularity and seclusion

An ample and imposing structure

An apostle of unworldly ardor

An appreciable menace

An ardent and gifted youth

An arid dictum

An artful and malignant enemy

An assumption entirely gratuitous

An assumption which proved erroneous

An atmosphere of sunny gaiety

An attitude of passive impartiality

An authoritative and conclusive inquiry

An egregious assumption [egregious = outrageously reprehensible]

An elaborate assumption of indifference

An endless field for discussion

An enervating and emasculating form of indulgence

An ennobling and invigorating influence

An entirely negligible quantity

An essentially grotesque and commonplace thing

An eternal and imperishable example

An exalted and chimerical sense of honor [chimerical = highly improbable]

An excess of unadulterated praise

An excessive refinement of feeling

An expression at once confident and appealing

An extensive and populous country

An habitual steadiness and coolness of reflection

An honest and unquestioning pride

An icy indifference

An idle and unworthy action

An ill-assorted vocabulary

An immeasurable advantage

An imminent and overmastering peril

An imperturbable demeanor and steadiness of mind

An implacable foe

An inborn and irresistible impulse

An incongruous spectacle

An incredible mental agility

An indefinable taint of priggishness [priggishness = exaggerated propriety]

An indescribable frankness and simplicity of character

An indolent surrender to mere sensuous experience

An indomitable and unselfish soul

An ineradicable love of fun and mystification

An inevitable factor of human conduct

An inexhaustible copiousness and readiness of speech

An insatiable appetite for trifles

An insatiable voracity

An inscrutable mystery

An intentional breach of politeness

An interchange of civilities

An intolerable deal of guesswork

An involuntary gesture of remonstrance

An irrelevant bit of magniloquence

[magniloquence = extravagant in speech]

An irrepressible and impassioned hopefulness

An irritating and dangerous treatment

An itching propensity for argument

An object of indestructible interest

An obnoxious member of society

An ominous lull and silence

An open and violent rupture

An outburst of impassioned eloquence

An unaccountable feeling of antipathy

An unbecoming vehemence

An undisciplined state of feeling

An unerring sense of humor

An unparalleled and almost miraculous growth

An unparalleled atrocity

An unpatriotic and ignoble act

An unreasoning form of coercion

An utterly vile and detestable spirit

And now I address myself to my task

And the like

Announced in a tone of pious satisfaction

Another thought importuned him [importuned = insistent or repeated requests]

Anticipated with lively expectation

Apparent rather than real

Appeal to a tardy justice

Appreciably above the level of mediocrity

Arbitrary assumption of power

Ardently and enthusiastically convinced

Argued with immense force and feeling

Arrayed with scrupulous neatness

Arrogance and untutored haughtiness

As an impartial bystander

As belated as they are
fallacious

As by a secret of
freemasonry

As odious as it is absurd

As ridiculous as it was
unnecessary

As we scan the vague
unknown

Assailed by poignant
doubts

Assume a menacing
attitude

Assumed almost heroic
proportions

At once epigrammatic and
arresting [epigrammatic =
terse and witty]

At once misleading and
infelicitous

At the mercy of small
prejudices

Attained by rigorous self-
restraint

Attended by insuperable
difficulties

Averted by some happy
stroke of fortune

Await the sentence of
impartial posterity

Awaited with feverish
anxiety

B

Bandied to and fro

Based on a fundamental
error

Beguile the tedium of the
journey

Bemoaning and bewailing
his sad fortune

Beset with external
dangers

Betrayed into deplorable
error

Bewildering multiplication
of details

Beyond the dreams of
avarice

Blended with courage and
devotion

Blind leaders of the blind

Blunt the finer sensibilities

Blustering desire for
publicity

Bound up with
impossibilities and
absurdities

Breathed an almost
exaggerated humility

Bred in the tepid reticence
of propriety

Brief ventures of
kindliness

Brilliant display of
ingenious argument

Bring odium upon the
individual

Brisk directness of speech

Brutal recognition of
failure

Bursts of unpremeditated
frankness

But delusions and
phantasmagoria

But that is beside the mark

But this is a digression

By a curious perversity of
fate

By a happy turn of
thinking

By a whimsical diversion

By common consent

By means of crafty
insinuations

By no means inconsolable

By temperament
incompatible

By the common judgment of the thinking world

By the sheer centripetal force of sympathy

By virtue of a common understanding

By way of rejoinder

C

Calculated to create disgust

Calm strength and constancy

Capable of a severe scientific treatment

Capacity for urbanity and moderation

Carried into port by fair winds

Caught unawares by a base impulse

Ceaseless tramp of humanity

Censured for his negligence

Championing the cause of religious education

Chastened and refined by experience

Checked by the voice of authority

Cherished the amiable illusion

Cherishing a huge fallacy

Childishly inaccurate and absurd

Chivalrous loyalty and high forbearance

Clever and captivating eloquence

Coarse and glittering ostentation

Coherent and continuous trend of thought

Commended by perfect suavity

Common ground of agreement

Complicated and infinitely embittered

Conceded from a sense of justice

Conceived with imperfect knowledge

Concentrated and implacable resolve

Conditions of unspeakable humiliation

Conducive to well-being and efficiency

Confused rumblings presaging a different epoch

Constrained by the sober exercise of judgment

Consumed by a demon of activity

Continuous and stubborn disregard

Contrary to the clearest conviction of his judgment

Couched in terms of feigned devotion

Credulous and emotionally extravagant

Creed of incredulity and derision

Criticized with unsparing vigor

Crude undigested masses of suggestion

Cruel and baseless calumnies [calumnies = maliciously false statements; slander]

Cynically repudiate all obligations

D

Daily usages and modes of thinking

Dangerously near snobbery

Darkly insinuating what may possibly happen

Dazzled by their novelty and brilliance

Debased by common use

Deep essentials of moral grandeur

Deeply engrossed in congenial work

Deeply moved as well as keenly stung

Deeply rooted in the heart of humanity

Defiant of analysis and rule

Degenerate into comparative feebleness

Degenerated into deadness and formality

Degrading and debasing curiosity

Deliberate and cautious reflection

Delicacy of perception and quick tact

Delude many minds into acquiescence

Dense to the point of stupidity

Descanting on them cursorily [descanting = discussion or discourse]

Devices generally held to be discreditable

Devious and perilous ways

Devoid of hysteria and extravagance

Dexterous modes of concealment

Dictated by an overweening partiality

Differ in degree only and not in kind

Difficult and abstruse questions [abstruse = incomprehensible]

Diffidence overwhelmed him

Diffusing beneficent results

Dignified by deliberation and privacy

Dimly implying some sort of jest

Discreditable and insincere support

Disdaining the guidance of reason

Disenchanting effect of time and experience

Disfigured by glaring faults

Disguised in sentimental frippery

Dispel all anxious concern

Displayed enormous power and splendor

Distinguish themselves by their eccentricities

Distracted by contending desires

Diversity of mind and temperament

Divested of all personal feelings

Dogged and shameless beyond all precedent

Dominated by no prevailing taste or fashion

Doomed by inexorable fate

Doomed to impermanence and transiency

Draw back in distrust and misgiving

Dreaded and detested rival

Driven towards disaffection and violence

Due to historical perspective

Dull and trite commonplaces

Dwindled to alarmingly small dimensions

E

Easy-going to the point of lethargy

Elementary principles of right and wrong

Embittered and fanatical agitation

Encrusted with pedantry and prejudice [pedantry = attention to detail]

Endless and intricate technicalities

Endowed with undreamed-of powers

Enforced by coercive measures

Enormities of crime and anomalies of law

Entangled in theological controversy

Entirely futile and negligible

Erroneous assumptions and sophistries

Espoused with extraordinary ardor

Essentially one-sided and incomplete

Eternally fruitful and stimulating

Evidently malicious and adroit

Evinces a hardened conscience and an insensibility to shame

Exact and resolute allegiance

Examples of terrific and explosive energy

Exasperating to the last degree

Excruciating cruelty and injustice

Exposed to damaging criticism

Exposing his arrogance and folly to merited contempt

Expressions of unrestrained grief

Exquisite lucidity of statement

Extraordinarily subtle and penetrating analysis

Exuberant rush of words

F

Facile and fertile literary brains

Faithfully and religiously eschewed [eschew = avoid; shun]

Fallen into the convenient oblivion of the waste-basket

Fanatical and dangerous excesses

Far off and incredibly remote

Fastidious correctness of form

Fate had turned and twisted a thousand ways

Fed by many currents from the long stream of human experience

Feigning a virtuous indignation

Fertility of argumentative resource

Fictitious and adventitious aid

Finely touched to the fine issues

Fit to stand the gaze of millions

Fits and starts of generosity

Fixed convictions of mankind

Flouted as unpractical

Foolish and inflexible superstition

Fostering and preserving order

Free from all controversial pettifogging [pettifogging = quibbling over insignificant details]

Freighted with the most precious cargoes

Frequently recurring forms of awkwardness

Fresh and unsuspected loveliness

From the standpoint of expediency and effectiveness

Full and tuneful diction

Full of ardent affection and gratitude

Full of presentiments of some evil

Full of singular freshness, insight and power

Full of speculation and a deep restrained excitement

Fumble and stumble in helpless incapacity

G

Gain the applause of future ages

Generous to a pathetic and touching degree

Give vent to his indignation

Giving an ear to a little neighborly gossip

Glances and smiles of tacit contempt

Gnawing at the vitals of society

Grace and gentleness of manner

Graceful succession of sentences

Gratuitous and arbitrary meddling

Greeted with unalloyed satisfaction

Grooves of intellectual habit

Growing sense of bewilderment and dismay

Guilty and baffled antagonists

H

Habits of unintelligent routine

Habitual self-possession and self-respect

Happy and gracious willingness

Hard-souled and joyously joyous

Haunted by blank misgivings

He affected neither pomp nor grandeur

He became more blandly garrulous [garrulous = excessive and trivial talk]

He declined the proffered hospitality

He dropped into an eloquent silence

He eludes analysis and baffles description

He glanced at her indulgently

He had the habit of self-engrossed silences

He harbored his misgivings in silence

He poured bitter and biting ridicule on his discomfited opponents

He spoke with sledgehammer directness

He suffers nothing to draw him aside

He took his courage in both hands

He turned on me a glance of stored intelligence

He was disheveled and untidy

He was inexhaustibly voluble

Heavily freighted with erudition [erudition = extensive learning]

Heights of serene contemplation

Her voice had a wooden resonance and a ghost of a lisp

Hidebound in official pedantry [pedantry = attention to detail]

High and undiscouraged hope

High-handed indifference to all restraint

His chin had too vanishing an aspect

His first zeal was flagging

His general attitude suggested an idea that he had an oration for you

His gestures and his gait were untidy

His mood was one of pure exaltation

His plea was irresistible

His tone verged on the ironical

His work was ludicrously perfunctory

Hopelessly belated in its appearance

I

I adjured him [adjured = command or enjoin solemnly, as under oath]

I am not without a lurking suspicion

I bemoaned my unlucky fate

I could almost allege it as a supreme example

I have somewhat overshot the mark

I lost myself in a reverie of gratitude

I made bold to retort

I must hazard the story

I was extremely perplexed

I will permit myself the liberty of saying

I would fain believe [fain = happily; gladly]

Illuminate with sinister effect

Immediate and effectual steps

Immense capacity for ceaseless progress

Immunity from criticism and control

Impartial and exacting judgment

Impatience of despotic influence

Impelled by strong conviction

Imperiled in a restless age

Imperious in its demands [imperious = arrogantly domineering]

Impotent outbreaks of unreasoning rage

Impromptu parades of noisy patriotism

In a diversity of application

In a fever of apprehension

In a frenzy of fussy excitement

In a frowning abstraction

In a great and fruitful way

In a high degree culpable

In a kind of confused astonishment

In a most commendable fashion

In a most impressive vein

In a position of undisputed supremacy

In a rapture of imagined ecstasy

In a secret and surreptitious way [surreptitious = done by clandestine or stealthy means]

In a spirit of friendliness and conciliation

In a state of mulish reluctance [mulish = stubborn and intractable]

In a state of nervous exacerbation

In a state of virtuous complacency

In a tone of uneasy interrogation

In a transport of ambitious vanity

In a whirlwind of feeling and memory

In accents embarrassed and hesitating

In alliance with steady clearness of intellect

In amazed ejaculation

In an eminent and unique sense

In an eminent degree

In deference to a unanimous sentiment

In extenuation of the past

In high good humor

In his customary sententious fashion [sententious = terse and energetic; pithy]

In its most odious and intolerable shape

In language terse yet familiar

In moments of the most imminent peril

In quite incredible confusion

In seasons of difficulty and trial

In spite of plausible arguments

In terms of imperishable beauty

In the dim procession of years

In the highest conceivable degree

In the local phrase

In the nature of things

In the ordinarily accepted sense

In the realm of conjecture

In the scheme of things

In the tone of one who moralizes

In the twinkling of an eye

In the world of letters

In tones of genuine admiration

Incapable of flashy make-believe

Incited by a lust for gain

Incomparable lucidity and penetrativeness

Inconceivable clumsiness of organization

Indulge a train of gentle recollection

Indulging a sickly and nauseating petulance

Ineffably dreary and unpicturesque

Infected with a feverish dissatisfaction

Infuse a wholesome terror

Inimical to true and determined principle [Inimical = harmful; adverse]

Inimitable grace and felicity [inimitable = defying imitation; matchless]

Injudicious and inelegant ostentation

Innumerable and incessant creations

Inordinate greed and love of wealth

Insatiably greedy of recognition

Insensibility to moral perspective and proportion

Insolent and riotous excess

Inspired by a vague malevolence

Inspirited by approval and applause

Instances might be multiplied indefinitely

Instantly alive to the slightest breach of decorum

Insufferable violence to the feelings

Intense and stubborn dogmatism

Intense sensitiveness to injustice

Intercourse with polished society

Intervals of respite and repose

Inveigh against established customs [inveigh = angry disapproval; protest vehemently]

Invested with a partial authority

Inveterate forces of opposition

Invincible jealousy and hate

Involuntary thrill of gratified vanity

Involved in profound uncertainty

Involving ourselves in embarrassments

Inward appraisal and self-renouncement

Irregulated and desultory education [desultory = haphazard; random]

Irrelevant to the main issue

Irresistibly impelled by conscience

Irritable bitterness and angry suspicion

It assumes the shape of malignity

It betrays a great want of prudence and discernment

It defies description

It dissipates every doubt and scruple

It enslaves the imagination

It extorted from him expressions of irritability

It gives one a little grip at the throat

It has been stigmatized as irrelevant

It has more than passing interest

It has seldom been surpassed

It imposes no constraint

It is a capital blunder

It is a common error among ignorant people

It is a consoling reflection

It is a mark of great instability

It is a staggering thought

It is always something vicious

It is an odd jealousy

It is an intolerable idea

It is impossible to resist acknowledging this

It is little more than a platitude

It is not consistent with elevated and dignified character

It is not wholly insignificant

It is notoriously easy to exaggerate

It is the common consent of men

It is unnecessary to multiply instances

It makes life insupportable

It must be a matter of conjecture

It occasions suspicion and discontent

It runs counter to all established customs

It was a matter of notoriety

It wears a ragged and dangerous front

It would be a fruitless and unthankful task

It would be superfluous to say

It would not seem an improbable conclusion

Its dominating and inspiring influence

J

Jealous and formidable foes

Justifiable in certain exigencies [exigencies = urgent situations]

K

Keen power of calculation and unhesitating audacity

Kindle the flames of genuine oratory

Knotty and subtle disquisitions [disquisitions = formal discourse]

L

Labored and far-fetched elocution

Laid down in a most unflinching and vigorous fashion

Lamentable instances of extravagance

Lash themselves into fury

Lax theories and corresponding practices

Lay hold of the affections

Leaden mood of dullness

Lend a critical ear

Lest the requirements of courtesy be disregarded

Links in the chain of reasoning

Little less than scandalous

Lofty and distinguished simplicity

Long-sighted continuity of thought and plan

Looking at the matter by and large

Looming large and ugly in the public view

Loose and otiose statement [otiose = lazy; indolent; of no use]

Lost in indolent content

Lovely beyond all words

Lucidity and argumentative vigor

Lulled into a sense of false satisfaction

M

Maddened by a jealous hate

Maintained with ingenuity and vigor

Manifestly harsh and barbarous

Marvelous copiousness of illustration

Marvelously suggestive and inspiring

Men of profound erudition [erudition = extensive learning]

Mere effects of negligence

Microscopic analysis of character

Mingled distrust and fear

Ministering to mere pleasure and indulgence

Minutely and rationally exposing their imperfections

Morbid and subjective brooding

More or less severe and prolonged

Moved to unaccustomed tears

My worst suspicions were confirmed

Mysterious and invincible darkness

N

Naked vigor of resolution

Naturally prone to believe

Necessity thus imposed by prudence

Nerveless and faithless folly

No more than brief palliatives or mitigations

Noble and sublime patience

Noisy torrent of talk

Not averse to a little gossip

Not so much polished as varnished

Noted for their quixotic love of adventure

Nothing could be more captious or unfair [captious = disposition to find and point out trivial faults]

Nothing remained but a graceful acquiescence

Notoriously distracted by internecine jealousies

O

Objects of general censure

Obscured beneath the rubbish of the age

Obsessed with an overweening pride

Obstacles that are difficult but not insuperable

Obviously at variance with facts

Occasioned by direct moral turpitude [turpitude = depravity; baseness]

Oddly amenable to the proposed innovations

Often employed promiscuously

Ominous and swift days

Omitting all compliments and commonplaces

On a noble and commanding scale

On sure ground of fact

On the edge of great irritability

On the horns of a dilemma

One of life's ironical adjustments

One of the foreseen and inevitable results

One tissue of rashness, folly, ingratitude, and injustice

Openly flouted and disavowed

Oppressed by some vague dread

Organs of party rage and popular frenzy

Our opinions were diametrically opposed

Our vaunted civilization

Outward mark of obeisance and humiliation [obeisance = attitude of deference]

Overcome by an access of misery

Overshadowed by a fretful anxiety

Overwhelmed with reproach and popular indignation

P

Painful and lamentable indifference

Palpably and unmistakably commonplace

Parading an exception to prove a rule

Paralyzed by infirmity of purpose

Paralyzing doubts and scruples

Paramount obligation and righteousness

Partial and fragmentary evidence

Passionately addicted to pleasure

Patently inimical to liberty

Patience under continual provocation

Peculiarly liable to misinterpretation

Peddling and pitiful compromises

Pelting one another with catchwords

Perfectly illustrated and exemplified

Perpetually excite our curiosity

Pierced to the quick

Pitiful shifts of policy

Plainly dictated by a lofty purpose

Pleading the exigencies of strategical interest [exigencies = urgent situations]

Plunged into tumultuous preoccupation

Pointed out with triumphant malice

Polished beauty of diction

Political storm and stress.

Position of titular command

Preached with a fierce unction [unction = exaggerated earnestness]

Precipitate and arbitrary changes

Predict the gloomiest consequences

Pregnant with a lesson of the deepest import

Presented with matchless vigor and courage

Princely generosity of praise

Prodigious and portentous events

Protracted to a vexatious length

Proud schemes for aggrandizement

Provocative of bitter hostility

Pruned of their excrescences and grotesque extremes [excrescences = abnormal growth, such as a wart]

Purged of glaringly offensive features

Pursued to a vicious extent

Q

Questioned and tested in the crucible of experience

Quickened into a stabbing
suspicion

Quickness to conceive and
courage to execute

Quite destitute of resources

Quixotically generous
about money

R

Radiantly and
transparently happy

Railed at the world

Rare candor and flexibility
of mind

Rare fidelity of purpose
and achievement

Rarely brought to pass

Reeling headlong in luxury
and sensuality

Regarded with sincere
abhorrence

Regulated by the fixed
rules of good-breeding

Religious rights and
ceremonies

Reluctant to appear in so
equivocal a character

Render null and void

Rent by internal
contentions

Repugnant alike to reason
and conscience

Resigned to growing
infirmities

Resist a common
adversary

Resting on some collateral
circumstance

Rhetorical and ambitious
diction

Rich and exuberant
complexities

Rigid and exact boundaries

Rooted in immeasurable
error and falsity

Roused to tumultuous
activity

Rude and blind criticism

S

Sadly counterbalanced by
numerous faults

Said with epigrammatic
point [epigrammatic =
terse and witty]

Salutary in the extreme

Salutary tonic of a free
current of public criticism

Sanity and quietness of
soul

Scorned as an
impracticable theory

Scornful of petty
calculations

Screen themselves from
punishment

Scrupulous and chivalrous
loyalty

See with eagle glance
through conventionalisms

Seem to savor of paradox

Seize the auspicious
moment

Self-centered anxiety and
preoccupation

Self-command born of
varied intercourse

Self-interest of the most
compelling character

Selfish and uselessly
recondite [recondite = not
easily understood]

Selfishness pampered by
abundance

Senses of marvelous
acuteness

Sensible diminution of our
comfort

Sensitive and apprehensive
temperament

Sentimental wailings for the past

Serve the innocent purposes of life

Set down with meticulous care

Shames us out of our nonsense

Sharp outbursts of hatred and bitterness

Sharp restrictions of duty and opportunity

Sharply and definitely conceived

She had lost her way in a labyrinth of conjecture

She took refuge in a passionate exaggeration of her own insufficiency

Sheer midsummer madness

Silly displays of cheap animosity

Simple and obvious to a plain understanding

Sinister and fatal augury [augury = sign of something coming; omen]

Skulking beneath a high-sounding benevolence

Slack-minded skimming of newspapers

Slavish doctrines of sectarianism

Slow and resistless forces of conviction

Smug respectability and self-content

Snatch some advantage

Socialized and exacting studies

Some very undignified disclosures

Something essentially inexpressible

Something stifling and over-perfumed

Spinning a network of falsehoods

Spiritual and moral significance

Staring in helpless bewilderment

Stealthily escaping observation

Stern determination to inflict summary justice

Stigmatized as moral cowards

Stimulated to profitable industry

Stopped as if on the verge of profundities

Strange frankness of cynical brutality

Strange streak of melancholy

Strangled by a snare of words

Strenuous and conscientious endeavor

Stretched out in dreary monotony

Strict and unalloyed veracity

Struck incessantly and remorselessly

Stupendous and awe-inspiring spectacle

Subject to the vicissitudes of fortune [vicissitudes = sudden or unexpected changes]

Subjected to the grossest cruelties

Subordination to the common weal

Subservient to the ends of religion

Sudden and inexplicable changes of mood

Suddenly and imperatively summoned

Suddenly swelled to unprecedented magnitude

Sufficient to repel vulgar curiosity

Suggestive sagacity and penetration [sagacity = farsighted; wise]

Suit the means to the end

Sullen and widespread discontent

Superior in strength and prowess

Supported by a splendid fearlessness

Supremely and undeniably great

Susceptible to every impulse and stimulus

Sustained dignity and mellifluous precision [mellifluous = flowing with honey; smooth and sweet]

Swamping every aspiration and ambition

Swift and vehement outbursts of feeling

T

Take root in the heart

Take vengeance upon arrogant self-assertion

Taken in their totality

Tamed and wonted to a settled existence

Tempered by the emotional warmth of high moral ideals

That way madness lies

The abysmal depths of despair

The accumulated bitterness of failure

The agonies of conscious failure

The air was full of the cry and clamor

The animadversions of critics [animadversions = Strong criticism]

The applause was unbounded

The best proof of its timeliness and salutariness [salutariness = favorable]

The bewildered and tumultuous world

The blackest abyss of despair

The blemishes of an extraordinary reputation

The bluntness of a provincial

The bogey of bad luck [bogey = evil or

mischievous spirit; hobgoblin]

The bounding pulse of youth

The brunt of life

The capacity for refined pursuits

The charming omniscience of youth

The cloak of cowardice

The collective life of humanity

The combined dictates of reason and experience

The companion of a noble and elevated spirit

The complaining gate swung open

The complex phenomena of life

The consequence of an agitated mind

The consequence of ignorance and childish assumption

The constant pressure of anxieties

The creature and tool of a party

The critical eyes of posterity

The dead and dusty past

The delimitation is sufficiently definite

The dictates of plain reason

The disjointed babble of the chronicler

The dull derision of the world

The dullest and most vacant minds

The dumb forces of brute nature

The dupe of some imposture

The eager pretentiousness of youth

The ebb and flow of events

The everlasting deluge of books

The evil was irremediable

The exchange of harmless amenities

The exertion of an inherent power

The expression was keenly intellectual

The facile conjectures of ignorant onlookers

The facts took him by the throat

The fitful swerving of passion

The flabbiness of our culture

The flaccid moods of prose

The flame of discord raged with redoubled fury

The flattest and most obvious truisms

The flippant insolence of a decadent skepticism

The foe of excess and immoderation

The fog of prejudice and ill-feeling

The frustration of their dearest hopes

The garb of civilization

The general infusion of wit

The gift of prophecy

The golden years of youth and maturity

The gratification of ambition

The grim reality of defeat

The hall-mark of a healthy humanity

The handmaid of tyranny

The hint of tranquillity and self-poise

The hints of an imaginable alliance

The hobgoblin of little minds

The holiest and most ennobling sensations of the soul

The hollowest of hollow shams

The homely virtue of practical utility

The hubbub and turmoil of the great world

The huge and thoughtful night

The hurly-burly of events

The idea was utterly hateful and repugnant

The idle of all hobbledehoys [hobbledehoys = gawky adolescent boy]

The ignoble exploitation of public interests

The imminent fatality awaiting him

The impulse of prejudice or caprice

The incorrigibility of perverse human nature

The incursions of a venomous rabble

The indulgence of an overweening self-conceit

The inevitable climax and culmination

The inference is inescapable

The infirmity and fallibility of human nature

The inflexible serenity of the wheeling sun

The ingenuities of legal verbiage

The inmost recesses of the human heart

The insipidity of indifference

The insolence of power

The irony of circumstances

The jaded weariness of overstrained living

The jargon of well-handled and voice-worn phrases

The jostling and ugliness of life

The lawyer's habit of circumspection and delay

The long-delayed hour of retribution

The lowest grade of precarious mendacity [mendacity = untruthfulness]

The makeshifts of mediocrity

The malarious air of after-dinner gossip

The mazes of conflicting testimony

The mean and frivolous affections of the idle

The menacing shadow of want

The mere fruit of his distempered imagination

The mere reversal of the wheel of fortune

The merest smattering of knowledge

The meticulous preciosity of the lawyer and the logician [preciosity = extreme over refinement]

The most absurd elementary questions

The most amazing impudence

The most exacting and exciting business

The most fallacious of all fallacies

The most implacable logic

The most preposterous pride

The multitudinous tongue of the people

The outcome of unerring observation

The outraged conscience of mankind

The overpowering force of circumstances and necessity

The overweening exercise of power

The panacea for the evils of society

The panorama of history

The pernicious doctrines of skeptics

The perpetrator of clumsy witticisms

The precarious tenure of fame

The precursor of violence

The pretty and delicate game of talk

The primitive instinct of self-preservation

The property of little minds

The prophecies of visionaries and enthusiasts

The proprieties of etiquette

The purse-proud inflation of the moneyed man

The question was disconcertingly frank

The ravening wolves of brute instinct

The remark was sternly uncompromising

The result of caprice

The rigor of the law

The sanction and authority of a great name

The severest shocks of adverse fate

The sharp and vehement assertion of authority

The sinister influence of unprincipled men

The speaker drew an indignant breath

The springs of human action

The staple of conversation

The stillness of finality

The stings of self-reproach

The straightforward path of inexorable logic

The strong hand of executive authority

The sum and fruit of experience

The sum total of her impressions was negative

The summit of excellence

The supernatural prescience of prophecy

The sweet indulgence of good-nature

The sycophants of the rich [sycophant = servile self-seeker attempting to win favor by flattery]

The taint of fretful ingratitude

The talk flowed

The target for ill-informed criticism

The tears welled up and flowed abundantly

The tediousness of inactivity

The tendency to evade implicit obligations

The ties of a common cause

The tranquil aspects of society

The tribute of affectionate applause

The ultimate verdict of mankind

The unbroken habit of a lifetime

The unimpeachable correctness of his demeanor

The unlicensed indulgence of curiosity

The unsophisticated period of youth

The utmost excitement and agitation

The vanishing thoughtlessness of youth

The vanity and conceit of insular self-satisfaction

The very texture of man's soul and life

The victim of an increasing irritability

The victorious assertion of personality

The virtue of taciturnity [taciturnity = habitually untalkative]

The voice was sharp and

peremptory [peremptory = ending all debate or action]

The want of serious and sustained thinking

The widest compass of human life

The wonderful pageant of consciousness

The words stabbed him

Their authenticity may be greatly questioned

Their indignation waxed fast and furious

Themes of perennial interest

There was a blank silence

There was no sense of diminution

They affected the tone of an impartial observer

They rent the air with shouts and acclamations

Thoughts which mock at human life

Through ever-widening circles of devastation

Through the distortions of prejudice

Thwarted by seeming insuperable obstacles

Time was dissolving the circle of his friends

Times of unexampled difficulty

Tinseled over with a gaudy embellishment of words

To a practiced eye

To be sedulously avoided [sedulously = persevering]

To prosecute a scheme of personal ambition

To state the case is to prove it

Too preposterous for belief

Too puerile to notice

Too sanguine a forecast [sanguine = cheerfully confident; optimistic]

Torn asunder by eternal strife

Totally detached from all factions

Touched with a sort of reverential gratitude

Transcend the bounds of human credulity

Transitory in its nature

Transparent and ridiculous self-importance

Treasured up with a timid and niggardly thrift

Treated the idea with lofty scorn

Tremendous exploits and thrilling escapades

True incentives to knowledge

U

Unamiable and envious attributes

Unbounded devotion and indulgence

Uncharted oceans of thought

Unconquerable fidelity to duty

Under all conceivable circumstances

Under the sway of arbitrary opinions

Undertaken under propitious circumstances [propitious = auspicious, favorable; kindly]

Uneasy sense of impending change

Unequaled simplicity and directness of purpose

Unexceptional in point of breeding

Unexpected obstacles and inextricable difficulties

Unfailing and miraculous foresight

Unfeigned astonishment and indignation

Unfounded and incredible calumnies [calumnies = maliciously false statements]

Unhampered by binding alliances

Universal in their signification

Unjust and unrighteous persecution

Unreasoning and unquestioning attachment

Unrivaled beauty and excellence

Unrivaled gift of succinct and trenchant speech [trenchant = forceful, effective, vigorous; incisive; distinct]

Unsparing industry and attention

Unspeakably alluring and satisfying

Unsurpassed in force and fitness

Unswerving and unselfish fidelity

Untiring enunciation of platitudes and fallacies

Unutterably trivial and paltry

Unwavering and unquestioning approbation [approbation = warm approval; praise]

Unworthy and ungenerous treatment

Upbraid ourselves with folly

Urgent warning and admonition

Utterly and essentially irreverent

V

Vast and vague aspirations

Vastly complex and far-reaching problems

Vehemently and indignantly repudiated

Venerable and dignified conservatism

Versatile and essentially original

Versed in the arts of exciting tumult and sedition [sedition = insurrection; rebellion]

Viewed in its general tenor and substance

Vigorous and well compacted

Violating all decency

Violent and unforeseen vicissitudes [vicissitudes = sudden or unexpected changes]

Vitiated by intolerance and shortsightedness [vitiated = reduce the value; corrupt morally; debase]

Vivid even to oppressiveness

Voracious and insatiable appetite

Vulgar eagerness for place

W

Warnings too pregnant to be disregarded

Warped by personal pretensions and self-consequence

We may parenthetically note

We must profoundly revere it

Weigh the merits and demerits

Welcomed at first with skeptical contempt

Well-concerted and well-timed stratagems

Whirled into rapid and ceaseless motion

Wholesale friction and discontent

Wholly devoid of public interest

Widely divergent social traits

Wield an unequaled and paramount authority

Wiser counsels prevailed

Withal decidedly handsome

Written in indelible characters upon his heart

Y

Yield to urgent representations

Z

Zealous in the cause he affected to serve

Other Books in the Writer's Skill Development Series

Available at Amazon and wherever books are sold.